Tejgaon Airport
A1-317
BANGLADESH
18th AUGUST 1974
DEPARTURE
IMMIGRATION

'Young man, you say you are going to England to study?'

'Yes, Sir.'

'And you will return home after completion of your studies?'

'Most certainly, Sir. I am returning to join my family enterprise.'

The entry clearance officer hesitated, staring at me in silence from behind his desk at Dhaka High Commission. I grew uncomfortable beneath his gaze.

'But how can I be certain?' he said finally, his tone still friendly but his words unsettling.

'Sir?'

'What if you like it in the UK? What if you want to stay?'

'No, Sir. It's already decided, Sir.'

He paused a second time, his eyes on me again.

'Young man,' he said: 'I can't say for certain that you will not return and that you will want to settle in England. I am obliged to take your word for it. Since all your papers are in good order, I therefore cannot refuse your visa.'

He stamped my passport and handed it over. 'Here is your entry clearance.'

'Thank you, Sir,' I said, accepting it with a trembling hand.

It was 6 August 1974. I was 19 years old. Within two weeks, on 18 August, I left Bangladesh for the first time, bound for London.

THE SUNDAY TIMES · FEBRUARY 19, 2006

IMMIGRANT BRITAIN

Migrants are some of Britain's most enterprising people. **Dan Drilsma-Milgrom** looks at the 250,000 ethnic businesses that contribute £18bn a year to the economy

Brick Lane millionaire: Muquim Ahmed

...quim Ahmed (47)

...Ahmed came from ...sh in 1974 to study ...ng at the South East ...college. After two years of ...he started helping his ...port goods from Britain ...and to Bangladesh. ...ss was good and he ...d into property, buying the ...na in London's Brick ...was a millionaire at 26 ...into electrical wholesaling, ...expanding his property ...s elder brother. ...n, based in Bangladesh, he ...ts worth at least £30m. He ...coming a leading ...owner through his ...g Cafe Naz chain, which ...ix sites in Britain with ...another three next year.

Estates Gazette **Rich List 2005**

Muquim Ahmed:
Self-made man

Earl of Cadogan:
Inherited estate

The week Old and new money meet in *EG*'s Rich List   6...

Muquim Ahmed
Pride of Bengal Award 2024

Curry life

TIKKA WEEK
NOT A DAY!

Muquim Ahmed
Hard-Slog Millionaire

ASIAN JEWEL AWARDS
Lloyds TSB

Entrepreneur Excellence Award

The Lloyds TSB Entrepreneur Excellence Asian Jewel Award celebrates the achievement of those Asian men and women who have taken the risk and set up their own businesses and are now making a success of their chosen enterprises.

2

About the Author

Muquim Ahmed is a stalwart of the Bangladeshi/British community, symbolising the entrepreneurial spirit of perseverance, dexterity, and persistence. Known to many as highly motivated, ambitious, idiosyncratic and inquisitive, he had the Midas Touch – success wherever he ventured. His multiple businesses over half a century ranged from currency exchange, travel, wholesale distribution, import and export of electronics goods to cinema, music production, shipping, restaurants, industrial bakery and ready meals. Today his focus is on property. But life as a businessman is never without its challenges. There were times when everything he touched seemed to go up in flames. Misfortunes such as the BCCI (Bank of credit & Commerce) failing in 1991, the liquidation of London and Provincial Factors in 1993, the fire that destroyed his warehouse in 1994, the Brick Lane bombing that almost killed him in 1999, and his major banker – Habib Bank Ltd – closing its UK operations in 2005 all came thick and fast. But despite these disasters, Muquim never wavered but marched on regardless. "Have courage, resources and determination to overcome your predicament." Winston Churchill

Dedication

This book is dedicated
to my eldest brother Moin
who devotedly nurtured me
to be who I am today.

Acknowledgements

I want to express my gratitude to my Editor Marnie Summerfield Smith who during the course of time became a family friend. Her vast experience and knowledge strengthened my resolve and style of writing with precise diction and choice of words.

I am ever so grateful for Marnie's enthusiastic encouragement to reveal my adolescence which was indeed my formative years. The tradition and deference instilled by my parents and the schools which I attended – these narratives emphasised by Marnie probably has made this book more interesting.

I want to thank my soulmate, my wife Farzana whose relentless persistence in formatting my manuscript which would otherwise be difficult to relate.

I am grateful to Rushi Millns for proofreading the book and enthusiastically making some of the phrases politically correct. I remain grateful to her.

My publisher Chris Day of Filament Publishing has imbued in the process certain changes and additions that has desirably exalted my book and its applications.

I am in debt to Nahas Pasha of "Curry Life" Magazine whose valuable input and suggestions have helped me a long way. He has always stood by me in matters of community issues. A big thank you.

MIRACLE ON BRICK LANE

**A story entwined with the evolution of the
Bangladeshi Community in East London**

by

Muquim Ahmed

Published by
Filament Publishing Ltd
14, Croydon Road, Beddington,
Croydon, Surrey CR0 4PA

+44 (0)20 8688 2598
www.filamentpublishing.com
Book Layout by Ana Celia Silva

ISBN 978-1-915465-70-2

Miracle on Brick Lane
by Muquim Ahmed

Contents

Preface 11

Chapter 1 - Miraculous Escape 13

Chapter 2 - Immigrant 1974 21

Chapter 3 - Early Days 25

Chapter 4 - War of Independence 43

Chapter 5 - Opportunity Knocks 45

Chapter 6 - Bank of England 55

Chapter 7 - Mount Mascal Farm 59

Chapter 8 - Amazing Brick Lane 63

Chapter 9 - Naz – Historic Cinema Hall 69

Chapter 10 - My Businesses 81

Chapter 11 - Family Life 99

Chapter 12 - Victories and Victims 111

Chapter 13 - Cambridge University Debate 115

Chapter 14 - A Cool Million 121

Chapter 15 - The Phoenix Rises from the Ashes 129

Chapter 16 - Pressing Ahead 135

Chapter 17 - Sylto Plc 145

Chapter 18 - Institutional Failures 153

Chapter 19 - Innovation in the Food Industry 159

Chapter 20 - Quantum Securities Limited 183

Chapter 21 - British Bangladesh Chamber of Commerce 189

Chapter 22 - Misapprehension 201

Chapter 23 - Queen Mary University 205

Chapter 24 - Political Affiliation 213

Chapter 25 – Second Chance 231

Chapter 26 – Origin 235

Chapter 27 – Leadership 239

What the Press says 246

APPENDIX 256

ACCLAMATION 270

INDEX 282

Preface

It was total serendipity that I found myself at the heart of my community. Before the Bangladeshis arrived in the 1970s, Brick Lane had been the epitome of success for many communities including the Huguenots, the Jews and the rest.

And it became the epicentre of all my enterprises and initiatives. Naz Cinema, Glamour International, Milfa Travels, Milfa Shipping, Milfa Sterling Exchange, Café Naz, Pandora, Asian Post, Notun Din, Sylto Distributing Co., and Sylto Plc. They all paved the path for me to become the first Bangladeshi millionaire at the heart of East London. Historically, the immigrants that made their fortunes in Brick Lane, Spitalfields and Shoreditch would eventually move to leafy suburbia. But to date I still maintain a foothold in Brick Lane.

Writing my memoir – my personal story and that of my community and how they are woven inextricably – is intended to inspire. I want to motivate the next generation to aspire and achieve as my generation has done. Through enterprise, initiative, politics, science, and law, Bangladeshis in Britain have achieved great heights. We have four parliamentarians in the house of Commons – Rushanara Ali, Tulip Siddiq, Rupa Huq and Apsana Begum. Baroness Pola Manzila Uddin in the house of Lords and Luftur Rahman, the Executive Mayor of Tower Hamlets Council. We have many doctors, scientists, King's Councillors, City highflyers, High Commissioners and Ambassadors in the British foreign service. All these achievements should motivate us to excel more.

My community has come a long way from where we were, yet we want to continue to ascend – the sky is the limit!

UK Parliament Hansard

April 26th 1999

Lord Williams of Mostyn

'My Lords, with the leave of the House, I should like to repeat a Statement made by my right honourable friend the Home Secretary in another place'. The Statement is as follows:

'With permission, Madam Speaker, I should like to make a Statement about the bomb explosions in Brixton and Brick Lane'.

'Last week on Saturday 17th April, the explosion in a busy market street in Brixton injured 39 members of the public and three police officers. This Saturday, at about the same time, another improvised device exploded in Brick Lane in East London, injuring six people. In both cases no warnings were given'.

'I know that I speak for the whole House in expressing my deep sympathy for those injured in these blasts, for their families and friends and our admiration for the very prompt way in which the police, fire and ambulance services responded'.

Chapter One
Miraculous Escape

1999

The blast was so intense that it seemed the whole world was crashing down on me. Buildings shook. Windows shattered. Debris flew everywhere. Dark, black smoke filled the sky. Panic gripped those caught in the explosion.

It had happened again, a second attack that month — a second nail bomb attack on an immigrant community in the heart of London. It was Saturday late afternoon, 24 April 1999, on Brick Lane, a street famous for its curry houses, a vibrant, bustling area at the east end of the capital, the hub of the city's Bangladeshi community.

A week earlier, a similar bomb had exploded in the centre of Brixton, injuring 42 people. A one-year-old boy was left with a nail lodged in his skull. Fortunately, no one died, but not for the want of trying — there was a racist on the loose, willing to unleash violence and mayhem on the minority communities. The thickly populated immigrant community in the East End of London was his next target.

Rashmi, my then wife, had called and asked me to meet her and our daughter Monique at Milfa Travel, 21 Brick Lane. This was our travel shop, 30 feet across the road from my famous restaurant Café Naz. I was sat in the window of Café Naz when she called and walked over to meet her, striding past the red car parked outside.

I had barely put my foot through the door of Milfa Travel when the bomb went off. The earth shook. I felt the entire building above Milfa

Travel was going to crash down on me. As the force of the tremor hurled me to the ground, I instinctively turned around and saw a huge fire ball shooting up into the sky. The blast tore off the boot of the red car where the bomb had been. It flew up into the air that was now thick with billowing black smoke.

Windows everywhere were shattered. Shrapnel rocketed — bits of metal, nails, shattered glass; the debris blanketed the entire area.

Pedestrians on either side of the road had been thrown to the ground by the force of the blast. A man had blood gushing out of his thigh. Others suffered lacerations from shattered glass. One of the worst injuries I saw was suffered by Emdad Talukder, who some years later was awarded an MBE for opening a fostering and adoption centre for the Muslim community in Tower Hamlets. His head had been split open by a two-inch piece of flying glass. A doctor we only knew as Dr Huq was visiting a relative in Brick Lane at the time, and Mr. Talukder maintains that he would have bled to death had it not been for the medic.

Police were on the scene almost instantly. As confusion and mayhem set in, you could hear them shouting:

'Nobody move...'
'Everyone stay where you are...'
'Stay inside and shut your doors...'

But even though the police tried desperately to take control of the situation, those caught up in the blast were frantic.

Nobody knew what was happening. It was chaos.

Monique, who was five at the time, was terrified, crying, shaking and dribbling. Rashmi was in a state of shock. She had been thrown to the ground by the colossal force of the blast but managed to cling on to our precious Monique and did her best to comfort her.

Police cordoned off the area in a matter of minutes. For safety reasons, no one could leave the area. Monique was becoming more hysterical. We could not comfort her. I begged a policeman to let me take her to a safer place. I wasn't allowed. We had to stay put. The bomb blast affected her deeply. My little Monique was totally traumatised. This horror and commotion must have affected her subliminal mind. For a while afterwards, she would wake up crying in the middle of the night. Sudden noise would startle her, she would be apprehensive and start crying. She was later put in a special psychological care unit at her Westlodge private infant school for a considerable time.

Monique's trauma affected me emotionally. At times I could not comfort her. I felt frustrated. I also suffered commercial losses. The force of the blast was so ferociously powerful, that it blew the door of Café Naz inwards, swept through the interior and smashed into the 3ft reinforced concrete wall at the back of the dining hall. It ricocheted off the wall and tore back through the room until it hit the front window. Fortunately, this was made of laminated safety glass, so it didn't break but bulged outwards, ballooning into the street. It was such a strange sight that people came to take photographs of it.

Although six people were hurt, miraculously nobody was seriously injured, and no one was killed. The council offered financial assistance to everyone affected.

A House of Lords delegation headed by Lord Levison came to visit Café Naz, to show empathy and support to the community, and to encourage us to remain strong, united and unwavering in the face of this racial attack.

PAGE 4   **THE MIRROR**, Monday, April 26, 1999

THE BOMBI

MIRACL

Restaurant boss tells how he escap

ANGER: Oona yesterday

Britain will not give in to racists

By OONA KING
Labour MP for Tower Hamlets

By CHARLIE BAIN, GRAHAM BROUGH, ADAM McGUIREAN AND JONATHAN HUTTER

MILLIONAIRE restaurant owner Muquim Ahmed escaped the Brick Lane explosion by seconds, thanks to a phone call from his wife.

SAFE: Ahmed with his wife and children

STATEMENT BY THE COMMAND COUNCIL OF THE WHITE WOLVES

codeword:

statement begins:

Notice is hereby given t all non-whites & jews(defined blood, not religion) must perm ently leave The British Isles before the year is out

Jews & non-whites who main after 1999 has ended will be exterminated.

When the clock strikes midnight on 31/12/99 the W Wolves will begin to howl, when the wolves begin to the wolves begin to hunt. You have been warned.

HAIL BRITANNIA!

statement ends

BRAVE: Dr Haq helped a bomb victim

EVIL: The White Wolves sent this message of hate to newspaper

Gushing

BRICK LANE

THE MIRROR, Monday, April 26, 1999   PAGE 5

MILLIONAIRE

...ast with just seconds to spare thanks to wife's phone call

BRICK LANE E.1.
ব্রিক লেন

AFTERMATH: A pall of smoke rises into the sky from the burnt-out shell of the car inside which the Brick Lane bomb exploded.

FROM PAGE ONE

measures." Police were probing a range of threats, added Mr Venom.

He said: "They're terse and uncorroborated, but we're treating them seriously."

Last Monday, Asian journalists in Brick Lane were told in a C18 phone call "Remember Brixton – you're next."

Anti-racist campaigner Suresh Grover says he passed a letter from Combat 18 to police on Thursday. It listed seven sites for future bombings – including Tower Hamlets, the borough which covers Brick Lane.

It also threatened schools, hospitals and businesses in the Irish Republic" and "Irish Catholics".

But Mr Grover alleges police are unable to find the hand-written note, postmarked Portsmouth and the Isle of Wight.

Since then yesterday's bomb a caller alleging to be a member of C18 phoned police from a pay phone in New Malden, south west London, claiming responsibility.

Police accept both blasts have been aimed at blacks and Asians, possibly as a result of the inquiry into the racist killing of black teenager Stephen Lawrence.

But they do not know if C18, another extremist group or a lone madman is behind them.

More than 100 people in mainly Asian Southall have offered to patrol streets.

● Voice of The Mirror – Page 6

MENACE OF THE WOLVES

By GRAHAM BROUGH and ADAM McGIBBON

NEO-NAZI terror group the White Wolves are named after their territories, it emerged yesterday.

Mike Whine, of the Board of Jewish Deputies, said: "They may comprise only half a dozen people but you do not need many to carry out an act of violence.

"Their letters are fairly amateurish in terms of their phraseology but the danger is very real because the people whom we know to be involved in the group have a history of violence.

"They first emerged in the fascist organisation Combat 18 several years ago and are named after a Serb terrorist group that was terrorising Kosovans.

"Some people from Britain and Germany had gone as vol-

unteers to Serbia and brought the name back with them.

"It featured in racist literature distributed a few years ago."

When the Wolves broke away from Combat 18 in 1994 they released a 15-page "manifesto" full of race-hate.

Gerry Gable, editor of the anti-fascist magazine Searchlight, said: "They are intelligent in a perverse way.

"They may not be involved in the usual fascist activities like stirring up football violence."

In recent weeks up to 25 people have contacted the Jewish Deputies after receiving scribbled death threats from the Wolves. A vile warning from the hate group was among chilling threats issued before Saturday's explosion in Brick Lane.

Asians at the Eastern Eye newspaper office nearby had a menacing phone call last Monday in which a member of Combat 18 said: "Remember Brixton on Saturday – you're next."

A message also arrived from the Wolves saying non-whites and Jews in Britain after this year would be exterminated. The stencilled sheet turned up the day before the Brixton bombing.

Eastern Eye editor Siddartha Shrivsami passed it on to police.

He said: "Next week it could be Golders Green that's hit."

WRECK: Brick Lane bomb car...

THE MIRROR

The opposition leader at the time, William Hague, also visited Café Naz and condemned this racial atrocity. Because that's what it was — a race attack.

A week later, on 30 April 1999, a bomb containing 1,500 nails exploded at the Admiral Duncan pub on Old Compton Street in Soho, where the customers were mostly gay. Seventy people were injured. Three sadly died.

The following day, police raided a house in Cove, Hampshire where they arrested David Copeland, and discovered explosive materials. They also discovered Nazi memorabilia and newspaper clippings of the bombings. Copeland, 22, was a self-confessed Nazi. He said he wanted to 'set fire to the country and stir up a racial war'. He had tried to do this by leaving the Brick Lane bomb, hidden in the black sports bag, on the pavement of Hanbury Street. He had meant to leave it at Petticoat Lane, during Sunday market, when thousands of people would have been milling around.

Luckily, he got his days mixed up. He came on a Saturday instead. He found the area deserted. Instead of taking the bag home, he left it on the pavement of Hanbury Street.

A passer-by found it and thought it was a builder's forgotten tool bag. He put it in the boot of his red car, intending to drop it at the police station. He drove down to Brick Lane police station, parked his car outside Café Naz, and went across to the police station next to Milfa Travel to see if it was open to hand over the supposedly lost tool bag. Moments later, carnage. The bomb could have gone off while this man was driving the car.

But neither he nor I were destined to die that day. There is an old Bengali saying: Rakhe Allah Mare Ke. It means man cannot destroy when Allah wants to save. David Copeland could not do that on 24 April 1999, despite his hateful efforts. In June 2000, more than a year after the bombings, he was handed six life sentences and told he would spend a minimum of 50 years in jail.

Many of us from the immigrant community came close to losing our lives in 1999. Had it not been for my wife's timely phone call, I may well have been killed. I became a victim of a terrifying form of racism, pure hate for the immigrant. Racism, a distaste for another race in some form or another, emanates from paranoia. A fear of difference. This manifests in bigotry. Racism and prejudice have always existed between white and the black, Muslim and Hindu, Christian and Jew, and also within those groups. But it is the will and determination to extinguish these hates, when they raise their nasty heads, that is the essence of multicultural society.

Respect for life and human dignity must be at the heart of existence. This philosophy is ingrained in all religion with the intention of making the world a better place so that we all can live in harmony.

Bangla Town gate to Brick Lane

Chapter Two
Immigrant

1974

'Young man, you say you are going to England to study?'

'Yes, Sir.'

'And you will return home after completion of your studies?'

'Most certainly, Sir. I am returning to join my family enterprise.'

The entry clearance officer hesitated, staring at me in silence from behind his desk at Dhaka High Commission. I grew uncomfortable beneath his gaze.

'But how can I be certain?' He said finally, his tone still friendly but his words unsettling.

'Sir?'

'What if you like it in the UK? What if you want to stay?'

'No, Sir. It's already decided, Sir.'

He paused a second time, his eyes on me again.

'Young man,' he said: 'I can't say for certain that you will not return and that you will want to settle in England. I am obliged to take your word for it. Since all your papers are in good order, I therefore cannot refuse your visa.'

He stamped my passport and handed it over. 'Here is your entry clearance.'

'Thank you, Sir,' I said, accepting it with a trembling hand.

It was 6 August 1974. I was 19 years old. Within two weeks, on 18th August, I left Bangladesh for the first time, bound for London.

There remains a belief – perhaps a myth – on the Indian sub-continent that if a person is to succeed in life, he must have a higher qualification from the mother of all nations, the United Kingdom.

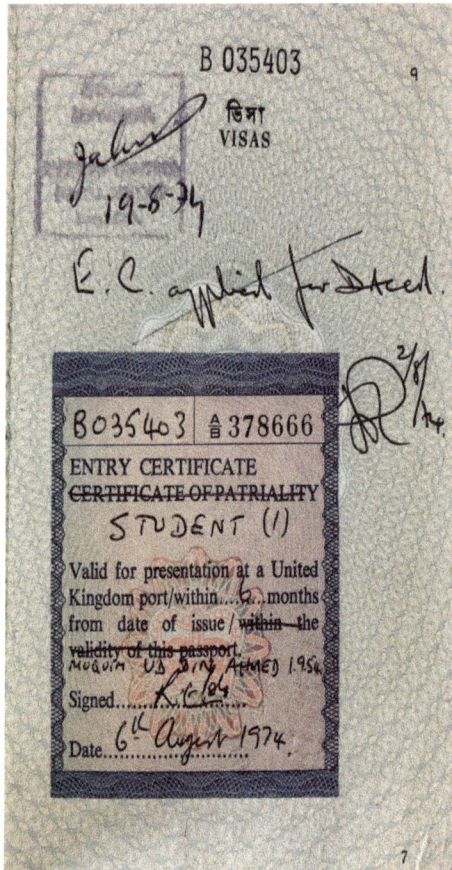

Whether such a belief is fact or fiction, there is enough evidence to suggest there's more than a grain of truth to it. The elite of our society – the leaders of our nations, the army generals, the 'best' doctors and the 'best' lawyers and accountants – were all educated in Britain. My parents certainly believed it, insisting that their youngest son's final education should be in England. My eldest brother, Moin, already in London at the time, secured a place for me to study engineering at Southeast London College of Technology (SELTEC), Lewisham, on the understanding that I should return home with the acquired knowledge to run Tito Industrial Engineers, our machine tool factory in Bangladesh.

I dreamt of the day I'd return home to Bangladesh with the education that would change the trajectory of my life and that of my family. That day never came either. It seems that man behind his desk at Dhaka High Commission had a point after all. His prediction did come true, I did not return.

The student became the immigrant.

Muquim Ahmed with student friends of MC College, Sylhet, Bangladesh 1970

"Preparation is the infallible element in winning the battle of struggle in life."

Chapter Three
Early Days

I was born in 1954 in Sylhet to Haji Mubarak Ahmed and Begum Omarjan Bibi. My sister Rokiya Begum was 18 years older than me; my two brothers, Muslehuddin (Muslim) and Moinuddin (Moin) were 21 and 23 years older than me respectively. I was an unexpected child, it's fair to say. I recall thinking that everyone around me was a giant compared to me and as I got older it would occasionally cross my mind that I was adopted, which of course I wasn't.

When I was very young, my mother lived between our Sylhet town house and our village home, but she spent more time in the village as that was really her world where she managed the household and entertained on behalf of my father. Consequently, I was mainly in the care of one of our servants – Harish Ali – and my brother Moin, which is why I consider my brother to be the person who brought me up. In addition, in 1959 when I was five, Moin married Nurun. Since they didn't have children for quite a few years, Nurun really babied me. I would fall asleep in their bed and then, when my brother came home, which was often late, he would carry me into my own bed. This was a bed he had custom made for me, not a full-size bed. I was an affectionate child, and I loved all the attention.

Once, when I was around four years old, Harish Ali and I strolled into Lamabazar, a small crossroad market, about half a mile from the town house.

But when we returned home, we discovered he had lost the front-door key. He cried buckets and prayed to Shaha Jalal, a saint in Sylhet Town, for help to find the key. An hour later, Moin arrived to bring Harish some much needed relief. After supper when Moin was putting me to bed, he found the key in my back pocket.

As I got older, Madhovi Ghose, Moin's friend and our next-door neighbour, would escort me to Shishu School for infants on her way to the Government Girls' School. Shishu was within the compound of the girls' school. I think Madhovi taking me to school and sitting me on her lap is my first memory.

Before I was born, my parents lived in the town house so my brothers could continue their studies at Raja G C High School, Sylhet. And by the time I was born, my father had already packed up his business and retired. He was thinking about settling in the town house for good and by the time I was of school-age, my father had sold all his village properties and permanently settled in Sylhet. Our father helped Moin and Muslim to establish businesses – a travel agency called Pakistan Overseas Express, and a ready-made garment store called Eastern Fancy Store. Within a few years, Muslim opened another shop in Hassan Market (a shopping center built by Sylhet municipality in 1950s). Moin extended his travel agency by opening few more branches.

In 1960, when I was six, and as a result of a disagreement with Moin, Muslim moved to London. And in 1961, we had a new house built. Called Mubarak Monzil, it was built in Shibgong, a mile and a half away from Lamabazar. Tons of timber was brought in from the hilly regions of the Chittagong Hill Tracts. Picked up from the train by trucks and ferried to the building sites, the logs were then sawn into different length and sizes. Many men were engaged to build the house; a local architect helped to design and build it.

I became one of the first students to attend the Blue Bird School, a co-educational kindergarten, when it was established in 1961. The school was situated in a building with a corrugated tin roof on the hilltop opposite the Manikpirer Tila (mountain). It was the first English-medium school established by the elite in Sylhet for their own children. The renowned philanthropist and businessman Aminur Rashid, owner of Jugo Bari, a weekly newspaper, and also owner of Rashid Tea Estate, was among the people who sponsored the school. There were a few English Memsahib (white ladies) who were the teachers at that time, notably Jill Khan, the first headmistress.

Students in my class included Niser, Rafi, Tauhid, Zafar and Momen – the brother of Yamin Choudhury, the famous freedom fighter from Sylhet. Harold Rashid, Tahera Rashid and Shamim Uddin were also founding students. They were children of prominent families of the town and remain friends of mine today. Zafar is in Canada and Tahera Rashid has now returned from the USA and settled in Dhaka. Shamim is the sister of my childhood best friend Sajjad Hayat whose husband Safwan Choudhury is probably now the richest person in Sylhet. Safwan owns a few tea estates, composite textile mills, and many other enterprises including Bank Asia.

Aged seven, I became embroiled in a fight at the playground. I broke Tauhid's tooth (which was loose anyway). I remember the detention to this day – I had to kneel and hold my ears between my legs for a whole period, approximately an hour. I also truanted and was getting mixed up with a local gang.

Due to my behaviour and truanting, my family felt they had no choice and in 1963, after three years at the Blue Bird School, I was sent as a boarder to Our Lady Fatima Cambridge School in Comilla, a district town 150 miles from Sylhet.

I was only nine at the time and at first, I was very sad to have been sent away from home and cried at night. I missed everyone and again wondered if I was adopted.

Our Lady Fatima Cambridge School was a foundation co-education school, a convent school renowned throughout the whole of Pakistan, run by American nuns. Tahera Rashid, Sajjad Hayat, Faisal Rashid, Ivan, Harold, Eva, Sabiha, Akthari and Ferdous Rahman were my classmates there and to this day, I keep in touch with some of them.

Boys and girls from all around the then Pakistan were sent to this school. From 1963, when I started there, to 1965, the principal of Our Lady Fatima Cambridge School was Sister Mary Leo. The school building was a huge structure, housing the hostel on the first and second floors. Boys up to the age of 10 were taken as boarders before 1963 but then the school started taking older boys.

The school was expanding so fast that it commissioned a separate hostel for boys. This resulted in the sourcing and establishing, in 1963, of living quarters at De Launey House, an estate consisting of a few acres of land, two huge lakes and a mansion consisting of around 40 rooms. One part of De Launey House was turned into dormitories while the other was kept for private use.

The kitchen was detached from the main house, with the capacity for six to eight servants to work together and serve the masters through a passage that led to the dining areas in the main property. Phil De Launey lived there at that time. He had nothing to do with the educational side of things but ran the hostel. He married a local woman.

De Launey House was designed to mimic the manor houses of the English countryside.

The grand mansion sat in the middle of a 10-acre plot with the main gate. There was a majestic bamboo hedge alongside the Macadam Road, the lakes, the playing fields and beyond the agricultural land on either side.

There were garages for automobiles at the back end of the property. These had probably been stables and cow sheds at one time. We were told that the De Launeys also had elephants for hazardous journeys and transportation through jungles, common at that time.

The front of the manor house had gigantic steps leading up to the extended veranda which dominated the front of the building. This facade and the main building were constructed on raised ground probably back filled some five or six feet high. The back of the building also had steps but not as grand as the ones in the front. There were two rows of about 10 steps attached on the sides.

The lake on the front of the property was right opposite the entrance steps and across the road. It had a pair of concrete benches that made steps into the lake. At the back of the house was another lake, but smaller, with similar bench steps into it.

During the summer, every Saturday in the front lake, boys were taught to swim – including me. There were two guides assigned to every six boys. Senior boys were allowed to swim in the lake behind the building. It was the older sister of Phil De Launey's wife who held me as I splashed my way to being able to swim.

During the summer holidays, Mr. De Launey allowed fishermen to cast huge nets into the lake to catch the fish. The fishermen no doubt paid well for this privilege. None of us boarders ever witnessed the catch, but we heard lots of gossip about it. De Launey house also had a lot of paddy fields. Rice and vegetables were grown, some of which was consumed by us boarders and the rest sold in the market.

There were exotic fruit trees, like olive, cashew nut, guava, amloki (gooseberry), mango, coconut, and many more which were rarely grown in other parts of the then East Pakistan.

The origin of De Launey Koti (house) is a fascinating story. Phil De Launey was probably the fourth or fifth De Launey to be living there when I was a boarder. His forefathers came with the British Raj, built this koti and then ruled over the district of Comilla. During the partition of India, Phil's only sibling Paul De Launey opted for the properties in England leaving Phil with everything in Comilla. De Launey house had many valuable artefacts including huge Chinese vases and classical black metal sculptures. Most notable of all these was the Master Bed, which was used by Lord Robert Clive – the Englishman trader who was the first to conquer Bengal in the Battle of Plassey against Shiraj ud Daulah the Nowab of Bengal in 1757. I understand this bed is in the Jadu Ghar (Dhaka Museum) and is a national treasure.

Because of Phil De Launey, the missionaries from America anchored themselves in Comilla and built the church and the missionary school. The missionaries' objective was, of course, to spread Christianity into the local needy population. The school was divided into two time zones. One starting at 8am and the other beginning at midday. The first was designed for rich people's children and the teaching medium was English – this was my group. The second group were taught in Bengali. White American nuns taught us in the morning session and indigenous Bengali teachers taught in the afternoon. The afternoon Bengali medium school was free.

There came a time when our rich fee-paying parents objected to the morning prayers which were mandatory in a Christian school and in 1965, Sister Mary Leo was deported by the then Pakistani government due to this and perhaps other reasons.

Sister Mary Joan of Arc took charge as the principal of the school. She was also our maths teacher.

Sister Mary Josepha was my class tutor. She was an excellent and compassionate teacher who instilled in me, and others, the foundation of the English language. She had an uncanny and unerring ability to understand what a particular student was good at. She had that unique ability to see if any, the innate talent possessed by her students. She took personal interest in me and gave me extra tuition for which I had to walk from De Launey house to school every Sunday evening. She was meticulous and stringent. I got spanked twice for not doing my homework. I must add here that the school was a ten-minute walk from the hostel.

Sister Mary Annett taught us literature in standard seven (age 13) and her teaching method was revolutionary. She encouraged us to pick a literary book from the library and then made us write a book report on it.

This report was to be in a book form with a hard cover with the outline and the moral of the story (if there was one) explained. We were also encouraged to comment on the style of writing. In the end, we created a sort of abridged version of the actual book. This method became the mainstay in our studies of English language and literature. We studied Shakespeare, Charles Dickens, Somerset Maugham, Pearl S Buck's The Good Earth, Leo Tolstoy's War and Peace, Daniel Defoe's Robinson Crusoe, Jonathan Swift's Gulliver's Travels and many more classics. If we were really struggling with a particular text, she would buy us the abridged version.

I was passionate about these books, the classics, and had a wonderful collection, which remains at the first home I bought in the UK – Mount Mascal Farm. I wish I read more these days. Perhaps I'll get back into it. I still wish I had studied even more literature at school than science, but there we are. So many of us can look back and wonder how things might have been different or wish that they were.

Something of which I am very proud is that every one of us was taught American penmanship style. This is also known as Spencerian script, based on copperplate script, which was considered the standard writing style for business correspondence prior to the widespread adoption of the typewriter. Platt Rogers Spencer, after whom the style was named, was inspired by the smoothness of pebbles in a stream to create a style of writing that could be written quickly and legibly for business purposes, as well as elegant letter writing. The logos of both Coca Cola and Ford Motors are written in Spencerian script.

As a result of this wonderful instruction, you can tell just by looking at my handwriting that I am from either Our Lady Fatima (OLF), or the other two missionary schools in Dhaka or Chittagong. The boys and girls educated in those schools acquired a foundation that propelled us into the world with a good understanding of English, maths, science and social subjects.

When I was growing up in the 1960s, the status jobs were to be a doctor or an engineer and from the age of 12 or 13, I wanted to be an engineer so that I could make things. I feel OLF had a great hand in forming my early persona and intellect, exerting a significant influence on who I have become today.

As a result, I have always believed it is important for children to receive a good education in their formative years – an education that infuses them with the moral boundaries and the customs and manners of the society in which they live. Students who graduated from Our Lady Fatima have successfully established themselves in affluent societies all around the world.

In 1967, after four years at OLF, I was sent to Dawood Public School in Jessore. I had been expelled from De Launey house – not the school, where I was considered a scholar, but the hostel where I was unruly.

The school and the hostel were different entities. Phil De Launey was the sole operator, and his decision was final. In all honesty, I was a bit of a fiery kid.

I had a fight with another pupil called Robert Hall and was once slapped by Mr. De Launey because I put a dead spider under the pillow of my roommate Faisal Rashid. I knew Faisal was frightened of spiders, but I did it for a dare, encouraged by the other boys.

I also balanced a shoe on the top of a door, which landed on matron's head. She was not amused. I had only been threatened with being hit once before, by Moin, for truanting. He had tied me up, ready to hit me with a stick but my mother caught him and stopped him. Phil De Launey only hit me lightly, but I fell to the floor and wouldn't get up when he told me to. I thought if I got up, he would hit me again. I was furious at Phil and took revenge on him by punching, and cracking, all the mahogany door panels on the hostel side of the manor. Blood poured from my knuckles as I did it, but I was determined to get even. My sense of justice played on my childish mind and compelled me to enact retribution. I still have a scar on my middle finger as a result. Moin was the main person I spoke to regarding my expulsion, and he was understanding overall and probably sympathetic, as were my parents.

Were these misdemeanours merely the natural energy and mischievousness of a young boy or some deeper, underlying issue? My guess, since I have been a very respectable adult would be the former. Not that I am any kind of pushover. I can only be pushed so far as people have occasionally found out. But I do consider myself a rational and calm gentleman and feel that it was Dawood Public School that moulded me to be the man I am today – disciplined, regimental, focused and resilient. No longer the unruly kid of De Launey house or the difficult child at Blue Bird School.

Dawood's school foundation stone was laid by Ayub Khan, the President of Pakistan on September 3, 1959. Ayub Khan seized the country in a coup in 1958 and remained in power until 1969.

Dawood Public School was founded by the great philanthropist, Sir Adamjee Haji Dawood Bawany, the man who funded the newly independent Pakistan government in 1947. Sir Adamjee funded over a dozen schools and colleges in Pakistan including a good number in the now Bangladesh. His business acumen was brilliant and his work ethic excellent. He was one in a billion and his conglomerates encompassed more than 40 operatives across finance. His root trade of consumer goods was world class with an empire that extended over several continents.

In 1927, the Burmese Government nationalised his industries as did India, later, and subsequently Pakistan (during Bhutto's administration). The Bangladesh government nationalised the biggest jute mills in the world – Admjee Jute Mills – which had 25,000 staff and thousands of looms. A huge living complex was built in Khalishpur, around the mills in Khulna, Bangladesh. King George VI knighted Adamjee in June 1938 and Pakistan honoured him on August 14, 1999, with the minting of a postage stamp.

Many thousands of us owe a great deal to this man who was born in Jetpur, Kathiawar, Gujarat, India on June 30, 1880.

Dawood Public School was a beautifully constructed building, with plenty of grounds, situated in the middle of Jessore Army Cantonment (barracks).

Nelson Gomes, the vice principal of the school, was a man of strong virtue and formidable disposition. He instilled into his students a sense of purpose and belonging, and a belief that we must strive and succeed in whatever we do and push forwards however bad the situation. He made his students independent thinkers. 'Take a situation, adverse or dreadful,' he would say, 'rein it in and bring it to your advantage.' He was a great teacher, and motivator, bringing out the best in a student by encouraging and hammering in the faith and belief that one can do it. He was strict and vociferous but meant well. We were all respectful and fearful of his indomitable character.

Dawood Public School, Jessore

His teaching methods sought to instil self-discipline, self-sacrifice and dedication to duty.

Not everyone was a fan of Mr. Nelson and there was a plan by senior boys, one night to wait until he was in the room, then switch the lights off, pounce on him and beat him up, perhaps kill him. I had learned my lesson in De Launey house and didn't want to join in, even though Mr. Nelson had hit me with a ruler for poor spelling. The plan was in full motion when just as the lights went out, the principal Lilly Khan's car came up the drive, her car lights hit the room and ruined the plan. It all came out in the open and three boys – the gang leaders – were expelled. I had learned my lesson and obviously kept my distance from the trouble.

Literature wasn't held in as high esteem at Dawood as it had been at the convent, and I missed it. But extra-curricular activities were paramount in this school's philosophy and sports were compulsory, which made me very happy as I could spend my energy physically.

The school was divided into two teams, Green House and Red House, to encourage competition. I belonged to the Red House. The school uniform was grey half pants (long shorts) and white shirts and a striped, blue tie. The house distinction was wrapped round a flap on the shirt's shoulder or the shoulder of the kamis on the girls' uniform. We played all sort of sports: football, cricket, baseball, volleyball, badminton, table tennis. On sports day we participated in javelin, shot put, long jump, marathon, high jump, pole jump and so on. There was also a Scout troop, which was part of the curriculum.

The school bus picked up the boarders at 7.45am and deposited us at school 15 minutes later ready for assembly at 8am. There were around 50 of us. School finished at 1pm and we would return to the hostel for lunch, having been given time to freshen up. In the dining hall, which was also a theatre of learning, everyone took up their respective seats. When a bell rang, we all sat down.

A second bell would ring, and we would all shout 'Bismillah Hir Rahman Nir Rahim', meaning, 'In the name of Allah, The Most Gracious and The Most Merciful' (like saying grace), and then start eating our food. It was the duty of a senior boy to read while everyone ate quietly.

After reading for 10 minutes or so, and stopping at the end of a chapter, the bell would ring again for everyone to be at ease and continue eating and chatting freely.

After lunch, everyone would disperse to their dormitories to retire for the afternoon and nap (like Spanish siesta). Then, at 4.45pm, an usher would ring the bell for everyone to get ready for compulsory evening sport, which began at 5pm.

You had to dress in the correct sporting attire, which was dictated by the school's uniform rules. After getting dressed, everyone queued up in front of their dormitory and in an orderly manner marched towards the three playing fields which were close to the dormitories. A bell would ring again at 6pm to end the activities, then another ring would indicate we should shower and prepare for evening studies at 6.30pm. Between 6.30pm and 7.30pm, it was homework time.

Mr. Nelson would be at hand to help most of the time, although sometimes senior boys would help juniors. Dinner was served at 8pm. Boys would be required to be in hostel uniform: full khaki pants, blue shirt and red tie. A senior would read a book or speak on a topic of current affairs. We attended mosque at Arifpur Rail gate every Friday afternoon for Jumma prayer which was a stone's throw from the hostel.

I loved the sport at Dawood and in addition, I was given the opportunity to learn boxing, just me and two other students.

One of our teachers was a former boxer in the army and spotted my natural skill. I was the best out of the three of us and I was really good at defending myself and getting out of the way quickly!

This came in handy when one senior boy, due to the fact that I wore glasses, called me blind.

I asked him not to, but he repeated it three times and pushed me and pushed me, until I couldn't take any more and punched him. I was in trouble for hitting a senior boy, but Mr. Nelson understood the provocation and let me off the hook.

I was so precocious, so steadfast and so regimental in my pursuit of studies and extra-curricular activities, that I was chosen to be the school and hostel captain a semester early. My obedience to teachers, my attitude, ability and skill to manage and command, convinced both Lilly Khan and Nelson Gomes that I was worthy of such an appointment.

Lilly Khan, the school principal, made a lasting impression on my life. She was a remarkable woman who received the Presidential Award from Ayub Khan – the then President of Pakistan – for turning Dawood Public School of Jessore into the best teaching school in the whole of Pakistan. During her retirement and residence in the United Kingdom in the 80s, she was awarded the MBE from Queen Elizabeth II for her social action in the community.

During my final year in Dawood Public School, I was given the task of running the school for a week. I sat in the corner of Mrs. Khan's office and acted as the principal. This was an incredible experience, valuable beyond words. Giving assembly, meeting parents and sorting out an incident in the playground were the highlights of the week – all of which took place under the watchful eyes of Mrs. Khan.

Social responsibility, compassion and care for the poor was at the top of Mrs. Khan's agenda and she instilled these philosophies into her pupils.

One way in which she did this was to create a programme to help the people who lived in the villages that surrounded the hostel, which was at the border of the cantonment at Arifpur Rail gate.

At the end of the month after Friday prayers, boys were divided into 10 groups and chose 10 families in the village to help and guide them towards prosperity.

My group, five of us, were assigned to a young family who needed to buy a gunny – a tool with which to grind rice. We helped this family organise their household and used our own pocket money to buy them the rice grinder.

At the end of term, the groups reported on their experiences and the progress made by the relevant families. The class tutor collected the reports and submitted them to the principal to contribute towards the results of the annual award. I received the all-rounder championship certificate for the year 1969.

School Leaving Certificate

Throughout my school years, I would go home three or four times annually for a few weeks. It was always lovely to see my family and they were kept up to date with my school news since I wrote to them quite regularly. Sometimes during the holidays, I met up with other boarders including Sajjad Hayat whose father was the divisional manager at a tea estate in Sreemangal.

Perhaps because I was born so many years after my siblings, I did have a sense of being an outsider. But overall, I am so grateful for my time as a boarder, away from my family. I learned resilience and to rely on myself. If my wife Farzana goes away for a few days now, I don't have to worry – I can cook (albeit nothing complicated) and fend for myself.

For this reason, despite my initial sorrow at being separated from my family at the age of nine, I did want to send my own children to boarding school. I wanted my son Miraj to learn American penmanship like I had. But my wife Rashmi wouldn't hear of it, so there we have it.
Her viewpoint was that she'd had children and wanted to be with them. Who was I to argue? I had chosen a strong woman who, like my mother, knew her mind and her viewpoint and would not be shifted from it.

Dawood not only helped me to build my character through knowledge, leadership and awareness of social responsibility, but it also forged me to become self-confident, steadfast and unwavering in my aims and objectives. Not to be shy and selfish but resourceful and astute, to have a positive disposition. These qualities became enshrined in me.

They have helped me throughout my life and encouraged me not to dither or deviate but to be determined, methodical and resolute in pursuit of my goals.

Madam Khan, Sir Nelson and the other tutors played a superb and unique role in shaping us all at Dawood.

'Brave and strong, persistent, and bold
Focused and determined shall never fold'

After passing my Secondary School Certificate (SSC) in 1970 with four letters – distinction and national scholarship – (appdx 256) from Jessore Board, Dawood Public School, I was admitted to MC College. I left Dawood with many honours.

The College was just half a mile from my home in Sylhet and the first college in the Sylhet Division. It was established in 1892, making it the seventh oldest college in Bangladesh. Since its creation, it has played an important role in the educational, cultural and political spheres of Greater Sylhet. It is affiliated with Bangladesh National University and in 2000, the college won the national award as the country's best educational institution.

Raja Girish Chandra Roy of Roynagar in Sylhet established the college and named it after his maternal great-grandfather, Murari Chand Roy. Originally there were four teachers and 18 students. It was located beside the present Raja GC High School in Bander Bazar. At the beginning, it was a proprietary college funded by Chandra himself. The original college building collapsed in 1897 in the Assam earthquake.

Though Chandra survived the quake and ensuing devastation, it made him financially vulnerable, and he had to beg the government to take over the college. They did so in 1908 and on April 1, 1912, the college become fully government administered.

In my first year, I was elected as the sports and common room secretary of the Chandra League, a student organisation founded by Bongo

Bhandu Sheikh Mujibur Rahman, the first President of Bangladesh, who later became prime minster and was eventually proclaimed the father of the nation. I passed my HSC examination with distinction securing average star marks (appdx 257). I then continued my education HSC and honours in Physics at MC College from 1970-74 (appdx 258).

And then, with my formative years behind me, an excellent education for which I will always be grateful, a family background of excellence in business and the determination to succeed, on August 18, 1974, I travelled to the United Kingdom to pursue my engineering studies. In the UK at that time, class and race continued to stigmatise in subtle and in not-so-subtle ways. I had been upper class in Bangladesh and now, I could tell, by virtue of being an immigrant, I was very much lower class. It was, in some ways, quite a shock to my system and something that no doubt many immigrants and refugees experience all over the world to this day.

However, in my opinion and experience, in the UK with the election of Margaret Thatcher, the grocer's daughter, in 1979 – just a few years after my arrival, the class system was shattered, and meritocracy was proclaimed as the order of the day.

Thatcher liberated people and made upper class men like Michael Heseltine feel inferior and humble. For me, her election to power indicated that the sky was the limit. As I write, our Prime Minister is Rishi Sunak. A British Asian Hindu man who was born in Southampton to Southeast-African born Hindu parents of Indian Punjabi descent – incredible!

Chapter Four
War of Independence

I n 1971, when war broke out, my hometown was bombarded along with countless others. I was studying at MC College, which closed as a result. Lots of my classmates went to India to join the Mukti Bahini – the freedom fighters. My parents would not let me go to India, but instead sent me to the interior of the country to Hushenpur. This was far from the reaches of the Pakistan Army, who were plundering, killing and raping indiscriminately in as many towns as they could.

Hushenpur could only be reached by boat. My parents refused to leave their home but I went along with Moin, Nurun and their children. On that journey, I vividly remember seeing a sight which to this day, still fills me with sorrow, disgust and horror – a corpse floating in the river. The man's body was bloated, and he was still wearing his clothes. A heinous crime by the Pakistan Army. We witnessed this terrifying scene as we were escaping by boat from Sylhet town, along the river Surma.

My father no longer had properties in Burhampur which he had entirely sold in the early fifties to settle in Sylhet town. We had nowhere to go than to Hushenpur - the village home of Nurun's family. Her father owned lots of land and had a large bungalow. We were housed there, along with other relatives and people made homeless by the war, who fled from Sylhet town. There was barely a soul left in the towns.

In retrospect on October 15, 2022, two United States congressmen placed a proposed resolution in the house of representatives.

They urged President Joe Biden to consider recognising the atrocities committed by the Armed Forces of Pakistan, in the Bangladesh Liberation War of 1971, as crimes against humanity, war crimes and genocide. The bi-partisan resolution was proposed by Rep Chabot (R-Ohio) in association with Indian origin Rep Ro Khanna (D-Calif). The eight-page resolution entitled "Recognising the Bangladesh Genocide of 1971". It is estimated that up to 3 million of my countrymen, women and our nation's children were massacred.

The National Martyr's Memorial in Savar, Bangladesh

Chapter Five

Opportunity Knocks

– My Early Business Ventures
1974

When I left Bangladesh, I was so excited and overwhelmed with emotion. I was going to England to study! A place where our great leaders, doctors and lawyers had received their higher education. I had read so much about London, not least the adventures and pursuits of Sherlock Holmes created by Arthur Conan Doyle, which was a favourite novel when I was young. It was Charles Dickens and Shakespeare country, and I couldn't wait to see it with my own eyes instead of merely my imagination.

In a way I was sad too. I was leaving my parents behind, as well as my nieces, nephews, friends and relatives. I had profound respect and honour for my parents. I was brought up in the culture of deference and reverence.

They all came to see me off at the airport. I flew from Sylhet to Dhaka where Moin came to see me safely on my flight to London Heathrow. Due to Moin's connections, the captain of the aircraft knew me and spoke to me. We were a well-connected family and Moin was influential in the travel industry.

Muslim who had been between Bangladesh and London for 14 years by this stage met me at arrivals. He was so excited and gave me a huge hug before we got into his Austin Opal car. It was August, but I was freezing cold.

But cold as I was, I was staggered at the beauty of the country, which was so intensely green compared to home. A totally different climate, of course. Muslim and I went straight to his house. He had married Sokina in Bangladesh in 1969 at my father's house Mubarak Monzil. And now they lived with their children in a flat above their grocery business, Deshi (meaning home country) Store, in Hessel Street, East London, well known as the former home of London's main Jewish market. Sokina had prepared a banquet of Bangladeshi delights to make me feel at home.

Those first few days I had to acclimatise to the cold air, and Muslim would tuck me in tightly each night, ensuring I had enough blankets. I had packed my autograph book that all my school friends had written friendly and encouraging messages in – it was something everyone did back then. And my nicest shirts and trousers (also in my suitcase were some items from my mother for Muslim and his wife).

Muslim took me shopping, in Whitechapel, for a suit and a Sherlock Holmes style overcoat that I wore faithfully for 12 years. He also gave me some great advice to start reading a newspaper to increase my vocabulary and to ensure that I knew what was going on. I chose The Times and have been faithful to it, daily, ever since – until Covid, when I didn't want anything carrying germs to come into the house. So, I now get my news from Sky TV.

A few days after my arrival, Muslim took me to Southeast London College and paid my fees of £440. It was such a comfort to have my older brother beside me, knowing exactly what to do and I was extremely excited to be studying again. Speaking English which I was fluent in, thanks to my English medium education, came in handy and helped in my lectures at college. The Bangladeshi education system was not recognised at the time, so the college put me on the Ordinary National Diploma (OND) course.

It was all old stuff I knew, which I explained to my teacher Mr. Fitzgerald, so he put me on the Higher National Diploma (HND) course.

Once in the UK, it didn't take me long to realise that this was a country where opportunities to prosper and progress were way beyond those of my home country. Britain was and always will be the Land of Opportunities. An open society, a meritocracy, where you can arrive with nothing and through hard work and sheer determination make it to where you want to be. When determination meets opportunities, the sky becomes the limit. And boy, was I determined!

My zeal for enterprise knew no bounds. Side by side with my studies I began helping my brothers; Muslim in Deshi Store, his shop, and Moin who was importing various commodities and white goods into Bangladesh from various countries. We organised letters of credit from English banks to suppliers in Holland, Italy, Japan and Malaysia who would then ship the products to Chittagong port in Bangladesh. Business was soon so good that Moin established a clearing house and distribution centre in Chittagong.

The birth of our new nation – Bangladesh, in 1971 – was borne out of nine months of fierce war, the sacrifice of millions of lives and destruction of our infrastructure. The devastation meant that we had to import everything. There was an acute shortage of food and commodities. The challenges of this new nation afforded new opportunities. Many of us became exporters and importers out of sheer necessity. Moin saw the benefit to himself and to the nation of importing these various products and commodities, which were much needed to sustain the economy.

In Bangladesh there was the government's import-export board, of course, which did most of the essential imports; but some items were left to individual entrepreneurs, the private sector. Transport essentials such as buses, trucks and cars were all in great demand.

The government allowed the import of goods through the wage earners scheme. Those living in the United Kingdom could use their wages — pounds sterling — to import into Bangladesh. This benefited the government because it did not have to spend its foreign currency reserve on bringing those goods into the country.

The United Kingdom played an important role in this, as it did during the independence of Bangladesh, by being the first country to recognise it as an independent country. British banks were opening back-to-back letters of credit for goods to be imported into Bangladesh. In those days, other foreign banks were reluctant to accept letters of credit from Bangladeshi banks. Moin was importing essentials such as sugar, spices, palm oil and so on into Bangladesh and Muslim organised the money from the wage earners here in the United Kingdom. It was a family affair – any arguments of the past were forgotten long before.

So, every day after my lectures at Lewisham College, I would rush home to help at Deshi Store. It was open from 8am to 8pm, seven days a week. I would also help at weekends, fitting in with my college course work whenever time allowed. It was a busy, hectic time, and not just for me. Sokina would also be called upon to help in the shop on top of looking after the children Minhas, Yasmin and Matab, my nephews and niece aged one, three and five respectively. She also washed, cleaned, cooked and maintained the flat. I enjoyed the children's company and remembered going with them to London Zoo and Madame Tussauds. Deshi Store had two other staff, Jillu Miah and Towahid Ali.

I will go into more detail on the import and export business and Deshi Store later.

People are constantly striving to establish themselves, to grasp the moment, that opportunity, to flourish and prosper, to gain stability and achieve success. The migrant strives more than most, pushing their quality of life to new heights. But no matter how hard they push and how much they attain, the migrant still feels displaced, driving them on to achieve that little bit more.

Almost 50 years on from my arrival in the UK, as a British citizen and the first Bangladeshi millionaire, I feel both at home and yet still like a migrant and therefore slightly inferior. It's best to be honest about these things. Something in my biology, I suppose.

 My cells know they are far from home and that all things given, I can never, quite truly belong. In addition, the decades of colonial rule live within my genes – causing me to feel less than my fellow white man – even though I know it's not true that I am less than anyone who has been born in Britain.

There were so many rules that my great grandfather, for example, lived under – such as where he could and could not sit.

Many years after my arrival in London, I went for lunch with Oliver Letwin, who was asked by David Cameron his policy advisor at the time, to take me out for lunch. All because what I said at the dinner with David Cameron, Morgan Stanley, Lord Sainsbury and others, 'how the home grown terrorist problem could be resolved'. Oliver during the lunch told me that due to his forebears' experiences as displaced Jews, he still feels a certain sense of being an outsider and reassured me that it's dying out as the generations go on. That was quite some years ago now and perhaps he wouldn't be able to speak so confidently today, with the rise in antisemitism.

Today, I am happy with life and take it as easy as possible, but still striving, promising my children that I will leave them a comfortable endowment. They are doing well in their own right; they don't even need what I will give them, and they certainly don't ask for it. It's just in me.

RT HON OLIVER LETWIN MP

HOUSE OF COMMONS
LONDON SW1A 0AA
020 7219 3000

25 November 2006

Muquim Ahmed
Conservatives of Bethnal Green &
  Bow Association
46-48 Brick Lane
LONDON E4 6RF

Dear Mr Ahmed

Thank you for your kind letter of 10 November.

It was a delight to meet you for lunch – and I found the conversation most illuminating. I shall never forget your description of the insurance problem!

With best wishes.

Yours sincerely

Oliver Letwin

OLIVER LETWIN

Private Secretary: Mrs Angela Charles
Tel & Fax: 01308 456891   e-mail: charlesa@parliament.uk

My father made a success of life and he and my brothers set me up. I have gone above and beyond their wildest dreams and now I want to do the same for my son and daughter.

I do sometimes wonder what my grandfather, who sadly died young of cholera, would think of my lifestyle and that of my children. I'm sure he would be amazed, and I hope he would be proud.

However, in my early days in London, I was the quintessential aspiring migrant. I saw the opportunities and embraced them wholeheartedly. I kept in touch with my parents, writing letters, and through phone calls.

Part of an immigrant's life in any country is to support their families back home. Sending money back to our often-destitute relatives is a responsibility we willingly take on board. I was fortunate that my parents were well off, rather I had money transferred to me in London.

Within a year of my arrival in London my brothers bought another shop.

This one was at 48, Brick Lane, complete with a self-contained two-bedroom flat on the first floor. Moin came to the UK for a while, then he left for Bangladesh, leaving me to set up the shop, a proposed textile business, and move into the flat at 48, Brick Lane. It was wonderful having my own place. I still went to Sokina's for dinner each night as she and Muslim had agreed that they would make an extra plate for me every day. He decreed that wherever he was, there should be food made for me, and I was very grateful.

There was a significant moment when I had the BT engineers arrive at 48, Brick Lane to put in phone lines.

They were British white guys, and as I came down the stairs to show them what was required, they said to me, 'You own all this? But you're so young?'

And it was at that moment that I thought, wow, the shop and the flat, this is all mine. I'm doing well!

However, I couldn't continue with the planned textile business envisaged by my brothers. With my studies and duties in the import company, I simply didn't have the time for a venture that required my full attention if it was to succeed. I explained to them, and we decided instead to sell film videos, magazines and music cassettes, which would complement Naz Cinema, which was next door. Our opening hours were structured to coincide with screenings at the cinema, which also made it easier for me to fit in around my lectures.

We named the shop Glamour International and had a full-time employee, Jabber Miah, who was an honest, sincere worker. He manned the shop quite efficiently but sometimes needed supervision.

At the end of the day, I would balance the till and take account of the stock.

So, life became rather overwhelming. My days were busy, full, and demanding. I would leave the flat at 8am to make my 9am college lecture. On my return at 5pm, I'd join Jabber Miah at the shop, where a new employee, Jasim Uddin, was by now running the travel company. All three of us would work long into the evening.

I knew I had a big decision to make, carry on stretching myself between my studies and work or quit college and get fully involved with the family businesses. I feared the opportunity to make money would not come again.

'I can always go back and sit the final exam next semester,' I told myself. But that next semester never came. And I became more involved with the family business.

Cinemagoers were soon flocking into Glamour International, with the records, cassettes, magazines and other goods selling fast. Moin was regularly sending Bangladeshi magazines, newspapers and books on the flights from Dhaka for us to sell in the shop. With business booming, I began developing the travel agency in my spare time, arranging flights for those visiting Bangladesh.

I would take bookings from friends, relatives and the public and pass them on to the approved agent of the national airline – Biman. Moin had previously dabbled in this market in UK with his Crimson Travels agency at 118 Mile End Road, London, until he had to close it and return home to attend urgent matters. Author Shahagir Bakth Faruk, in his book Bari to Basha, mentions Crimson Travels as being his first employer in the UK.

Moin was a true entrepreneur. His imagination and nose for ideas were remarkable. He could grasp what the market demanded and then seemingly with little effort create a business catering for exactly that.

It never took him long to make it sustainable and profitable before he moved on to the next challenge.

He started shipping second-hand Bedford trucks from England and re-conditioned cars from Japan into Bangladesh, something again that I helped him with. I will go into more detail on all these business ventures later in the book.

I had some good friends at college, most of whom were from Sri Lanka one was half Irish. But I didn't socialise much, I was too busy.

I did meet some Indian guys from Fiji who were at the college on scholarships. Their country provided them with accommodation and four of them shared a house at Courtland Avenue off Sidcup Road in Lewisham. My friends threw me a birthday party, a year after my arrival on the weekend closer to my birthday on September 1st at my Fijian friends' house.

At the time I was going out with a Sikh girl, but her parents wanted her home by 9pm, which was when the party was just going to get started. I went alone and there was Rashmi - a beautiful 18-years-old – a tantalising, unpretentious beauty stood before me. She was full of grace and charm; her imperceptible smile won my heart. I fell in love with her immediately and we danced the night away.

Our chemistry worked. I was fortunate to marry Rashmi. She was not only pretty and compassionate but a practical woman. She helped me with the business and supported me whatever I ventured into. I would be travelling abroad trying to procure new products to be ahead of the market and she held the fort. She managed the finance of the businesses while I concentrated on the expansion.

The adage "Behind every successful man stands a steadfast wife", is true.

Chapter Six
Bank of England

B efore 1979, when the newly elected Tory government abolished Exchange Control, which controlled how much money you could transfer abroad, Commonwealth workers in the United Kingdom could send up to a maximum £2,000/year to their families and dependants back home.

Bangladeshi people faced difficulties in sending money to their dependents in the early 70s, because most of us habitually did not hold accounts in British clearing banks. In those days wages were paid in cash. Relationships and transactions with Pakistani banks were boycotted by Bengalis after the war of independence in 1971. To send money to Bangladesh was very difficult after the war.

Seeing an opportunity in 1975, I applied to the Bank of England, through National Westminster Bank, for a Collection Account. The application process was complicated and cumbersome. Initially the Bank of England required me to complete a Form DE (declaration of earning). This Form DE was filled, and money was remitted, and the laborious process of filling forms went on for more than a year. But finally, after fulfilling all the requirements, on May 9, 1977, I got the approval of the Bank of England to operate a Collection Account through NatWest (appdx 260). The declaration form DE was not required to be kept as a record for each remitter, but due diligence under the supervision of NatWest Bank was imperative.

This licence allowed me to collect up to £2,000 per year from a worker in the UK and send it on his behalf to family in Bangladesh.

This was done through the Wage Earners' Scheme, first introduced in 1974 by the Bangladesh government, which provided incentives to Bangladeshi nationals working abroad to send their earnings back home through official channels.

The Collection Account worked brilliantly for Bangladeshis here in the United Kingdom. Money was deposited into my account, which was automatically transferred to the external account from where it could be remitted anywhere in the world, enabling the Wage Earner's Scheme to pay for the import of commodities and essentials into Bangladesh. Through Moin's business connections in Bangladesh, I acted as an agent for direct payment to those companies who were shipping products into Bangladesh. Millions of pounds sterling was sent to the country and paid for the goods under the scheme. The venture became so successful, I had to employ two full time staff to keep records for the Bank of England to meet the compliance and run the transactions smoothly. The difference between this and my other enterprises was that I did not need any capital, only honesty and trust. My family had a good name in the diaspora, as well as in Bangladesh, which helped me tremendously.

The bank charged a nominal transaction fee, we charged a remittance fee, and I earned a decent commission out of these transactions. I was fortunate to accumulate enough to buy the lease and then the freehold of the Naz Cinema.

Unfortunately for my enterprise but evidently for the fortune of the country, the exchange control which was introduced in 1939 was abolished in 1979. Nigel Lawson, financial secretary to the treasury, persuaded the then Conservative Chancellor Geoffrey Howe to debar exchange control after 40 years of its existence.

The late Chancellor Lawson is regarded as an important architect of privatisation and deregulation of financial services in Thatcher's era.

National Westminster Bank Limited ♻

Eastern Branch 130 Whitechapel High Street London E1 7PS	Please address your reply to the Manager Your ref
	Our ref FGN/SC/I
Telephone 01-247 6606	Date 16 July 1979

TO WHOM IT MAY CONCERN

<u>Our Account - H M AHMED - M U Ahmed Collection Account</u>

We write to confirm that the total cash paid into the above account for the year ending 31.12.78 was £6,338,794.39.

We also confirm that this money was transferred to our external account in the name of H M Ahmed.

G B BLAKE
Manager

It was never my goal to be a businessman, an entrepreneur or a millionaire. I wanted to be an engineer to create and manufacture consumer products, but since my life took a different turn, I wanted to be the best at whatever I did.

This should always be the belief: faith should be the motivator and then you can excel in whatever you do.

So, when opportunity knocks open your door wide, float freely, let the wind help your sail for the wind might not be there for long.

One of the principle,
I always try to follow in my life is:
"When opportunity knocks open your door wide,
float freely, let the wind help your sail, don't let
the squall deviate you from your destiny."

Chapter Seven
Mount Mascal Farm

Between 1974 when I arrived in the UK and 1981 when I bought my beautiful home, Mount Mascal Farm, North Cray Road, London for £130,000, everything I did made a profit. I had £40,000 in my deposit account and borrowed £90,000 from the bank. In those days, you could get a mortgage even if you weren't British. I got the mortgage via my friend Ruksana who is half English and half Bangladeshi. I bought insurance from her boss Gordon and because I did that, he asked his son-in-law, who was the manager of a branch of Halifax, if he would give me a mortgage. I got it! Can you believe it? Nowadays, it isn't possible. But back then, people did things via personal connection and trust. £90,000 was the maximum he could lend at his discretion.

I was still living in 46-48 Brick Lane when I bought Mount Mascal Farm. I had been looking at houses for two to three years. In December 1980, Peter Dayal who supplied me with LCD watches suggested I look at Chislehurst. He was quite posh, and his wife was English, they lived in Chislehurst. He took me to see some properties there. I told him my maximum budget was £100,000. After we had seen some houses, he took me to an estate agent called Alan de Maid, and I saw Mount Mascal Farm in the window. I loved it and wanted to see it. Rashmi told me, "I won't marry you unless you buy me that house!"

But that's another story. Because, in 1977, three years after I arrived in the UK, having left college to work for the family business, the college would not apply to the Home Office for an extension of my visa (appdx 259).

A deportation order was out on me in the beginning of 1977. I had to leave Britain within eight weeks. I had been seeing Rashmi for more than a year by then and she was also working for me. To resolve the problem, it was decided that she would marry me so that I could stay. Rashmi was born and brought up in Kenya and came to England at the age of 11. We arranged it all – her roommate was a witness – simple and effective, and in March 1977, we were married at Westminster Registry Office. Then I sent my passport and marriage certificate to the Home Office and after some time, they gave me unconditional leave to remain.

I married quite early, admittedly. I was just 23 and Rashmi was even younger at the age of 19. She was young and beautiful, one in a million. She was Gujrati Hindu, and I was Bengali Muslim and, in those days, this was considered a forbidden union. In addition, nobody could know that Rashmi and I were married because she had married before her older sister, which was not socially acceptable.

So even though we were officially married when we viewed Mount Mascal Farm, we acted as if we weren't, which is why it was bought only in my name.

When I came to register Mount Mascal Farm, I was £2,000 short on expenses. So, Rashmi added her savings, and her sister Dipti gave us £500.

In March 1981, after we had bought the house, my family didn't want Rashmi and I living in the house if we weren't married. So speedily we had another ceremony at our new home, at which only Rashmi's parents and my brothers were present. For Rashmi to be married to me she was required to convert herself to Islam and so she became Rashma. We spared her parents this part of the ceremony – not that it mattered as we'd already had the registry office marriage. My parents knew the situation.

I am a liberal Muslim; I respect all religion. 'Lakum de lukun olia din' which in Arabic means: you carry on with your religion, I carry on with mine. Rashmi was amicable and we loved one another.

After the Muslim wedding, in March 1981 at Mount Mascal farm, a month later we travelled to Bangladesh and my father arranged a huge wedding reception for us there. Rashma as she was supposed to be called was treated like a princess. We got straight off the plane and into the family-owned car – no customs or checks. This was not unusual for an affluent family well connected in those days. Our luggage and passports followed later, brought by a customs officer. Rashmi was thrilled to be treated in such a special way.

Back home at Mount Mascal Farm, we were young and full of life. We worked hard and enjoyed financial comfort. For 15 years, until we had our children, Rashmi and I pursued many different enterprises entirely together. We speculated and accumulated wealth and prosperity.

We sometimes lost it too, but Rashmi stood by me and supported whatever initiative I ventured into. She had the luxury of having a maid at home. Moin arranged for a Bengali maid from Bangladesh. In those late 70s it was easy to arrange for domestic help from the Commonwealth countries.

We also had a beautiful garden. Two acres cultivated by a Scottish gardener called Alex Brown, recommended to me by my neighbour. Mount Mascal Farm has a beautiful garden on a hill top. It took me 42 years to build that garden. Whatever gardening I have learned, I learned from Alex and the rest from Monty Don, the BBC gardening guru.

I love to collect plants and the more I do, the more I learn that a garden is an infinite process – forever evolving.

The beauty is of course in the eyes of the beholder. I find comfort and solace in looking after plants – a world of peace and tranquillity I can dive into, escaping the stresses and strains of business.

Not long after we moved to Mount Mascal Farm, I decided to buy a Rolls Royce albeit second-hand because that's more sensible with cars. I went to Hanwells in Southall and traded in my Bentley. I took Rashmi with me as she was excited that we were buying a silver Rolls Royce.

I wish I could remember what it cost. It was a status symbol at the time, perhaps beyond my means. But I loved the car and felt fantastic, like a king, as I drove it away from Hanwells. Having a car like that doesn't appeal to me now. I don't need status symbols as I feel secure in what I've achieved. I'm content and not one of those people who can never have enough.

'The world has enough for everyone's needs,
but not everyone's greed.'
Mahatma Gandhi.

Chapter Eight
Amazing Brick Lane

B rick Lane has always welcomed immigrants. French Huguenots, stigmatised by oppressive laws and facing severe persecution, fled France in the 17th century and settled in the East End. Most were master weavers and based themselves predominantly in the Spitalfields area. The area became a hub for weaving, tailoring, and thus the clothing industry developed exponentially from here. You can learn about those early settlers at the exhibition at 19 Princelet Street, but the Suitcases and Sanctuary exhibition also depicts other migrants who made this part of London what it is.

Immigrants continued to arrive, and they provided labour, semi-skilled and unskilled. The Irish came in the 19th century, as did the Ashkenazi Jews. Jewish immigration continued into the early 20th century. Then the Indians and Bengalis arrived in the latter part of 20th century, Bangladeshis made up the largest group of recent immigrants and we made a success of it.

We have had the first Bangladeshi MP representing Bethnal Green and Bow - Rushanara Ali and another of my compatriots Lutfur Rahman was elected executive mayor of Tower Hamlets. We had three other members of parliament by 2020, Tulip Siddiq, Dr Rupa Huq and Apsana Begum. Most Bangladeshi immigrants to Brick Lane were from the Greater Sylhet region.

We shaped Brick Lane, and Brick Lane shaped us.

It is a vibrant part of London, the heart of the East End certainly during the 19th century.

The famous Brick Lane Palace Theatre stood here. This later became the Mayfair Cinema, then the Odeon, and then, of course, Naz Cinema and Café Naz. It is a historic place, too. The bricks used to rebuild the buildings in East London (gutted by the Great Fire of 1666) came from the brick fields in Spitalfields, hence the name Brick Lane.

The Sunday market at the end of Brick Lane, like the ones on Petticoat Lane and nearby Columbia Road, dates back to a dispensation given by the government to the Jewish community in the 19th century. Prior to that, there were no Sunday markets due to the Sabbath being observed by the Jewish community and the Christian's Sunday mass.

Rachel Lichtenstein's 'On Brick Lane', first published in 2007, describes the intricacies of the life in and around Brick Lane: from the Huguenots to the Jewish refugees of the 19th century to the 20th century Bangladeshi community. She methodically depicts the early lives of the Jewish immigrants, her ancestors, how they lived and worked in Brick Lane. She included in her dictum, Stephen Watt's Brick Lane Poem which includes mention of Pola Uddin (later made a peer in the House of Lords), Shamim Azad, Tassaduk Ahmed and Dan Jones. She also mentions Café Naz as the sixth port of call in her walking tour of the area.

Monica Ali's 'Brick Lane' told the story of upheaval within a family that came from Mymensingh District, Bangladesh in her 2003 novel Brick Lane.

A film followed in 2007 starring Indian actress Tannishtha Chatterjee. Both the book and the movie provoked controversy among the community for its portrayal of Bangladeshis in the area.

The early 1970s were a period of squalor in Brick Lane. It was rundown and derelict, a neglected slum. The Bangladeshis then were so desperate for housing that they began squatting in unoccupied houses, as depicted by Shabana Begum in her book "Sylhet to Spitalfields" But much of the degradation was swept away when Tower Hamlets Council built new homes, specifically to house Bangladeshi families in and around Brick Lane. By the late 1970s, Brick Lane had become predominantly Bengali, the new immigrants replacing the former Jewish community who had suffered a great deal over the decades. During the 1930s, Oswald Mosley and his black-shirted fascists marched into the East End, and their aggression culminated in riots and the Battle of Cable Street.

The Bengali immigrants who were mostly male initially, later brought their families into the relative safety of UK government after the war of Bangladesh Independence in 1971. Tower Hamlets soon became the hub for the new families. And with the rag trade based in the East End, the new immigrants found work in those Jewish-run businesses.

During the 1980s and 1990s there was even more of an influx of Sylheties into the area through marriage and settlements. Men deciding to bring their family in the UK. A new sophisticated Bengalis started to emerge by then. With this new community came cultural and religious requirements.

A French Protestant church, built in 1743, became in 1819 a Methodist chapel, and then in 1898, Spitalfields Great Synagogue, which was to become later the Great London Mosque – a place of worship for us. Wealthy Bengalis such as Tayebur Rahman, Abdul Motalib Chowdhury and I were at the forefront of fundraising to buy the building.

This one-time great synagogue at the corner of Fournier Street and Brick Lane became the Great London Mosque, which continues to serve the Bangladeshi community.

As well as hardship and success, the community faced tragedy when on 4 May 1978 Altab Ali, a 25-year-old Bangladeshi textile worker, was murdered when walking home from work with bags of shopping. It was the day of the local elections, and according to friends, Mr. Ali intended to do some cooking before heading out to vote. He never made it.

The young man who had left Bangladesh for a better life in 1969, bumped into three white teenagers. They stabbed him to death in St Mary's Park off Whitechapel Road. Two of his murderers were 17, the other 16, and they admitted that they had no reason at all to attack Mr. Ali; they did not care who he was. They murdered him because of his race. They were found guilty of their crime.

The National Front was standing in 43 council seats the day Altab was murdered. It was just over 30 years since Mosley and his Blackshirts had marched on the East End. People had had enough. Things had to change. Mr. Ali's racially motivated murder triggered protests. Ten days after he was killed, 7,000 people marched behind his coffin.

Marching to Downing Street, we urged the government to address racism in east London. I was one of the marchers, a motivator at the meeting held at the Brick Lane Mosque.

Altab Ali has gone down in the annals of history as a martyr. Some are born great, some people acquire greatness, and some have greatness thrust upon them. Altab Ali, sadly for him and his family, experienced the latter.

St Mary's Park, where he lost his life, had a new entrance archway installed in 1989 — a memorial to Mr. Ali and all victims of racist violence. Nine years later, the park was renamed Altab Ali Park.

My businesses of remittance (sending money overseas), money exchange, travel agency, shipping, personal cargo, cinema, musical shows, music production, video rental, cassette and record production, VHS films, amusement arcades, radios, watches, twin cassette players and stereo headphones – the shop and finally the wholesale distribution of electrical and novelty goods housed in the 20,000 square foot warehouse in Chicksand Street helped me to become the biggest distributor, importer and exporter among the UK's Muslim community.

This is the story of iconic Brick Lane, where all my enterprises made their first debut and magically, made me the first Bangladeshi millionaire in the UK.

Boishakhi Mela - Bengali New Year Festivities at Brick Lane 1980s

The lives of people in Brick Lane
has changed so much:
"The early 1970s were a period
of squalor in Brick Lane,
it was a rundown and derelicts -
a neglected slum"

Chapter Nine
Naz – historic cinema hall

1978

When I bought the Naz Cinema for £130,000 from Manu Bhai Patel, I believed I had bought a piece of East End history. During the 1960s and 1970s, Naz Cinema in the East End of London was the entertainment hub for Indo/Pakistani/ Bangladeshi people in the United Kingdom. In the 1950s, it was the Odeon, before then the Mayfair Cinema, which opened in 1936, and prior to that it was the Brick Lane Palace Theatre. It was a stunning space with 1,700 seats, a huge balcony, ornamental walls and an orchestra pit.

Owners Rank shut the Odeon in 1967 and sold it to Manu Bhai Patel, who renamed it the Naz Cinema. He was a tycoon with business interests in Kenya. He owned Naz Drive-in Cinema in Nairobi. Drive-ins were popular at the time: you drove into a huge field and watched a film on a big screen along with your family.

In 70s London, there was not much entertainment available for the people from the Indian Sub-Continent, except for the BBC's Nai Zindagi Naya Jeevan programme on Sunday mornings. It was normal for a man to live and work here leaving his wife and children back home, so he could be very much alone with not much to do during his leisure time.

The United Kingdom suffered a shortage of labour after the Second World War, so the government issued work visas to the Commonwealth citizens, who were invited to come to do menial work and drive the UK's buses and trains.

Men came from the Indian sub-continent to work and earn and to return home after a period of hard work. Indian cinema halls showed Bollywood films which played an integral part in keeping these men entertained.

Naz Cinema, under our ownership, became an entertainment hub for the Bangladeshi community. Palaseum Cinema Hall, located in Commercial Road, was much smaller than Naz Cinema.

We established a cassette/music record shop and an amusement arcade in the building. At that time too, Bangladeshi-owned restaurants were flourishing all around the country. Men working in those so-called Indian restaurants would get one day off in the week. They would invariably visit Naz Cinema to meet friends. Nirala Restaurant stood opposite Naz where they would have their lunch. They would spend the day loitering in my shop Glamour International buying cassettes and records of their favourite singers or movies.

After watching a movie at Naz Cinema, they would go back to work.

Kuti Miah, known as Kuti Bhai, who established Kuti's Restaurants in Southampton and is now a hugely successful businessman, was among the men who made use of the cinema, the shop, and the nearby restaurants. 'I would come to Naz Cinema to watch a movie and spent all my week's earning to buy records and cassettes from Glamour International,' he said. Although a spendthrift at the time, and a millionaire in his own right. Kuti Bhai used to have an employee in the 1990s called Rishi Sunak, who became Chancellor of the Exchequer of Great Britain and then Prime Minister.

I ran the cinema for more than six years. It was a straightforward business model.

You hired a film from the Indian Film Distributors in London, then screened it. Rumour had it that many elderly single Bangladeshi men would rather pay 50p to watch a movie at Naz than pay for heating in their room. Besides showing Indian movies and late-night Chinese sub-titled films, I also imported Bangladeshi movies, along with the rights, and then transferred them onto VHS cassettes to sell.

We also had live musical shows at Naz. Famous singers came from Bangladesh to perform. Stars such as Runa Laila, Shanaz Begum, Sabina Yasmin, Fakir Alamgir, Shafali Ghose and many other national singers and performers from Bangladesh took to the stage at the Naz in the late 70s. Later, we had a 4-track studio built where we recorded and produced cassettes and discs. We distributed records by the likes of Shefali Ghose, Himangshu Goswami and Kari Amir Uddin throughout the United Kingdom. Himangshu Goswami settled in the United Kingdom and now lives in London with his wife. They have three sons and a number of grandchildren.

Amiruddin is a renowned Bangladeshi folk singer from Sylhet in North-Eastern Bangladesh. When he performed at the Naz, the hall was packed out with 1,700 fans, most of them originally from Sylhet.

Some fans who could not get seats were allowed to stand in the foyer, and listen to the melodious spiritual folk music, that connected their soul with the creator. These folklore, known as Baul songit (music) are universal, the themes are of the creation of humanity and the Creator.

We also promoted wrestling nights for the EastEnders.

Many local grapplers who moved on to the professional circuit made their debuts on the stage at Naz.

The imagination knows no bounds; dreams do turn into reality. When I came to England and I was living in Hessel Street with my brother, I used to walk to Naz to watch Indian movies. I would feel sad each time I walked home, remembering how back in Bangladesh, I would go with my friend Faisal Rashid. His family was very wealthy and owned the Dilshad Cinema in Sylhet, so we would always be collected by car. I felt, on those walks home from Naz, that I had really gone from the upper echelons of society to the bottom.
And yet, here I was, four years after my arrival, I became the owner of this huge hall; a historic great monument. How fortunate can you be!

But all good things come to an end. The traditional cinema halls were starting to wane in the face of an onslaught from large multiplexes that began to spring up during the 1980s. I spent £18,000 on a new industrial boiler (I could have bought a semi-detached house with this amount in 1978), and then one year later we were forced to close. That was the end of Naz Cinema.

Naz Cinema 1984

To revive this dead enterprise in the mid 80s, I devised a super plan. I applied to Tower Hamlet Council for change of use. At first the Council refused my application. But when I lobbied - they realised that this was going to be a huge restaurant with 500 seats that would employ dozens of people from the community and would serve the nearby financial district. Dick Chaney and his 12 colleagues from the planning department visited Naz Cinema. Councillor Barrister Ashique Ali and Nurul Huq visited with them too.

The council planners were amazed by the presentation made by my friend of 40 years, architect Milan Babic, showing the propose modern and stylish premises with elegant ambience. Paul Bisley was the leader of the council then. He came across as a forward-thinking man.

Finally, I got the planning and started to build the restaurant. First, I needed to level the floor. Cinema flooring is raked, sloped upwards away from the screen, to give all cinema goers a clear view. This needed dismantling and the chairs had to be removed. One day when we were inside the hall, a guy walked through the open door and said, "I am John and I have my van and men just outside. I can give you £500 for those discarded metal armed chairs." A Gypsy approach – here today, gone tomorrow!

I thought I was in luck as I was going to get rid of the chairs and make some money too. "Of course, you can." I said.

John and his men instantly started loading his van. It took him the whole day and they returned the next day and filled the van again. When he was finished, he came over to me.

I thought he was going to give me the money but instead he said he was going to go and get it from the Bank. Innocently I let him go. I waited, and waited but sadly he never came back.

I went to the police; I could not even give them the van details. I learned a big lesson in life: do not trust strangers - safeguard your own interest first. A bird in hand is worth two in the bush.

I moved on and employed Din Builders to build the restaurant at the cost of £110,000. The chairs and table and the kitchen fit- out were to be quoted separately. The work was proceeding at full speed. When halfway through the project Mr. Din Muhammed sacked his foreman.

Banglatown Cafe Naz

The work stopped for a week or so then Mr. Din employed new people. After a week or so into the job there was a fire which destroyed most of the finished work. The police asserted that it was arson. Was it the foreman? It seemed possible. Mr. Din did not continue, and I could not carry on with the project either. I sold the cinema hall to a Akther who was a big leather merchant, and he then sold it to a developer. I bought back some of it and the foyer. The developer built 23 flats and named it the Odeon Court.

I should point out that in the late 70's the council had a core strategy for Brick Lane. Aesthetically and socially, they did not want just one trade in Brick Lane, they wanted mixed amenities for people. Brick Lane had Clifton Restaurant at one end and Sweet & Spicy at the other. The initial permission for restaurant usage of the cinema relaxed the rules which paved for the congregation of restaurants in and around Brick Lane.

In the late 90s, Brick Lane became more famous for the restaurant trade than the historic rag trade. The closure of Naz Cinema was not the end for the name Naz.

I write about this in more detail later, but during the 1990s, I turned the cinema foyer into the Café Naz restaurant and created a national chain of Indian restaurants, with its main branch in the heart of Brick Lane.

Café Naz was praised by food critics as one of the best Indian restaurants and the most reasonably priced. I believe that Café Naz's success was due to the fact that it was in such close proximity to the City. It provided excellent cuisine with West End flair, ultra-modern ambience, its interior design including a fine stainless steel and sand blasted glass façade with a stunning glass staircase.

The success of Café Naz in Brick Lane was so overwhelming that Bengalis from across the country sought to claim a piece of this success. Small factories and textile shops on the street quickly turned into restaurants.

At one point there were more than 60 Bengali restaurants in and around Brick Lane. I will tell the story of Café Naz in more detail later, but for now, it is fair to say that it played its part in making Brick Lane the curry capital of England. I ate there every day, in the afternoon, whatever the staff had and sometimes from the buffet. We had an incredible selection of 15 to 20 dishes each day. Other times the chef made me whatever I asked for.

But eventually, Brick Lane became a victim of its own success. It succumbed, perhaps, to the influx of Bengalis who were desperate to get a bite of the cherry, and there were not enough customers to go round. But I am glad to have planted that seed, and I have been acknowledged as the one who truly launched this culture of food on Brick Lane. In fact, Estate Gazette, the publication for commercial property, described me in 2005 as The King of Brick Lane.

A great honour, but difficult to live up to.

King of Brick Lane Muquim Ahmed found himself buying properties as he created his restaurant and food empire. And these assets have helped his fortune weather the lean times. Piers Wehner reports

Muquim Ahmed is the unofficial King of London's Brick Lane. Over the past 30 years, the 51-year old Bangladeshi-born restaurateur and property investor has bought half of the buildings on the street, and his flagship, Café Naz, is still the most high-profile eatery in the area.

It is a persona that Ahmed enjoys playing. "Do you want me to look serious, or bling-bling?" he asks our photographer as he poses in his Bentley – while ensuring that his Rolex is visible below the cuff of his Savile Row suit.

Ahmed, who came to the UK in 1974 to study "and then just stayed", is a man at ease with his wealth. "If all the people in this country were rich," he says, "the country would be rich," before launching into a glowing appraisal of Thatcherite economics.

But this is not to say that Ahmed doesn't have a social conscience. Far from it. He may have signed a strongly worded public letter during the last election, criticising the Labour government's tax policies, but he doesn't resent paying the tax itself.

"The way I think of it, the government, and the people it supports, is the major stakeholder in my companies," referring to the 40% or so tax he pays. "Then there are the banks, because they have the debt, and then there is me. I am a minority shareholder, really."

Ahmed's main business interest is food. As well as the famous Café Naz, he has restaurants in Cambridge, Hor-

Because of this, Ahmed has benefited from the steadily rising values in east London. He bought his first property, the land and factory in Brick Lane where he set up Asian Foods, in 1976 for £40,000. It is now worth, according to a recent valuation, £1.6m.

"But I never intended to become a property investor," he says. "It just happened. I bought things only out of necessity. At the moment, I am buying a bakery because

> **"I am buying a bakery because I need a factory. I don't want to buy it, but I am forced to because it is the only way to get my factory"**

sham, Cardiff and the City, and owns the food producer Asian Foods.

But Ahmed also runs a plethora of other companies and investment vehicles. His property portfolio, which comprises around 50 buildings, is split between a dozen different companies, with names such as Tower Hamlets Investment and Quantum Securities.

"I spread it around a bit," he says. "I like to keep things in separate smaller companies because it is more tax efficient." One day he plans to streamline the structure – which would no doubt make things easier for the compilers of the *EG* Rich List.

Although food is his business focus, property is where Ahmed holds most of his wealth. The portfolio is scattered across England but, he says: "Brick Lane is the centre."

"It's where my offices are. It is my home, really. It's where I came when I first moved here. It's where I set up my businesses," he says.

The week
Muquim Ahmed

I need a factory. I don't want to buy it, but I am forced to because it is the only way to get my factory."

Nevertheless, Ahmed has done some straight property deals, and has done rather well out of them. In 1976 he also bought Brick Lane's Odeon cinema for £125,000, changing its name to the Naz Cinema. In 1981 he sold it to a residential developer for £375,000.

Another building in his portfolio, a former glass factory which is now home to half a dozen of his companies, is being eyed by developers. It lies just by Canning Town station in east London. When Ahmed bought it two years ago, it cost him £725,000. Now that it is on the outskirts of the Olympic Games CPO area, and therefore part of the biggest regeneration in the UK, he is getting offers for twice that amount.

Ahmed also owns his restaurant, Café Naz, where he has served "proper Indian food" to some of the crème of British politics , photographs of whom adorn his office walls.

The restaurant was partly destroyed six years ago, when a nail-bomb planted by neo-Nazi terrorist David Copeland exploded, injuring 13 people. Ahmed escaped with his life thanks to a phone call from his wife that sent him across the road just seconds before the bomb went off.

Ahmed's business also had a narrow escape, and survived thanks only to his property investments. In 1994 his business empire began to fall apart. A fire at one of his warehouses turned from a disaster into a catastrophe when he found out that his insurance company had gone bankrupt. Even though his banks "were very kind", they still wanted their money.

"I mortgaged all my properties," he says. "Because I had them, I could pay the bank. If I didn't have property I would have gone out of business."

"That is my advice to any young businessman. Buy property. Buy it, then forget about it. One day, it will help you."

Rich list rank

263

£38m

Muquim Ahmed
Naz

*"Some of the vouchers intended for West Pakistan
under the quota were redirected
to recipients in Sylhet.
Perhaps the result was the mass exodus which
became the Sylhet stronghold in the
United Kingdom"*

Chapter Ten

My Businesses

Pandora

When I became the owner of Naz Cinema, I inherited two gaming machines with it. As the cinema only operated at weekends and on Mondays, these machines were not collecting enough revenue to justify their custom duty payment. So, I decided to open an arcade crammed with these gaming machine at 48 Brick Lane, which was next door. I named the arcade Pandora, after the tale of Pandora's Box which I read at school. A perfect metaphor.

I applied for the licence from Tower Hamlet Council, who inspected the premises and granted us the initial 12 machines, which could be operated from 10am to 8pm. In the beginning all the machines were hired monthly, but I decided later to buy the machines. This did not work out, however, because the machines were not rotated, and the punters were not eager to play on the same ones over and over. They wanted new games, new challenges, so I resorted to renting again. And once more, the gamblers were happy. But perhaps a little too happy. They spent a lot of time on the machines. The place became quite busy. That was when I decided to double the number of machines from 12 to 24. Of course, I had to pay excise duty annually for each machine which was substantial.

For the operation to run smoothly I needed an attendant to give change to the punters. £200 in 10p coins was kept as a float at the kiosk with the attendant. The place would run itself. Occasionally when a machine stopped working, the attendant would call for an engineer, but that was the extent of his role. Income from these machines was fool proof. The change attendant had a £200 float. At the end of each day, or first thing in the morning, all the money that had been given to the attendant by punters for him to change up was collected by me. I would then take this money equating to £200, then open the machine and collect all that had gone into them and give £200 back to the attendant. I was collecting a significant profit every day.

Although this was a relatively lucrative business, I had to take other issues into consideration. Bengali men were getting addicted to these machines. On Friday nights, after receiving their wages from the tailoring factories, they would come to the arcade and gamble almost all their money. Although there were winners, many were going home broke.

One Friday night I met a man. He was clearly distressed. I asked him, 'What's the matter.' He said: 'Bhai Sab (respected brother), I have no money to go home, nor have I any money to buy food for my children.'

I realised instantly that I had his money. He lost it to me and to those who won on the machines. I gave him two £20 notes and told him that he should try and give up this habit and not to come to the arcade again since he has no control over his addiction. This incident affected me, and I thought that morally and socially this could not be right. Gambling machines are designed so that the owners and the skilled punters always come out on top. Within a month of meeting that man, I shut down the operation. Some of my punters were not happy. They took their custom elsewhere, to another arcade near Aldgate underground station.

The local community leaders and the mullah from the local mosque were grateful.

Milfa Travel

Milfa Travel, the travel agency I established here in the United Kingdom, in 1975, was Moin's legacy. The name Milfa derives from mills and factories, places that produce goods. I wanted to become an engineer producing consumer goods, but I had to carry the name forward. Milfa was a good name for many of my businesses.

It was because of my brother's involvement in the travel trade, that I decided to call Milfa Travel by that name too. Our father had helped Moin establish Pakistan Overseas Express in the early 50s. A shop was bought in the newly constructed Hasan Market opposite Sylhet District Court. The business was immediately successful due to Moin's impeccable and friendly attitude and within a few years he opened other branches – one in the Station Road, Sylhet and the other in Moulvi Bazar.

Most of those who travelled from Sylhet to the United Kingdom in those days did so through Pakistan Overseas Express.

There were three other approved IATA agents in Sylhet district, but Moin's was the most popular. He made a lot of money sending people to England through the voucher scheme, a system generated by the Pakistan government to supply the manpower shortage in the United Kingdom.

Some of the vouchers intended for West Pakistan under the quota were redirected to recipients in Sylhet. Perhaps the result was the mass exodus which became the Sylheti stronghold specifically in Tower Hamlets. Migration from Bangladesh increased when, after the war of independence in 1971, single men started bringing their families to the safety of UK.

We received a major boost in 1976 when, after Salauddin Ahmed was posted from the headquarters in Dhaka to London as Biman-Bangladesh Airline's country manager for the UK and Ireland, Milfa Travels became the airline's passenger sales agent. Milfa Travel really flourished then and almost half of the business of Biman-Bangladesh Airlines went through us. This good relationship with the airline continued for many years during the tenure of other country managers such as Kamal Syed, Jalal Ahmed, Omar Faruk and others.

There were other approved agencies in London: Asia Express, Surma Travels, Jonata Travels and a few more who were not the approved agent for Biman. However, in the late 70s and early 80s travel agents in the UK did not make much money from ticket sales but from the remittances, shipping personal effects and so on. During this time, Biman's UK general manager, Yousuf Ali in London, and marketing director Salauddin Ahmed now based in Dhaka, devised a promotion to boost the airline's business. For every tenth ticket sold, the 11th would be free. As a result, all the agents made a lot of money.

Milfa Travel was a success. But in 2000, due to my involvement in various other businesses, some more lucrative than others, I gifted the company to my manager Mujibur Rahaman, who had served me diligently for a long time.

Milfa Travels is still trading as the approved agent for Biman-Bangladesh Airlines. The business is located at Montague Street, not far from where it was originally situated. Whoever runs it now, wherever it is based, it will always be my older brother's legacy. He was a true visionary, a man of charm with a positive disposition who opened the way for me to be a success in the UK. My other brother also did a lot for me. May their souls rest in eternal peace.

Milfa Shipping Ltd

Bangladesh was a ripe, emerging market in the 70s. The country's industries, manufacturing base and infrastructure were totally destroyed by the Pakistani army. After the war of liberation there was a huge demand for finished goods from the United Kingdom. Spotting an opportunity, and taking advantage of the Wage Earner's Scheme, I launched Milfa Shipping Ltd.

The business was heavily involved in exporting fridge-freezers, televisions and other goods into Bangladesh. We would pack the entire inner berth of a Bangladesh Shipping Corporation container ship with cargo and ship from Tilbury and Felixstowe. We also booked three or four containers for used Bedford trucks. Second-hand Bedford trucks were in great demand in Bangladesh, as were second-hand Toyota cars from Japan. Those travelling home to Bangladesh in the 70s and 80s would order a TV and a fridge to be shipped to Chittagong port, saving money by taking advantage of the duty-free rules such as the Wage Earner's Scheme. Others would order a second-hand car to be shipped from Japan. But often the TV and refrigerator, or the car, were not meant for their family. Most of my compatriots working in the UK at the time were from the villages of Sylhet, where there was no electricity, so a fridge or a television set was of no use to them. But they would take advantage of the tax concessions and declare 'A' form on disembarkation. This would enable them to import household items duty-free and a second-hand car at the discounted depreciation rate. Those could then be sold in Bangladesh on the open market.

There were other operators in the field at the time. Ehasan Enterprises and Modern Stores were my competitors in the market. Hawke Spares were sending Bedford trucks and second-hand engines in great numbers to Burma Haje, a businessman in Chittagong who controlled the Bedford truck business in Bangladesh. We were also buying second-hand Bedford trucks from different garages in and around London then shipping them to Chittagong as chassis only, thus saving on shipping cost. We were not in direct competition with Burma Haje who later became my nephew Tipu's father-in-law.

This was a big business at the time. Thousands of refrigerators and televisions were shipped from UK, Holland and Japan to Bangladesh including the trucks, and cars and buses from other ports. Business was so good that Moin established Milfa Clearing and Forwarding Ltd in Bangladesh. Customers could order a TV and a freezer in London and take delivery in Sylhet. Milfa's offices in Sylhet would also help individuals sell their TVs or freezers on the open market in Bangladesh. Dhaka Stadium Market became a hub for buying and selling of these imported household items.

The wholesale purchase of these products from manufacturers directly gave me the impetus to go into the distribution of these goods in the United Kingdom and in 1978, I opened Sylto Distribution. Sylto Distribution delivered anything from television and radios to wallets, cassettes, calculators and watches, all around the United Kingdom. This was a big step for me. Previously I had provided for my compatriots and now I was distributing similar household goods throughout the UK.

Milfa Air-Cargo Ltd

Milfa Air-Cargo, a separate entity to our shipping arm, was created so we could cargo goods to Bangladesh through Biman-Bangladesh airline. A licence was required to transact business. Therefore, Milfa Air-Cargo – an entity separate from shipping was created which had to provide a Bank Guarantee of £15,000 to Biman.

Air-Cargo customs clearance was done at the Dhaka International airport. In those days there was no air custom facilities anywhere else in the country. After customs clearance, incoming cargo from London would be sent to Sylhet via either domestic flight or by road with the goods in trucks and lorries.

At the time, the Bangladesh government ran the Wage Earner's Scheme, under which British-Bangladeshis could take as a baggage allowance, a fridge/freezer and a television without paying any tax, as I have mentioned. If someone in Bangladesh imported these goods, they would face a duty of 120 per cent. There were other personal items one could also take into Bangladesh without paying any tax, like cassette players, radios, record players, torches, toasters etc.

As I've stated before, a wage earner in the United Kingdom could also send home £2000 a year through home remittance scheme or use this money to import commercial items by paying regular duty.

Bangladeshis in the UK would invariably choose Milfa Air-Cargo or Modern Stores to send back home their excess baggage. If you booked your baggage through Milfa Air-Cargo before departure it would cost you 99p per kilo, but if you carried your goods when travelling, it would set you back by £15 per kilo – a big difference. No wonder, then, that passengers would choose to send suitcases packed with gifts they bought for their relatives in Bangladesh via cargo than pay excessive amounts that was probably more expensive than the gifts they were carrying.

Milfa Air-Cargo would also send thousands of bottles of whisky and brandy to Kathmandu, Nepal. In those days, Biman was the cheapest route for cargo to the country.

Glamour International

In 1975, a year after my arrival, I was entrusted with Glamour International, a ready-made garment business which was set up by Moin. It was a business familiar to our family as, in the 1950s, our family owned a ready-made garment outlet called Eastern Fancy Stores in Sylhet. Muslim started this shop before he came to England in 1960 where he set up Sabina Saree Centre in Hessel Street. Glamour International would complement Muslim's business, but Moin had to return to Bangladesh due to business commitments before things got going.

That left me in charge. I was a student and as I said, it was difficult for me to study and run the business as it was. The East End at the time was the heartland of the rag trade, but I was no expert. I was, however, a music fan. I loved listening to cassettes and records.

So I fitted the shop at 48 Brick Lane and stocked it with Indian records and cassettes, and magazines. Perhaps what transpired did not complement Muslim's business, as planned, but as mentioned, it did complement the Naz Cinema next door, which showed Indian films. We kept the name chosen by brother Moin, Glamour International. It suited the shop's fares: film magazines such as Stardust, Cinema World and others promoting Bollywood gossip – very apt. The record and cassette business were a bumper success. Men living alone, working odd hours, enjoyed simple entertainment to fill their empty lives, so they loved the music.

Glamour International became busier; we had to employ new staff. Shahagir Bakth Faruk in his book Brick Lane: Bari to Basa, which portrays his life in Brick Lane, explains that Glamour International, where he worked, became central to the Bangladeshi community. It became a hub for the Bengalis, especially with Naz Cinema being next door. Faruk, known as Faruk Bhai, was our manager at Glamour International. Under his supervision the business supplied whatever people travelling to Bangladesh needed.

They purchased gift items, radios, torches, two-in-one cassette players, Seiko 5 watches, briefcases, trunks and suitcases. We also had the sister companies upstairs, which supplied tickets for travel, remittance — run by Jasim Bhai — and provided cargo shipping facilities, managed by Mohith Choudhury. Faruk Bhai was assisted by Fazlur Rahman in the busy shop and Hassan Bawa ran the music shop in the basement.

Faruk Bhai wrote that Glamour International was the only shop in the country owned by a Bangladeshi immigrant that provided a complete service to our diaspora community. Whatever anyone needed when travelling home from the UK, Glamour International provided it.

My mission was not the shop alone, which was doing fantastically well with Faruk Bhai managing and Fazlu Rahman assisting.

I had to manage the other enterprises as well. Hassan, the person who was running the cassette and video shop downstairs also helped me to record the music of the artists who came from Bangladesh to perform at Naz Cinema. I was more interested in distributing these recorded cassettes and discs all around the country. This was by far a more lucrative and profitable venture.

Cassettes were very popular in the back of house – a restaurant's kitchen - because a cassette player could be handled easily. Record players did not suit a busy kitchen environment. The devotional divinity folk songs of Kari Amir Uddin would play while chefs cooked delicate exquisite dishes for the English clientele. So, the demand for cassettes were huge.

To fulfil this demand, I created a makeshift four-track recording studio. An Akai recording system with 12-track mixing console and four microphones were set up in the basement of 48 Brick Lane. Night after night, songs were recorded on spool and transferred into master cassettes. The Otari Duplicating System produced six so-called slaves. The cassettes would have details of the songs on the sleeve and would be sold all around the country. We also produced SP and LP records for performers such as Himangshu Goswami, Shefali Ghosh and Kari Amir Uddin.

Glamour International forged a reciprocal business link with Dhaka Records in Bangladesh, and from them we acquired the rights to show their Bengali films, such as the ever-popular Rupban Rohimbadsha, throughout Europe.

In the 1980s, the decline of cinema shows due to the popularity of VHS, and the growth of out-of-town movie complexes, enabled Glamour International to go into the video rental business. The restauranteurs continued coming to Brick Lane and their staff gathered at Glamour International to meet and rent films.

Glamour International also ventured into video machine rental. It was a vibrant and busy time.

Rank, Granada, Thorn EMI – the national brands in the 80s were busy with TV rentals and video machine rentals. Blockbuster was the big video film rental company, always packed with customers renting films, like they would do a book from a library – except paid. Glamour International was too minute compared to the national brands but independently it was also renting video machines and videos of the Bollywood films to the Bangladeshi, Indian and Pakistani community.

Around this time, there was The Music Channel Ltd, in which Thorn held 50 per cent shares and Virgin 45 percent (Yorkshire TV the remaining five). Richard Branson bought Thorn's shares for £1, then sold half of them for £3.5million. In less than a week Richard turned an investment of just £1 into a profit just over to £4.5m – a miraculous occurrence – right place, right time. And it was this deal that launched Virgin into the league of global communication.

I didn't know who Richard Branson was at that time, but our lives began to mirror each other in interesting and coincidental ways. I had a £4.1m loan from Lloyds Bank to buy a string of properties from Allsop Auctions, which launched me into the property business (more on that later). I followed his footsteps unknowingly as I became involved in recording music, producing discs and running a cinema.

He bought The Scala and I bought The Naz, both of which were also used for live shows, both of us had a record shop, ran mail order, and were involved in publishing – he had Event magazine, I had Notun Din and Asian Post. I had a travel agency he had Virgin Atlantic. Richard started with an old Bentley which he gifted to Mike Oldfield of Tubular Bells fame. I started with an old Bentley too.

Richard sold bootlegs of Island artists in Virgin shops and so did Glamour International selling audio cassettes records by Indian singers in the basement of 46/48 Brick Lane. Richard recorded songs in his Farmhouse studio, I recorded Bengali songs in the basement studio of 48 Brick Lane. Richard was hounded by HMRC Customs. I was hounded by Home Office Immigration.

On one occasion, I had an immigration raid at one of my premises. One of the immigration officers, who was white but foreign, was being very aggressive and I told him, "You don't speak to me like that. I was here before you and I've got more a grip on this country than you have. I pay taxes and your wages, so don't be so rude. You've come to do your job, so do it and do it professionally."

I had one illegal immigrant, but he'd provided me with fake papers. How was I to know? That man was removed, which was a shame because I really liked him and wanted him to work for me.

Richard was a millionaire at the age of 23, I was at 25 but not too far behind. He is dyslexic. So am I. He married Kristina Tomassi in 1972, at same age as me when I married Rashmi Bakshi in 1976. He was born four years earlier than me!

If I had known him, I would have considered him a mentor. He is certainly my idol – an idiosyncratic maverick.

When I was deeply involved in the entertainment business, artists were sponsored and flown in from Bangladesh. Live shows were performed in the Naz Cinema every week. The troupe would travel all around the country performing in town halls and their songs would be recorded in the basement of 48 Brick Lane. Cassettes and discs would be produced and distributed. I have kept some of these as memorabilia at my offices in Canary Wharf.

Milfa Record (Disc)

Milfa Sterling Exchange T/A Wall Street Forex

On 28 September 1999, I established Milfa Exchange House, which was the first exchange house in the UK to have arrangements with Dhaka Bank and Uttara Bank to pay in taka on our behalf to the wage earner's family or nominee, once we credited their sterling correspondence account in London. Milfa Exchange would pay into its nominated UK bank in sterling, then the bank in Bangladesh would pay the equivalent in taka.

After almost a year, the Bangladesh government through its central bank, relaxed its foreign exchange rules allowing Bangladeshi banks (maximum establishing cost £300,000) to open exchange bureaus in UK to collect and send sterling into their nominated account (corresponding sterling account) which the Bangladeshi banks maintained in London. Then the sterling equivalent in taka, which fluctuates daily, would be forwarded to the families or dependents in Bangladesh by the bank whose sterling account has been credited. This meant the pound sterling would remain in London to the order of the bank who was paying from its kitty in Taka to the nominee or to the wage earners' family in Bangladesh. This credited pound sterling in London would be used as foreign exchange by the Central Bank of Bangladesh when mitigating its foreign currency reserve.

Milfa Exchange opened with pomp and ceremony. Kiosks were built and a proper banking environment was created so that customers coming in to send money home would feel secure. Farhat Ali Khan, Abid Hussain and M. Khan, three retired bankers who were friends of mine, were hired to run the business. Compliance, however, was tightened by the Bank of England.

This made it difficult for me, as an individual with other businesses, to run a foreign exchange bureau.

After running the business for five years I sold it to my partner (in that business) Asghar Patel Bhai, the owner of Wall Street Forex which had branches all around the world.

Bangladesh Bank, the country's central bank, relaxed its rules and allowed local financial organisations to open exchange houses here in the United Kingdom. Prime Bank and IFIC Bank bought two properties (leasehold) from me in Brick Lane, transactions from which I gained substantially.

All the Bangladeshi exchange bureaus here in the United Kingdom are predominantly engaged in transacting remittance for the immigrant community. A great source of income (foreign currency) for Bangladesh: external payments.

Milfa Sterling Exchange T/A Wall Street Forex Brick Lane

Historically, at that time I had effectively provided the products and services that were necessary for the Bangladeshi community in London.

Some of these were unique and exceptional, others appropriate to the demands of the time. This I could do because I was fortunate to be in the right place at the right time. Necessity is the mother of invention, as the saying goes. I was given the challenge and I availed the opportunities.

As already mentioned, the United Kingdom in the 1950s and 1960s was short of labour. The country needed workers from the Commonwealth to run its factories, drive its buses and its trains. Thousands of people from Sylhet came to the UK to fill up those vacancies through our travel agency.

Summing up all these activities, it can be said that my brother Moin saw and took the opportunity, as thousands from Sylhet used our travel agency Pakistan Overseas Express to travel to the United Kingdom and start a new life. All three of us brothers had launched enterprises that revolved around helping those who travelled from Sylhet to UK. Moin helped in the '50s and '60s, and Muslim and I did the same in the '70s and '80s, providing services and products to this diaspora. Our family likes to think that we played a vital part in the movement of Sylhetis from Sylhet to London.

But by the latter part of the 1980s, the time was ripe for me to move to centre of the stage, stepping away from the periphery where I was working within the community. Having gifted my travel agency to Mujibur Rahman, who was my manager for a considerable time, I gave the video and cassette business to Abdul Rob. Faruk Bakth, who worked for me, opened Shahanan Music Centre at the other end of Brick Lane.

Farhad Husssain, another one of our employee opened a music shop in Drummond Street. Jasim Bhai established an identical travel agency to Milfa Travels.

I wanted to make room for emerging entrepreneurs from the community. Many proprietors and entrepreneurs came forward and took my place, sometimes with more intensity and skills that were more fit for purpose. I moved away from primarily serving my own community, and expanded my businesses further afield.

Miraj at Cafe' Naz with his school friends posed with me,
ready to take over the new world

Queen Mary University, Honorary Fellowship – with (from left) Mitu Ahmed, Miraj
Ahmed and Minhas Ahmed, 2009

Nottingham University – at Miraj's
Graduation Ceremony, 2012

With Monique & Henry, 2018

Chapter Eleven
Family Life

There came the time when Rashmi started to have the urge to have a child. Unfortunately, she had several miscarriages but finally – after enduring a pregnancy while confined to bed for nine months – she delivered Miraj on the 16 January 1991.

Miraj came into the world naturally but with his mother heavily sedated with a strong dose of epidural injected into her spinal cord. I had been told to hold her tight and still for the injection and that if she moved, she might be paralysed for life. I was so overwhelmed with anticipation and fear that I almost collapsed. The doctors sensed my exhaustion and stress and sat me down and gave me a cup of tea. It was Wednesday at 3.45pm when Miraj came into the world making a little cry. Rashmi's intense pain and exhaustion seem to have dissipated. We were thrilled and full of joy.

Miraj was a very precious child. He was the baby we had wanted for 15 years. We loved him to bits. Rashmi was still working alongside me, so Miraj had an English nanny called Pauline Summers and an educated Bengali nanny called Shumi Begum from Bangladesh. Shumi married an Englishman later and settled in England with her two grown up daughters. It was Moin who really believed it would be best for Miraj to be exposed to the two cultures.

Two years later, on August 30, 1993, Rashmi gave birth to Monique. She had been due on my birthday – September 1 – but arrived a day earlier via Caesarean section after Rashmi went for a routine check-up and the consultant decided to operate immediately. Monique was suffocating inside the womb for some reason but thankfully arrived safely. We were so grateful to have our tiny and beautiful daughter safely with us.

Family Photo as appeared in The Mirror, Apr 26 1999

I am a naturally affectionate person, so when it came to my children, I cared deeply for them both. Miraj would follow me everywhere, even out into the snowy garden when I was working. Of course, I was very busy with work, but one thing I always did was put Miraj to bed and tell or read him fairy tales, then stay until he was asleep. He particularly enjoyed The Twelve Dancing Princesses, Jack and the Beanstalk and Little Red Riding Hood. One of the special memories I have of their childhood is taking them to Walt Disney World in America when they were two and four.

Miraj really suffered with earache due to air pressure on the flight, and I was frantic to find a solution. Miraj was a bit possessive of me, really, and Monique was closer to her mother, I think, at that time. Today, I am grateful to be equally close to both.

I was able to send them both to private school, after which they attended Russell Group universities.

Miraj works in finance and Monique in accountancy, both for international companies, and are successful in their own right.

After I moved to England, I went to Bangladesh to visit my family almost every year. I could travel for free, first class, because I had the travel business. Because I worked such hard, long hours, when I arrived at my parents' home, I would just sleep for the first few days. It was a relaxing time for me. I was able to switch off. My parents knew how hard I was working because I wrote home to tell them, and I was often spoken about in the home community as a result of my success in business.

When I was a student at SELTEC, Lewisham College, London, I was given some great advice by a teacher called Mr. Patrick Fitzgarald who taught us Production Engineering. He told us, 'You're studying Production Engineering. If you want to be a production manager, you must be able to switch off. If you can't switch off when you go home, then you'll kill yourself. Do your job as best you can and then go home and relax.' I took his advice. Practically, it did make sense to me.

My mother visited me twice in the UK. I was able to arrange the flight for free, as well as for my father who came once.

They would stay for quite a while. They both saw Mount Mascal Farm – my father was here for The Great Storm of 1987 as were Rashmi's parents – I was in Hong Kong. A huge tree came down and hit the garden wall at the bottom of our land. Fortunately, we were insured.

When my mother came to stay in England, because she wasn't comfortable with Rashmi, who didn't speak Bengali, she would stay with Sokina.

She came when my children were born, and she spent time with them and visiting relatives in other areas of London.

In 1990, when my father was dying, I visited him three times in Bangladesh. The third time I went, I took my sister's son Mitu with me and when he said, 'Nana' (grandpa), my father looked at him and miraculously smiled. To this day I remember that magical smile and derive immense pleasure picturing it in my mind. My father must have loved Mitu - his grandson profusely. As I flew home from this third visit, my father died while I was in the air. It was January 27, and he was 91 years old – a remarkable age. Moin said he would hold the burial to wait for me, but I told him, "No, don't do that. I want to remember him the way he was. I don't want to see him being buried." He was buried in Shah Jalal Darga Sharif – a special place for the elite members of society. We could have afforded to bury my father there, but they gave him the honour of being buried there for free. Because he was a stalwart of that society.

So many people were sad about my father's death. They congregated to pay their last respects to him – even his mechanic, the people he sold his businesses to and his retired drivers. He was a good man, and fair in his business dealings. He was trusted by people to look after their money, like a personal bank. He would put the money in his steel safe and give it back exactly intact as they gave him to store.

My father's death was a huge loss to me, and I felt deeply sad, even though I was relieved that his suffering was over. Here in London, Habib Bank's manager and staff at Whitechapel branch came down to Mount Mascal Farm - my home, to convey their condolences.

By this time, my brothers and I were no longer working together, which suited us. Moin was living in Bangladesh and said he would divide my father's property when our father died, but unfortunately, he did not keep his word. I feel he was influenced by his wife who probably out of necessity was protecting her children's future.

I was fine about it, I had enough of everything I needed. The only thing I wanted was an old wooden box that had belonged to my grandfather. It had been used as a safe and my father slept on top of it. I have it now – it lives in my office.

But Muslim was furious and fought Moin every step of the way. Sadly, Moin and Muslim never reconciled, which as anyone who has been through this sadly common situation knows, is totally awful. Previously, I had always taken Moin's side in any disagreement, along with my father. But I had to side with Muslim on this occasion and helped him as best I could. While he was in Bangladesh dealing with everything, Muslim caught Hepatitis B and died in November 1996, just six years after my father. He was only 56, the poor man. His wife partially blamed me for allowing Muslim to go to Bangladesh.

My father died the year before my son was born, so sadly they did not get to meet. I feel that my father's soul came back to me through my son as he and Miraj are so similar.

My father was brought up by his mother Julika Bibi as my grandfather, Dinar Uddin Ahmed, died when my father was only five. He died of cholera, an infectious disease rampant in 1905 in the villages of Karimgonj, Assam, India. My grandma was a tenacious, resilient and a loving person. I remember her vividly as an affectionate granny, always trying to feed me more.

Since my father and my grandma lived in a village, it is quite remarkable that he managed to make enough money to move us - his family, from the village to the town – a step up.

I didn't get to spend a great deal of time with my father, but the time we did spend together was very special. He had a favourite chair, similar to a deckchair, which was on the veranda on the back of the house I grew up in. He would sit in it and smoke a hubbly bubbly pipe and tell me stories. I loved to sit and listen. My father always had a calming effect on me.

Even as an adult, when I was in the UK, if I was in difficulty with business, I would telephone my father and he would calm me down. Moin, although he loved me, did not have the same soothing effect on me. My father had a slow and gentle voice. Moin spoke very quickly. But my father was a man of inner peace.

Haji Mubarak Ahmed was an extraordinary and incisive man. He was tall in stature and my father had gravitas. He was a great communicator and had a gift for organisation and mastered the art of managing people. He employed dozens of people and had them working together as he wished, very effectively.

There is a story he told me that will always stay with me.

One of my father's employees said to him respectfully, 'Haji Sab why are you paying Rajab Ali five rupee and me only three a month?'

My father said, 'Very well, let me explain Altab Miah. But first go and check the stable and check the size of the litter our dog Tila has given birth to.'

Altab Miah ran to the stable and came back quickly to say there were six cute puppies.
'What is their gender?' Asked my father.
'Sorry Haji Sab, I will have to go and check.
He came running back to say there were four female and two males.
'Very well, what are their colours?'
Altab Miah ran again only to come back and say two red and four white.

'How many has floppy ears and how many straight?'
By this time Altab Miah was exhausted and thought Haji Sab was making him work too hard. But dutifully he ran, huffing and puffing to check their ear position. 'Three floppy and three straight, Haji Sab.' My father at last said to Altab, 'You are exhausted my son. Come and sit by my side.'

He then summoned Rajab Ali who was busy doing something else at the far end of the field.
'Salaam Haji Sab, what do you want me to do?' asked Rajab Ali.
'Can you go to the stable and check the litter Tila has got?'
Rajab went and came back to report.
My father said, 'How many?
'Six.'
'What gender?'
'Four female and two males.'
'What colour?'
'Four white and two red.'
'What about their ears?'
'Three floppy and three straights.'
'Thank you, you can go back to your job.'
When Rajab was gone my father said to Altab, 'Now you know why Rajab gets more money.'

I apply this allegory to my life whenever the opportunity arises and accept the fact that people are born with different aptitudes and abilities. Some can be more gifted than others and must be valued as such commercially. I believe in the grammar school system, because I think exceptional students and people should be elevated. The state should help those who are naturally bright.

I can see the lesson of Tila's puppies in my life every day. Currently, I have builders working in the garden. The end result of their work is excellent, but I can see that some workers other than the master builder are simply not being efficient and precise.

The most important things I learned through my father are faith and contentment. He had faith and was contented. I have been inspired by his faith and I do my outmost to be contented. Whatever happens, it is God's will and I must accept it. Momentarily I may feel depressed after a loss but then I pick myself up and say, 'It was meant to happen. It was my destiny, and I must march on regardless'. My father would say patience is a virtue and I try to follow that.

My father was also amiable and a modest man, humble in his disposition. He was excellent at reading people. Farsighted and progressive, he made enough money to be able to move from Sunamgonj village into Sylhet town to educate his children and enabled him to help Moin and Muslim to have independent businesses in the newly opened Hassan Market, (Sylhet) in the 50s.

Even after his retirement, my father ran our textiles and garments shop called Eastern Fancy Store at 197, Hassan Market after Muslim left for London after a futile trivial quarrel with Moin in 1960. My father ran this shop for over seven years, until due to arthritis he had to sell it and start a transport business – a fleet of buses and trucks which he could run from home – Mubarak Monzil, Shibgonj, Sylhet. He continued supporting the family including his grandchildren and all while Moin was chasing much bigger dreams and Muslim was in London running his own things. My father had pragmatic and astute business sense. He established a source of income by setting up businesses for my brothers before building the beautiful grand house in town - Mubarak Monzil.

My father rose up the affluent social ladder of his community, my brother Moin doubled his fortune and became an elite in Sylhet. While I in comparison did the best I could in my diaspora community in London.

Yasmin, my Mother and Matt - 1991

My Mother 1989

My Father 1989

My mother – Haji Omarjan Bibi – had a personality which can be encapsulated in a nutshell. She was fiery and sharp! But she also had immense energy and was extremely compassionate and caring. Anybody in difficulties, financial or otherwise would go to her for help, and invariably she would find a solution.

She loved people and enjoyed being the centre of attention. This can also be described as her having enjoyed feeling superior to other people and giving them money, which she would get from me in the latter part of her life. If I didn't give her money, she would borrow it from a friend and tell them, "Muquim will return it to you." And to save her honour, I would capitulate every time. The same with her gold bangles. She would give them away then tell me she didn't have one, so I would have to send a replacement. It makes me laugh to think of it. She shouted at my father a lot. He wouldn't respond, which made her more furious at times and that she would be compelled to raise her voice and shout at him for attention – an unforgettable woman.

My mother, Omarjan was short compared to my father, but beautiful and fair. They were like chalk and coal. I have her complexion but my father's features. I also like to think I have my father's fortitude and grace and my mother's aptitude and charisma.

She was affectionate and caring. She would melt at someone's predicament and would go out of her way to help. My sister Rokiya Begum was married into a comparatively rich family. Over time misfortune befall my sister. My mother brought up my sister's children. They lived in her house and did their schooling in Sylhet.

Conspiciously, she loved Muslim over Moin but mysteriously she hung on to life till Moin returned from a trip to Singapore and then passed peacefully in his arms.

My Brother Moin, Muslim and my son Miraj, 1991

Me and Miraj

Miraj & Daniel (Brother Muslim's Grandson)

I lived away from home most of my life but when I was at home, my mother loved me to bits. She made sure that I had plenty of vegetable and fruit in my diet. I can't remember my mother ever cooking for the family but she made sure that there was a variety of food on the table. She was responsible and ran the household effectively.

Our parents brought us up in a culture of deference and an obsequious disposition with the moral boundaries and the customs and manners of the society in which we lived.

Clockwise: Brother Moin, Bhabi Nurun, Father, Bhabi Sokina, Brother Muslim, 1988

"There is no time for denunciation when conflict raises its nasty head. But reconciliation, harmony, sacrifice and understanding is necessary for a family to survive, progress and prosper."

Chapter Twelve
Victories and Victims

Immigration has certainly played a vital role in my life and those like me who chose to come into this country. The Brick Lane bombing was a dark moment and there have been other experiences that have not been as life threatening, but challenging and stressful.

Five years after the bomb attack, I found myself under attack from within my own immigrant community because of a misunderstanding over a letter I wrote — not for the last time. I endured a vicious physical attack from within my own community, which I will detail later in the book. But there is no doubt that I have been a controversial figure quite often. Many times, I have tried to stand up against injustice, unfairness, and subjugation and this has caused me pain and discomfort.

In 2004, the Entry Clearance officer at the British High Commission in Dhaka refused Sector Base Scheme (SBS) visas for hospitality workers from Bangladesh, even though the Home Office had provided the work permits. Several of my restaurant workers were among those who were refused entry. I wrote to the British High Commission appealing against the decision, stating that the visas should not be refused because the applicants are poor and would probably not return to Bangladesh when their visa expired.

But something went wrong, and the letter (appdx 262) was spun — to my detriment.

The Entry Control Officer (ECO) declared publicly that the reason for refusing the visas was because, 'Muquim Ahmed the President of British Bangladesh Chamber of Commerce said that these SBS scheme workers will not return home after expiry of their visa'. What I actually

Euro Bangla Weekly Journal

said was that it wasn't the British High Commission in Dhaka's job to refuse Sector Base Scheme (SBS) visas. People may well not return home, but that should not be the concern of the High Commission. It is the law of the land (home office) that should compel them to return.'

The Bengali newspapers in the UK made a huge fuss out of this. The story was published in almost all the ethnic papers. It was reported on the front pages that the British High Commission in Dhaka was refusing clearance to SBS scheme applicants because I warned that they would not return after their visas expired. This was not the case. I was appalled.

I had passionately argued in my letter that the scheme was designed for unskilled workers who were suited for menial jobs, and therefore they would be poor. David Blunkett, home secretary at the time, had introduced the scheme to let the destitute in the developing countries to come to Britain to do the jobs the indigenous population refused to do. The scheme might have been fundamentally flawed but it was not for the ECO to refuse applications by claiming that I had said the workers were poor and would not return. This was not what I was saying.

This caused havoc in the Bengali community in the United Kingdom. People were up in arms and the misunderstanding threatened my life. Obnoxious phone calls and abusive encounters in shops and Bengali restaurants made life unbearable.

The fact that I was a prominent member of the community kept the headline writers busy. The newspaper Euro Bangla led the way in hounding me. Week after week they harried me with stories until I finally succumbed and agreed to compensate a few workers who had been refused entry due to the misquote by the immigration officer. It cost me a few thousand pounds.

Fortunately, an appeal against the ECO's refusal reached the immigration courts in UK in the nick of time. The adjudicator allowed the SBS scheme applicants entry and made clear that I had been misquoted by the ECO.

 The British High Commission apologised to me, and this brought the emotional fiasco to a close (appdx 266)

Thankfully some members of the community were supportive and saw that my views had been taken out of context. G U Choudhury, then president of British Bangladesh National Council (appdx 267), was among those who stood by me and helped me through the ordeal. Barrister Anis ur Rahman OBE, a community leader, defended me on talk-shows on community TV programmes.

As the saying goes, evil thrives in darkness. I was arguing with the ECO that he could not refuse entry to my prospective Café Naz staff, who had already been given permits by the Home Office. I had clearly stated that the ECO could not refuse visas to my staff on the basis that they were poor, and because he thought that they might not return. But the way it was spun, and that it was I who had warned that they would not return, caused me embarrassment and pain.

Confusion and misunderstanding can happen in life, but one should have the tenacity and perseverance to prevail. Most times, a bright day comes after a dark night.

Chapter Thirteen

Cambridge University Debate

After the devastation of Brick Lane bombing and the difficulties of the imigration SBS (Sector Base Scheme) letter, here I am in 2006 being asked to participate in a debate at the Cambridge Union. A member of a diaspora, a boy from a small town in Bangladesh, invited to step on to a stage where great statesmen had stood since the union was established in 1815.

This was the stage where Eden, Baldwin, Churchill and Roosevelt participated in debate. Proudly in 1947, the first Indian Prime Minister J L Nehru addressed the Union.

The motion that evening Thursday, 18th May 2006 was 'This House Would Place A Limit On Immigration.' Alongside me arguing against the motion stood Catherine Fieschi of the think-tank Demos, and Phillip Cole, principal lecturer in Applied Philosophy at Middlesex University and author of Philosophies of Exclusion.

For the proposition were Sir Andrew Green (later Lord Green), founder of campaign group Migration Watch UK, lawyer and former Tory parliamentary candidate Sangeeta Sidhu and Peter Hitchens, author, broadcaster and Mail on Sunday journalist. I had to make special arrangement with Alyson Thompson , President Elect, of Cambridge Union for a seat at the high table for my friend Shahagir Bakth for dinner, who accompanied me to Cambridge that day.

Below, is the extract of my speech from that debate held on that exceptional day:

THE CAMBRIDGE UNION SOCIETY

EASTER TERM 2006 ~ 4TH DEBATE
~ THURSDAY 18TH MAY ~

THIS HOUSE WOULD PLACE A LIMIT
ON IMMIGRATION

Proposition:	Opposition:
SIR ANDREW GREEN Migration Watch UK	CATHERINE FIESCHI Demos
MS SANGEETA SIDHU Lawyer and Former Parliamentary candidate	MR MUQUIM AHMED Immigrant entrepreneur and Brick Lane Millionaire
MR PETER HITCHENS Author, broadcaster and journalist for the Mail on Sunday	MR PHILLIP COLE Principal lecturer in applied philosophy at Middlesex University, Author of "Philosophies of Exclusion"

PRESIDENT IN THE CHAIR:
ALYSON THOMPSON
(TRINITY COLLEGE)

"I begin by opposing the motion that there should be no limit on immigration.

Our society has changed, our needs have changed, our world has become a global village.

Travel and communication have become rampant; migration for better quality of life is inevitable.

Most of the developed nations are opening their doors to managed migration. Those nations who are not confident and resourceful are frightened and may shut their doors, but we here at United Kingdom are keen to enhance our work force to serve the nation.

Stelios Haji-Ioannou of [airline] EasyJet, who is himself an immigrant, said only recently that for an economy to be vibrant, you need people from another country who will work relentlessly to succeed because of their disposition.

Immigration is a vital part of the welfare of this country. The NHS is the biggest importer of migrant labour. Our national statistics show that 40 per cents of all nurses are immigrants and 30 per cents of all our doctors are immigrants.

America, the world power of today, the greatest nation on earth, the greatest success story of integrated migration, is a nation of immigrants. It is said that they have it in their genes to be energetic, vibrant, enthusiastic with an exceptional zeal to succeed.

As a nation we have some inherent problems. Our birth rate is falling, and our population is growing older. We desperately need younger people to man skilled and unskilled jobs and create wealth to support the pensioners. The Government functions on borrowed money. It has spent the wealth created by our forebears and now it needs young vibrant migrants to fill up the deficit which we acknowledge we have in our economy.

The Home Office is relentlessly trying to reform the Asylum and Immigration Bill. The right of appeal against refusal is to be abolished, which is certainly an awesome blow to social justice, a system we are so proud of. Immigration limit will hamper the economic growth, the growth and diversity of our nation.

A displaced individual will have to work that much harder to establish himself and, in that process, creates wealth for himself and hence for the nation.

The Government of today will have to be wary of the way they tackle the controlled migration issue.

The resultant cannot be a burden on the social welfare in anyway. It must be an asset for the nation.

We welcome inward investment into the country. Sometime Prime Ministers lobby for such investments. The Government of the day will have to pick and choose. The migrants, we will have to pick and choose as well.

The skilled migration scheme will enhance our society and enrich the Government's coffers. It is estimated that billions of pounds are generated from the Work Permit scheme for the Government.

Ladies and Gentlemen, I come from a sector — the catering and hospitality industry —known to have acute shortage of staff. The 'back of house', which is the kitchen, have chefs who are not paper qualified enough to fall in the skilled TIER systems.

Tony McNulty, the immigration minister, said that if proper certificates are provided then he assures the Entry Clearance officers should be sympathetic in providing the entry visas.

The immigration chief at the Home Office, David Roberts, came under fire after he told [John] Denham's [Home Affairs] Committee that he did not have the 'faintest idea' how many illegal immigrants were in the country.

We lost our Home Secretary [Charles Clarke] after the release of 1,000-odd foreign convicted criminals into our society.

Especially when one of whom committed a gruesome murder of a police officer. The Prime Minister Tony Blair was struggling last night in the Commons with such issues.

Ladies and gentlemen, immigration is a big issue, and we need to address it more directly — Our universities and colleges, our research and development programmes, should work side by side with politicians and come up with a solution which is pragmatic and realistic. We require skilled, qualified immigrants as and when we need them. We cannot put a 'limit' as society is constantly changing, and our need is varying all the time.

Therefore, we cannot have a set limit. Hence, I oppose the motion.

We draw as and when our need arises. 'Necessity is the mother of invention."

We won the debate. And after our victory, Phillip Cole wrote to me saying: 'I think the three of us made an excellent and formidable team.'

"We require skilled, qualified immigrants as and when we need them.
We cannot put a 'limit' as society is constantly changing, and our need is varying all the time.
Therefore, we cannot have a set limit.
Hence, I oppose the motion."

OBSERVATIONS

A COOL MILLION?

SEAN CAREY

EVERYONE in London's East End Bangladeshi community knows Muquim Ahmed. He is their youngest and most successful entrepreneur. The rumour is that he is a millionaire. The tag does not impress Muquim himself—a small, bespectacled man, aged 29, with a nice line in suits. He sees himself as a worker, rather than as a member of some remote financial aristocracy. "Who is a millionaire?" he asks. "Not me. I might have a big house, nice cars and a lot of money, but a millionaire is someone who has three or four million pounds in cash." He taps his fingers on his office desk. "Anyway I do not live like a millionaire. A millionaire can sit back and let other people earn the money for him. But I haven't come to that stage yet. I still work hard. Very hard in fact."

Muquim, the youngest in a family of three brothers and a sister, came to Britain at the age of 18 from the Sylhet district in the north of Bangladesh to study production engineering. He remembers vividly his first sight of London. "I had never seen anything like it. Such a big city. When I was coming along the motorway from the airport, I said to myself, 'My God, this is beautiful!' Beautiful? "Yes, beautiful," he replies. "Everything was organised. Have you ever been to Bangladesh? No. Ah, then let me tell you that it's all chaos. There's no system. Even driving a car is difficult. Not like over here. That's why I take my hat off to you people. You have systems."

Muquim claims that an engineer is what he really wanted to be. "I used to dream of it when I was a small boy. But in life it happens that what you want to be, you cannot be," he says cheerily. "You become something else."

So how did he become something else?

"Well, my eldest brother, Moin, had a travel shop at Mile End. It was quite a good little business. But then he decided to go back to Bangladesh, and go into import and export. So I was given the shop to look after. It wasn't so bad. I used to have lectures only a few hours a day, so I was able to look after the office and do my study at the same time. With the profits of that place, I bought a shop at Brick Lane [in the heart of the old Jews, now Bangladeshi, district of Whitechapel] a seven year lease, and started another tra agency. I had to work pretty hard. You se wanted the agency from Bangladesh A lines, but first I had to prove to them tha could give them the business—that I w closely connected with the community. Th watched me for about three months, and th they appointed me their agent. I think th were worried that I was so young. I was o 20 at the time. I think everyone thought I that. I remember some English people co ing to connect the phones in the office a one of them said, 'You're a bit young to o all this.' They were a bit shocked, you kno

These reactions taught Muquim that it v important to look smart and acquire the tra pings of success. "If you don't have a get-t people don't seem to trust you," he s matter-of-factly. It was what motivated h to dress in Cecil Gee suits costing £400 £500 a time, to drive a Rolls-Royce Sil Shadow—"A great car. You can't get bet than that, can you?"—and, three years a to buy a house in Bexleyheath that is equ ped with sauna, jacuzzi and swimming p and worth a cool half million.

The success of the travel agency allo Muquim to branch out. He went into record business in 1978. He brought over ists from Bangladesh, recorded them i small makeshift studio on Brick Lane, pressed records by hand. "For two year was okay," Muquim recalls. "I was mak £300 or £400 a week profit. Then I was hit piracy. But the thing that really sank record business was video." These were to ing times. Muquim put together some lig ning-fast deals. In 1980 he acquired the lea and then the freehold, on the huge but li used Naz cinema (a former Odeon) on Br Lane. He imported films from Banglade showed them on the big screen, and m videos of the same films on licence. "I making money twice over," he says.

The enterprise that launched him into big time and out of the ethnic business m was his insight into the wholesale trade was doing retailing in video and hi-fi equ ment, and I could see how much money people I was buying off were making thought, 'What am I doing buying fr them? Why not buy directly from who they're getting it from?' You see I am competitive that way."

Muquim's Sylto Cash and Carry has a tu over of £20,000 a day. He sells anything fr televisions and radio cassettes to wallets w calculators and watches. His customers co from as far as Scotland, Ireland Guernsey. "They come because I am chea he says. "They are mainly shopkeepers market traders who buy in bulk. It's no gc selling one watch at a time. Even if a frie

LTD

New Society April 1985

Chapter Fourteen
A Cool Million

If an immigrant like me can progress and prosper, anyone, with zeal and determination, can. A Cool Million, an article written by Dr Sean Carey, honorary senior research fellow in the school of Social Science, University of Manchester, outlines my hopes and aspirations, and my successes. I hope readers will be inspired. Carey astutely portrays my character — I am resilient, persistent and determined.

The £500 Cecil Gee suits and the Silver Shadow Rolls-Royce were not come by easily. But looking wealthy; looks alone, will not help. Commitment is of paramount importance. You must be able to perform. Like they say, it takes years to build a reputation but to lose one just takes a single gaffe. For a man to be successful, he must be dignified, trustworthy and amiable.

The secret of my success lay in my communication skills, and I was confident and determined. I had self-belief: I can do it. Another aspect of my success was that I was engaging. My mission was that the man across the table to me had to know he was dealing with a fair and conciliatory person.

To be successful, one must build goodwill in the market. You must be predictable and honourable. It's the same as a successful brand: same quality every time. You must have a reputation for fulfilling your commitments, no matter the prospects.

Having to deal with the Bank of England while setting up my Collection Account through NatWest helped me to establish my credibility.

SIAN TIMES Tuesday September 7 1993

PROFILE

ASIAN TIMES: BACKING ASIAN BUSINESSES

Bangladeshi 'Boy Wonder'

.D. GOVENDER meets a young
man who was born with a silver
spoon in his mouth, has conquered
and continues to conquer.

EBONAIR. SUAVE.
intillating. Youthfully
uberant, yet as wise
a Roman elder states-
in. An Empire builder
th solid foundations,
d many sizeable
hievements to his cre-
t, and with a lot more
pected of a man who
s the appearance of a
ill-groomed Vienna
oir boy, without any
ice of the customary
thlessness that one
sociates with powerful
oons.

lat's a potted sum-
ry of the Bangladeshi
y Wonder, Muquim
med, who made his
tune while still in his
enties. There are
iny astonishing Asian
ccess stories, but you
e not likely to come
ross an infant genius
Muquim's calibre.
He is worth many mil-
ns, certainly his elec-
nics company, one of
many interests,
ns over a prodigious
m, which the shy,
ing, but ebullient and
rmly cordial and ami-
le Muquim Ahmed,
uses to elaborate on.
summed up his atti-
de in an interview
th a journalist in
85: "Who, is a mil-
naire? Not me. I
ght have a big house,
e cars and a lot of
ney, but a millionaire
someone who has
ree or four million
nds in cash. Anyway
o not live like a mil-

lionaire. A millionaire
can sit back and let
other people earn the
money for him. But I
haven't come to that sta-
ge yet. I still work hard.
Very hard in fact."

Muquim Ahmed
uttered these words in
April, 1985, at a time
when he drove a Roller
and owned a house with
a market value of
£500,000. In September,
1993, Muquim's attitude
still remains as intelli-
gently modest, cautious
and realistic.

Muquim, who was
born in Bangladesh, was
educated in the best
English-medium private
schools in the country.
That accounts for some
of his very positive pub-
lic school mannerisms, a
virile confidence, a quick
and lively mind, the
ability to lead from the
front, coolness under
fire, a self-deprecating
air, an equable tempera-
ment and that most en-
viable attribute, sound
judgment of individuals.

His privileged
bourgeois family in-
sisted on a good educa-
tion for the bright and
cheerful boy, hoping
that he would join the
family electronics busi-
ness. They despatched
him abroad for further
studies after he had got
a BA Hons in Physics.
Muquim Ahmed arrived
in this country, aged 19
in 1973. He was aso-
nishingly frank and gen-

erous in his appraisal of
London. He was also
affectionately critical of
his own Bangladesh. He
recalled his first reac-
tion to the metropolis in
1985: "I had never seen
anything like it. Such a
big city. When I was
coming along the motor-
way from the airport, I
said to myself, 'My God,
this is beautiful. Beautiful? Yes beautiful. Ev-
erything was organised.
Have you ever been to
Bangladesh? No. Ah,
then let me tell you that
it's all chaos. There's no
system. Even driving a
car is difficult. Not like
over here. That's why I
take my hat off to you
people. You have sys-
tems."

He has his own "sys-
tems", which combined
with his extraordinary
brain, and his restless,
constructive energy, has
taken him a long way up
the road to success.
There are still a few
more peaks to climb, not
out of necessity, but be-
cause the man simply
enjoys the challenge.

While studying Pro-
duction Engineering in
this country, his ambi-
tion was to be an en-
gineer. Muquim also
acted as buyer for the

family firm in Bangla-
desh, which controlled
the fridge and tv market
in the whole country.
They were also sole
agents for Bedford
trucks.

While still studying,
Muquim took over his
brother's travel busi-
ness. The brother had
returned to his native
country to start an
export-import business.
With the profits from
the travel business, then
enjoying a colossal
boom, the student-

entrepreneur bought a
shop at 48 Brick Lane
and started another tra-
vel agency. Not bad for a
20-year old. He wanted
the Bangladesh Biman
agency for the area, but
his age was something
of a barrier. However
the wise chaps at Biman
did not write him off,
they watched his prog-
ress and soon found that
he was good for their
business and gave him
the agency.

It's one thing being a
prodigy, but another

Profile of Muquim Ahmed

Date of birth: Born Sylhet, September 1, 1954
Educated: Sylhet Government College. In London
added to to his BA Hons in Physics from Bangladesh,
the Higher National Diploma in Production Engineer-
ing.
Married: Rashmi from Nairobi, 2½ year old son. We have
just learned that Rashmi has presented Muquim with a
baby girl!
Favourite Food: "Very easy with food." Prefers home
cooking. Not fussy about Western or Eastern cuisine.
Had housekeeper for 8 years and she fed him entirely on
English food. Happily survived the experience!
Hobby: Fancies himself as a writer, and hopes to
surprise his friends with a novel.
Transport: Owns a Rolls Royce, a Porsche and a Merc.
Enjoys driving.
Likes: Disciplined people who are methodical and time
conscious. "Tempus fugit, time flies, but we should not
kill it."
Dislikes: Those who do not view life positively.
Favourite Colour: Blue

---

squaring up to the im-
age of maturity that
supposedly goes with
age. To compensate for
that, the quick thinking
Muquim hit on a sarto-
rial answer on the basis
that an immaculately
tailored gent cut a fine
and convincing figure.
Honorary Eastender,
though he was, Muquim
rejected the traditional
Arthur Daley style in
glittering suits, going
for the sober and conser-
vative Cecil Gee, which
at that time cost £500 a
go. And he acquired a
Silver Shadow Roller. "A
great car," he says, "You
can't get better than
that can you?"

Muquim became the
first to produce what in
the 70s were called re-
cords. Artistes from
Bangladesh were
brought over to record
the latest hits. These
sold extremely well. But
the pirates stepped in
and queered the pitch.
"But," he recalls, "it was
the emergence of the
video that dealt the
death blow to the record
business."

In 1980, Muquim
bought the freehold of a
former Odeon cinema in
Brick Lane, renaming it
Naz, the first Asian-
owned cinema in the
country. Films from
Bangladesh were given
big screen exposure.
Under licence, the ethi-
cally correct Muquim
made videos of the films.
He made money twice
over.

Then came the big
one. "I was retailing
video and hi-fi equip-
ment, and I could see
how much money the
people I was buying
from were making. I
said to myself 'What am
I doing buying from
them? Why not buy
directly from where
they're getting it from.'
You see I am very com-
petitive that way."

Thus was born Mu-
quim's Sylto Cash and
Carry which in 1980 had
a turnover of £20,000 a
day, considerably more
today despite the reces-
sion. His customers
come from all over Bri-
tain because he operates
on the unbeatable Asian
principle of: SPQR -
Small Profits, Quick Re-

turn.

There are other i
terests which are al
ticking over nicely. He
in publishing, impo
and export, amuseme
arcades, restauran
and retailing. All this I
the time Muquim w;
all of 30!

He was one of the lo
ers in the BCCI affa
For a while he was u
set, but then he put
behind him as one of th
bad cards that fate dea
from time to time. He
not just an optimist, b
optimism is sel
fulfilling because l
makes it happen th;
way. He loves convers
tion, he loves to lear
and has a boyish et
thusiasm for life. He
a most generous ho;
who takes his guest
business and social, '
the best restaurants
town.

Like Alexander th
Great, Muquim looks fi
new worlds to conque
He says: "Life is con
petition. It's all abo
the survival of the fi
test. I want to be th
first in my field. I wa
to direct the affairs
the first Bengali PLC i
this country."

His home in Bexley
tucked away in a mini
ture forest with tenn
court, swimming poo
sauna and jacuzzi. Th
lawns are as smooth ;
the green baize of a b
liard table, and ther
are a variety of interes
ing and intriguing tree
plants and flowers.

Although Muquim ha
a full-time gardener, h
is in charge and work
with his own hands. Th
business on Saturda
afternoon and the whol
of Sunday in the Englis
summer, which is enti
tely devoted to plantin
pruning, transplantin
and landscaping. "N
activity is closer to m
heart than gardening,
he says with, for th
first time, a fanatica
gleam in his eye. The
say that people wh
work with plants are
because of their close
ness to nature, calmnes
and serenity personi
fied. That fits the bil
where the good nature:
contented and very be
nevolent Muquim
Ahmed is concerned

THE DIPLOMAT AND THE TYCOON: Dr Yusuf, the venerable High Commissioner for Bangladesh, and the youthfuly, effervescent Muquim Ahmed at
a recent House of Commons reception.
Photo: Shah Ahmed Sadeque

Millions of pounds of other people's money were transacted, which helped to show that I was trustworthy and reliable. This gave me the courage to ask NatWest Bank to help me to buy Naz Cinema. I was able to do this with the commission I earned from these transactions.

In those days, banks were reluctant to lend to Asians, primarily because of the temporary nature of our residence in this country. The mindset was that we had come to the UK to earn money, not to settle, and we would soon return to our country of origin. I assured the bank, explaining that I was a marathon runner; I did not intend to give up halfway. I am here to adopt, change and flourish.

A bank manager needs a predictable, performing individual to lend money to, an enterprise that is profitable and can repay the principal and the interest. Even at an early age I grasped that philosophy and fulfilled those ideals so I could progress.

It is of paramount importance that our up-and-coming generation sow the seeds of trust and goodwill with the financial institutions they are dealing with. Commitment and punctuality are the essence of all transactions. It takes a lifetime to build the trust, but only a moment to destroy it.

In his profile of me titled Bangladeshi Boy Wonder, published in the Asian Times in 1993, GD Govender describes me as a man born fortunate. He wrote that I was of 'equable temperament, quick and lively mind and with the ability to lead from the front'. An enthusiastic analysis. But I like to believe that I am an incisive person, ardent and astute. I do perform well under pressure. When I was at high school, I would be involved in sports and games, managing and attending to other people's difficulties and differing abilities.

EAST LONDON Advertiser

TOWER HAMLETS · HACKNEY & INCORPORATING STRATFORD · NEWHAM · WEST HAM ADVERTISER

No. 5422   Friday, May 3, 1985   01-729 1414; Classified: 593 3100   18p

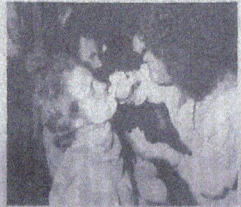

• Couple in homes sale fury... Page 13

VE DAY SPECIAL TURN TO PAGE 23

• A close shave for charity Page 8

THE EAST END'S 'MR MONEY'

I'VE MADE A MILLION'

BY KEN HAYES

TWENTY pounds, a suitcase of clothes and a fierce determination to succeed — that's all Muqim Ahmed had to start on the road to riches.

Today, just ten years after he arrived from Bangladesh, the softly-spoken, bespectacled 29-year-old businessman is a millionaire living in a £500,000 country house and driving a Rolls Royce.

The recipe for his success is a simple motto: "If you have the will to be a rich man, you will become rich."

Muqim was an 18-year-old student when he came to Britain to learn production engineering.

He's from Sylhet in north-east Bangladesh, home for all but a handful of the East End's 40,000 Asians.

"When I arrived, I thought all Britain was like the airport — air-conditioned," said Muqim.

"I soon found that wasn't so, but I did learn this country was clean, tidy and systematic. I'd had a good education at home and I wanted to succeed."

Muqim began working in his elder brother's travel shop in Brick Lane, seven days a week, 12 hours a day.

His travel business has grown, and he is now the ... ing the soundtrack — international shipping and a cash and carry business.

"Give me any situation and I will examine it and make the best of it," said Muqim.

He directs operations from a modest office in Chicksand Street, Spitalfields, sitting in an ornate green velvet chair at a glass-topped desk within easy reach of his "tools" — a single white telephone, a diary, a cheque-book and a calculator.

And July sees completion of the development at Brick Lane's Naz Cinema into an Asian community and social centre, combined with a unique Indian restaurant-cum-takeaway for businessmen, complete with Stock Exchange link-up.

He also has plans to buy a ...

ROYAL SEND OFF

• Prince Philip launches a sail of the century — See page 3

Occasionally I had less time for my own studies. But I did well in my final exams. My ability to concentrate and focus when needed helped me to achieve much more than my peer group.

Key Haynes in the East London Advertiser on May 3, 1985 wrote: 'Twenty pounds, a suitcase of clothes and a fierce determination to succeed — that's all Muquim Ahmed had to start on the road to riches.'

(I don't know why he wrote £20 as it was £5, which was all Bangladesh State Bank would allow you to take out of the country then.)

If you have the will to be a rich man, you will become rich.
It is the faith and determination and the capacity to weather life's ups and downs, being focused and resilient throughout, that will always win the day.

Life was tough in the East End of London. Race, creed, and colour played an important part in the day-to-day of our life. Sometimes I would come face to face with racism but I would absorb it and march on. One day I was waiting to pick up my father-in-law Shanti Lal Bakshi from Bethnal Green Underground Station. As soon as he got in and slammed the passenger door, some men appeared from nowhere and started punching and kicking the car and its windows. Luckily the windows were up, and doors locked. Frightened, we drove to the police station, which was only few yards from us. Noticing our distress, four policemen rushed to the station, but the perpetrators were gone.

A year later, 1976, I seem to recall, on a Sunday afternoon, I was strolling towards the Clifton, the famous restaurant, for my lunch. Clifton was on the other side of Brick Lane from me.

I was living in the flat upstairs at 48 Brick Lane in those days. I'd just passed Taj Store, the huge grocery outlet, suddenly the shutters along the street started coming down – a fearsome group of skinhead boys hurtled down Brick Lane towards me. They started throwing milk bottles. I was trapped. Instinct took hold. I screamed and threw milk bottles back at them. By God's will, from either side of the street, the shop keepers attacked the skinheads with broomsticks and shutter sticks. Luckily nobody was seriously hurt. I came out of it completely unharmed. What an escape!

There was the story in the newspapers next day that we, hapless Bangladeshi immigrants, were mercilessly beaten by skinheads. The opposite was true. It was the skinheads who was sent packing.

Racism for us took many forms, of course. We struggled to secure finance often because banks were not keen to handle coloured people's accounts and ethnic businesses were difficult to operate on the high streets. Bangladeshi people operated on the periphery of society. Yet I catapulted myself forward and succeeded in securing support from the bank and the multicultural society I was living in.

How? Hard work, good manners, determination, and positive attitude — and a belief in my own capabilities to survive progress and prosper.

For me a glass is always half full.

"Brick Lane 1978"

*"A fearsome group of skinhead boys hurtled down
Brick Lane towards me. They started throwing
milk bottles. I was trapped. Instinct took hold.
I screamed and threw milk bottles back at them.
By God's will, from either side of the street,
the shop keepers attacked the skinheads with
broomsticks and shutter sticks.
Luckily nobody was seriously hurt.
I came out of it completely unharmed.
What an escape!"*

EAST LONDON Advertiser

071-790 8822

THURSDAY, OCTOBER 27, 1994

30p

200 lose jobs after ordeal by fire

firefighters silhouetted against the flames: At the height of the blaze the jets of water were turning to steam.

Photo: London Fire Brigade

FLAMING HELL!

East Enders evacuated in £5m burn-up

BY JULIA HARTLEY-BREWER

TWENTY-five East Enders were evacuated to safety when their homes were threatened by a raging blaze which left a factory and warehouse gutted, £5 million damage and 200 people jobless.

■ Special report pages 6&7

EMALE P44 ■ LETTERS P20,21 ■ TV P31-34 ■ LISTINGS P42,43 ■ COURTS P14 ■ SPORT STARTS

Chapter Fifteen

The Phoenix Rises from the Ashes

October 21, 1994

A phone call in the dead of night woke me up. I checked the clock. It was 1.15am. I answered the phone, still in a daze. It was the police. At first, I thought the alarm had gone off in the warehouse, and the police were telephoning to alert me; it was normally the case when you were woken up in the middle of the night by a call from the authorities.

But there had been a fire. I had to hurry and get to the warehouse, let the services in to give them ease of access so they could put out the blaze. They said it was small and at the back of the building, so I quickly grabbed my clothes and drove off at speed to Chicksand Street. But to my distress, it was not a small fire. Huge flames engulfed the rear of the building on Heneage Street. It was, as the East London Advertiser described it later, a 'FLAMING HELL' - 5 million pounds damaged and 200 people jobless.

My first thought was for the people working in those factories housed in that part of the building. Fire brigade officers were too busy trying to control the flames to be concerned about the contents of the offices, despite, among others, Mohib Choudhury, Nahas Pasha, Tara Miah, Abdul Matin, Hamid Choudhury and Razzak Nana — who had their offices on the first floor — arguing with the brigade officer to allow them inside to salvage their belongings.

I also shared offices with my sister companies Notun Din (the Bengali News weekly) and The Asian Post in the adjacent building at Chicksand Street, most of which was occupied by Sylto Plc.

The police and fire brigade stopped occupiers entering their offices because of the fire. Tears rolled down Mohib's face. He was the editor of Notun Din. I could hardly control my emotions: my entire life's venture was at stake. The warehouse was full to the brim, ready for the Christmas trade. I was totally devastated. Before my eyes, the flames threatened to engulf the entire block. Officers comforted everyone and explained the danger to life, and that they were limiting and containing the fire where it was most intense. They were going to do their best to save some of the buildings, they said. Indeed, Sylto Plc's offices were among those saved.

Many who worked in those offices and factories were there, witnessing the blaze. They were comforting one another, wondering how this terrible thing had happened. No one knew at the time. The police were unable to confirm whether it was arson or accident.

I was so numb with pain and so disillusioned that I almost collapsed. My friend Hamid Choudhury, who lived in the flats opposite, took me in and made me a cup of hot coffee and said: 'It is all God's will. By His grace, the phoenix will rise again. Have faith. Destruction and commotion will come but construction and comfort will follow. Insha'Allah. It is all His will.'

More than a hundred spectators stayed until late the following morning as the fire still burned. Two fire engines were damping the flames as late as 10am in the morning. What a sight!

Where last night there had been piles of stock, there was now ash, carpeting the ground. Fire officers would not allow anyone to enter, even into the apparently undamaged front of the building; they feared that its foundation could be unstable. Apparently, the fire brigade made the ruins safe and then left. Some of us were desperate, we wanted to venture into the debris and look around to see if anything could be salvaged.

Clive Jennings, our company accountant, ordered that our part of the building should be boarded up. So it was.

The intensity of the blaze had been so great that the steel beam in the main building had been twisted, with no trace of the timber that bridged the floors. A four-storey skeleton of twisted steel stood where the warehouse had been.

Fire at Chicksand Street, 22nd Oct. 1994

At 10.30am, Sagheer Qurashi, Habib Bank's general manager in charge of the UK operation, visited the site. Our next door neighbour Abtar Singh, who had a cloth manufacturing warehouse, was kind enough to provide tea and coffee for everyone.

But it didn't help me; I was a depressed soul who by then thought life was not worth living.

Mr. Qurashi, however, was a great comfort. He assured me that Sylto Plc would have all the support it needed from Habib Bank. He would do everything possible to make sure Sylto got on its feet again and move forward, regardless of this great loss.

The bank's support and reassurance were very graciously accepted. Yet grief and sorrow overwhelmed me. It all came so suddenly; I got totally lost. I started having nightmares and losing sleep at night, suffering insomnia. Sometimes in the middle of the night, I would wake up drenched in sweat. Why should it happen to me? How can Allah be so cruel? The horror of the fire haunted me relentlessly.

I was battered but I like to think that I was not broken and thought, misfortune befalls but cannot last long, good fortune is bound to follow. One could only hope because hope keeps us alive. It was only a matter of time, surely, until things improved. Churchill urged resilience in the face of adversity; not fretting or indulging in despair. Of course, it is easy to say these things, be optimistic, but extremely hard when you have suffered such a blow. I went to Umrah, a mini pilgrimage to Mecca, and found it extremely comforting.

Trading from the burned warehouse was impossible, though the office block of Sylto Plc was almost intact. Mr. Qurashi, the General Manager of Habib Bank offered us a re-possessed property at Fournier Street. We moved quickly and started trading from there. Sylto Plc marched on despite this great misfortune.

Sylto Plc's insurance claim in respect of stock was £1.2 million and in respect of the Chicksand Street premises, which was personally owned by me, was of £1.5m. With the consequential losses, the claimed loss from the insurer amounted to over £3 million. The losses were reported to the insurers, NAF&G Fidelity SA. Everything seemed to be normal, and the claim was going to be settled. But the insurer appointed a forensic expert to the claim. The appointed forensic expert was snooping around to find clues as to how the fire had started. There was a clause in the insurance policy prohibiting the use of Calor gas heaters in any of the premises in the buildings.

There were five independent buildings, three facing Chicksand Street and two facing Heneage Street and we had a strict regime: none of us, or the tenants, could use portable gas heaters. This was stipulated in their leases. Because of this punitive clause, if a Calor gas heater was found in any of the premises, the insurance would become null and void. The forensic investigator was trying desperately to find a gas cylinder at the burnt site. We had also engaged an insurance assessor who has been taking photographs of the site to prove that there were no gas cylinders. The insurers were trying to wiggle out of paying. This confrontation went on for over a year.

Finally, when everybody's patience was in tatters, Sylto PLC was forced to engage solicitors Davies Arnold Cooper (DAC), the specialist insurance solicitors in the City.

After pursuing the claim for two years, everything came to a halt because NAF&G Fidelity SA declared bankruptcy.

Flaming Hell, indeed!

Trauma has taught me a virtue in life: no matter how hard you try, accidents can happen. One must accept the eventualities.

You may be flying high; you have the wind beneath your wings, yet a lightning can strike, and you are almost instantly senseless on the ground.

Consolation and encouragement do go a long way but yet you feel incapacitated, debilitated. You must pick yourself up. Difficult, yes, but life has to go on. At such time, Allah comes to your aid. Faith motivates you; you stand up and try to walk away from the tragedy.

I was like a tightrope walker, balancing high up between two mountains. I did walk with confidence and skill, but sometimes the wind changed direction unexpectedly and I slipped from the rope. I was dangled a thousand feet above the ocean, between the mountains; swinging between life and death. Still hanging, clutching with both hands to the rope, the lifeline. I have got to pull myself up for myself and for my young family, I told myself — a last grasp for existence.

Adrenalin kicked in. With all my strength I pulled myself up. Desperately, I clung on to life, managed to sit on the rope as it swayed due to the slightest motion of the wind. Yes, I was totally engulfed, burned, destroyed and devastated; but with sheer determination, and by the skin of my teeth, I kept my sanity.

Sometimes, you can be the cleverest, most industrious person, but because of debilitating circumstances, you can fail.

But it is the will and the zest for life that one hangs on to, and you climb and walk again. So, I stood up and said to myself: I have to march on regardless. Unfortunately, as I mentioned, my insurer went into liquidation. In the process, Sylto Plc lost again a huge sum of money in legal fees. I then had to file negligence claim against my broker, Miles Emblin & Co.

Another challenge, another walk on the tightrope for survival.

"With all my strength I pulled myself up. Desperately, I clung on to life, managed to sit on the rope and kept my sanity."

- *Muquim Ahmed*

Chapter Sixteen
Pressing Ahead

Publishing
The Asian Post

Recalling GD Govender's Bangladeshi Boy Wonder story, which appeared in Asian Times in September 1993, I set about convincing the acclaimed journalist to join my newspaper The Asian Post, which was established in 1992.

On 10 January 1995 we announced in the paper that 'GD Govender, Britain's most proterfeaturely outspoken and controversial ethnic columnist, joins The Asian Post where every week his elegant and penetrating prose is likely to cut to the heart of any matter he cares to deal with.'

Beside the Bengali news weekly, Notun Din — which you can read about further along — of which I was then the Managing Director, I established The Asian Post in 1992. It reflected primarily on life for British Asian society in the United Kingdom as well as what was happening in the Indian sub-continent. The newspaper had an independent editorial board headed by Executive Editor Abdul Montaqim, but it was always closely monitored by me because I knew that ultimate responsibility would lie with me should there ever be any claim against us, or a failure — I would be the one to bear the brunt.

Everything was going well. The workforce was growing. Readers enjoyed the content we produced. Our distribution network was expanding.

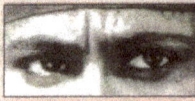

TAMASHA 27
The Bandit Queen has her eyes on winning an Academy Award

We Wish You a Merry Xmas and a Happy New Year!

FAREWELL TO ANOTHER YEAR
1994's movers and shakers... faces and places... all in this week's special review issue

HIGHLIGHTS
■ Indian condoms ...8
■ The rag trade...10
■ Visiting Lanka ...18
■ Careers...31

The

Asian Post 22 December- 9 January 1994/5 Volume III Issue 10 ■ 50p

ASIAN POST

Britain's First Class Asian Newsweekly

Asthma threat to East End Asians

A SIAN CHILDREN in east London are being born asthmatic as a result of their mothers inhaling pollutants found in numerous printing presses in the Docklands, where most of Britain's major newspapers are produced.

Multi-millionnaire media mogul Rupert Murdoch's company, News International, is claimed to be the main source of emissions of hazardous chemicals as it is the largest printing press in the area.

Rose Tilly, a former photo-journalist who is now leading a campaign against print pollution, said: 'Dangerous levels of various toxic chemicals used in printing are being released into the atmosphere.

"Numerous analyses which proved print chemicals analysed in national newspapers were also present in house dust, some in blood and urine samples."

The Docklands – which is in the London Borough of Tower Hamlets, an area with a high concentration of Asians – is the most concentrated area of print works in the world. The Times, Sun, News of the World, Financial Times, Daily Mirror and the Guardian all moved there after the once-desolate Docklands was designated an "Enterprise Zone" by the Conservative Government.

Since the mass migration by the press from Fleet Street to the Docklands, health experts have found that incidence of asthma in the area

EXCLUSIVE

has trebled.

The area around the Docklands print works are now home to the highest levels of asthma in Britain. The European Commission initially accepted a proposal by Ms Tilly that the United Kingdom had "failed to have regard for public health and safety", but then rejected it. Ms Tilly believes this is because of "vested interests".

Tower Hamlets has offered to arrange a meeting between Ms Tilly and News International where it would mediate, but she is not satisfied and is currently in the process of taking the council to court.

Ms Tilly is currently examining the possible legal ground on which to take the council to court. She believes it would be possible to sue the council for neglect, but environmental law does not seem clear enough and her first attempt last Friday to take Tower Hamlets to court failed.

She has the support of Asian women in the area. One Bangladeshi member of a Docklands women's centre said: "Bangladeshi mothers are giving birth to asthmatic babies."

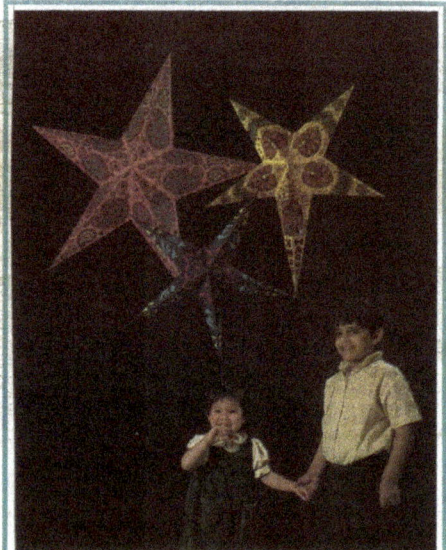

IT'S FOR THE KIDS: At least the V&A Museum unlike Channel 4 thinks of Asians – it has put on an Indian Christmas festival.*Turn to page 9*

Turn to page 9

A N INVESTIGATION into the inadequate protection given to the National Lottery's first Asian winner was announced last week amid much controversy over whether to publish his name or not.

A factory worker and a fam-

National Lottery to be investigated

ily man from Blackburn, the £18million winner left his home for fear of being hounded by the press after Lottery organisers Camelot failed to protect his identity. Camelot

had given away too many clues about the man who insisted on anonymity, and the press – led in this instance by the Daily Mirror – finally found out his identity.

The News of the World actually printed what seems like a wedding picture of the man and his wife, who have now gone to India. .

The Daily Mirror claimed

that they had the man's name, but would not publish for certain reasons. The Asian Post has it on good authority that the reason was that the man's family home is prey to racists, and publication of his name would have endangered their safety.

Asian Post Front Page 1994

6 THE LEADER Tuesday 10 January 199

ASIAN POST
Britain's First Class Asian Newsweekly

The democratisation of British Asian theatre

ASIAN theatre in Britain is a comparatively new development, emerging as it did well after the first generation of settlers established themselves as part of the British economic landscape.

With material security, the younger generation broadened their horizons and show an eagerness to carve out a territory for the community on Britain's cultural landscape.

While most first-generation Asians would opt for conventional professions and careers, younger ones are looking to music, theatre, writing and journalism for a living. Where theatre was concerned, however, it was – like the media and much else in this country – white dominated. Even roles designed for Asians and Africans were played by whites with browned and blackened faces.

Asian theatre in this country was spurred by a constructive resentment against their treatment by the mainstream theatre both in terms of employment and portrayal. The early and contemporary Asian theatre was not only concerned with the effect of racism on their lives, generational conflicts and the tragi-comedy that is the inevitable product of oppression, but they also brought to us some of the great classics of the Indian sub-continent. Some brave souls even interpreted Shakespeare from the Asian point of view and adapted Ibsen and Brecht for the Asian stage.

The Asian Post welcomes this wish for dramatic assertion on the part of our young, brave and resourceful actors, theatres, scriptwriters and directors. It goes without saying that publicity of whatever kind is absolutely indispensable for the development of any theatre, not just Asian and it is in this spirit that we congratulate Hardial Rai, the organiser of the discussion of the relationship between the British Asian Theatre and the Asian Press.

Mr Rai's lesson in humility deserves emulation by the controllers of ghetto tv and radio in this country; the latter seem not to want anything to do with the Asian press. The ghetto tv and radio bosses believe they are not accountable to public opinion. *The Asian Post* warmly welcomes this intelligent and stimu-

Non-Asian quibbles
From D. Vidal in Hounslow, Middx.

Dear Sir,
Happy New Year to you and your staff! May I say how nice it is to see your paper published in London, quality press is so unrepresented in the UK.

My only quibble with the news is that you askew the angle on an issue so that it loses its seriousness.

For example, in issue 10, your front page banner was "Asthma threat to East End Asians". Surely the fumes emissions etc causing the problem are equally applicable to the non-Asians in that area – or are we to believe that the emissions emerge and seek out Asian children only?

A further example appeared on Issue 9's front page. When I first saw the headline "Tories penalise Asian business", I thought the Government had introduced a tax designed for Asians only. Surely the measures will affect all small business?

Please maintain some impartiality in your reporting – as this will heighten your credibility and newsworthiness.

The Editor writes:
In the two stories you have highlighted, we felt we were justified in concentrating on the Asian angle, as our community is being disproportionately affected. We do accept, however, that non-Asians are affected as well, but we are here primarily to serve the Asian community, which – despite its economic and cultural contribution to British society – has little or no support or sympathy from media or Government.

Kid's stuff
From Shubash in Shepherd's Bush, London

Dear Sir,
Why not start a page for young people? When my parents bring home me or my sister Shobana. I am 11 and my sister is 13.We would like to read about other kids like us in this country and in others, such as India.

Miserly round-up
From Alexander Hoque in London

Dear Sir,
Your yearly roundup was so miserly and scant. Couldn't you think of any other notables in the world? For example Bhoutros Ghali (Flop-master General of UN),Suha Tawail who gave Yasser Arafat a heir (genetically legal), T.N.Sheshan who has set the example of giving a meaning to the election in the corrupt politics of India, etc., etc.

A very happy New Year anyway.

Sultan of Smut
From Samir Rai in Birmingham

Dear Sir,
I read with interest your feature on India's Jackie Collins, Ms Shoba De. I was pleasantly surprised to read that India could produce such forthright and assertive women as Ms De.

Who would have believed that this strikingly beautiful mother-of-six was once the founding editor of that bitchy fanzine, 'STAR-DUST', as well as a successful model?

Her analysis on sex and men were more or less spot on. Must say, they would probably raise a controversy or two!

I believe it is about time that the media, being a powerful organ of communication, should redress the prevailing stereotypical view of Asian women

diced brush of Western tabloids.

I am heartily sick to my stomach of reading about suffering Asian womanhood. Thank God for such women as Shoba De, who can articulate views about multi-dimensional and assertive women.

Keep up the good work on Asian women Asian Post, especially the intelligent and attractive ones, from the greatest admirer of feminine charm this side of the English Channel.

Bandit Queen
From Suky Singh in Coventry

Dear sir,
Your feature on the *Bandit Queen* saga exposed the wanton manner and hypocrisy of the Indian Censor Board.

Shekhar Kapur should be wreathed in laurels for painting a bold canvas of the Indian rural scene, and especially of the Indian caste system.

Indeed, *Bandit Queen* could be a turning point in Indian Cinema. The raw depiction of soul-destroying brutality and surprising nudity of the film are in no way inimical to the narrative of the film or the audience. They merely enhance the salient points in the film.

The Censor Board must be peopled by morons and perverse mentalities who have no sense of aesthetics, or understanding of the power of cinema, as a catalyst, to influence and change opinions.

Maybe this is what the Censors or the Government is afraid of – ie of the masses being roused into action. Of robust displays of assertiveness. India's democratic polity can be enhanced ten-fold if it maintained a climate of openess and free exchange of divorce

POSTBAG
Send your letters to the Editor,
The Asian Post, Asia House,
24-28 Fournier Street,
London E1 6QE

■ Editor
Muquim Ahmed

■ Executive Editor
Abdul Montaqim

■ Deputy Editor
Sajeev Sonny Azhakesan

■ Editorial Consultants
Neville Stack,
Nayeem Gahar,
Enayatullah Khan,
Muhib Choudhury

■ Publishing Manager
Linda Hatton

■ Advertising Manager
Lesley Tickner

■ Production Editor
Shahed Ali

■ Circulation
Jalal Ahmed,
Bahrul Hussain Babul

■ Contributors
Satish Advani,
Sanjay Patel,
Jaswinder Singh

■ Dhaka
Mahbubul Alam,
Former Press Minister B.H.C.
Washington

■ Delhi
Resident Editor I.K.
Gujral, Former Foreign Minister of India

■ Islamabad
Iqbal Ahmed

■ Colombo
Sunil Naidu

■ Washington
Tahera Rashid

Editoral
0171 377 6754

Advertising
0171 377

Asian Post Editorial Page
Editor: Muquim Ahmed

137

A couple of successful years had turned The Asian Post into a truly informative, entertaining, purposeful news weekly. The company reached national distribution through the distributor, Menzies. The operation was being run successfully. Money was coming in and the overheads were met with a bit of surplus.

But on the night of Wednesday 21 October 1994 the fire undid all we had done. Journalists working on the paper suffered the destruction of all their personal belongings, their computers, their notebooks — everything was consumed by this terrible fire. A sorrowful sight. But the determined and persistent Abdul Montaqim and his team stood tall and went to work. We accepted the generosity of Janomot, the oldest Bengali news weekly, only 50 yards away from the burnt site, which offered The Asian Post and Notun Din a space to operate from their offices. The editions of The Asian Post and Notun Din came off the presses with the full details of the fire on the front page.

Habib Bank Ltd, my various companies' banker, graciously allowed me and my enterprises to move into 24-28 Fournier Street. Luckily, the bank had this property empty so immediately all my companies and affiliated were housed into this 10,000 square foot office block. The office of The Asian Post was quickly setup. The name of the building was changed to Asian House. This mishap seemed like a blessing to all those who were employed by the company. New offices, new computers, private rooms for executives. Everyone was revitalized, and with renewed enthusiasm they set about printing an even better newspaper. It was now being published in full colour and with extra pages, bringing us up to 32 pages.

Moral support from the family was of paramount importance and I had that backing, and it helped to revitalise me and my struggling empire.

Muslim provided a loan of £50,000 and my brother-in-law Pankaj Bakshi gave another £50,000. I sold my Rolls Royce for £55,000 and I didn't mind at all – I needed to do what was necessary. This gave me the financial and moral impetus to reorganise my various enterprises. The Asian Post quickly succeeded in re-establishing itself more independently and the zeal and persistence of the team enabled us to march on at full speed. Montaqim was relentless. He and his team were self-motivated and inspired not to look back but to move forward, serving the cause and the community.

For two years, The Asian Post ran smoothly and successfully from Fournier Street. With the bank being co-operative, the paper became self-sufficient, thanks to the money coming in from advertising and sale/distribution. But Lady Luck would not hang around for long.

The bank started getting jittery because the insurance claim for the fire failed to materialise. After two years of intense litigation, the insurer, as I have mentioned, went bust, leaving my firms precariously exposed. The bank asked The Asian Post and all other companies to move out of Fournier Street. As always the banks are the friends when the sun shines.

The last edition of the newspaper came out on Tuesday, 16 April 1996 from its third and final home, The Brady Centre, 192-196 Hanbury Street, London.

Notun Din

In 1987 Notun Din ('New Dawn') came into existence under the intellectual auspices of Abdul Guffar Choudhury, a highly regarded Bangladeshi journalist, sadly he passed away at his London residence on the 19th of May 2022. Mohib Choudhury was the managing partner alongside a team that included Tara Miah, Manik Miah, Khurram Matin and Abdul Matin.

2 NOTUN DIN 28 October- 3rd November 1994 নতুন দিন-২

Managing Director	Chairman
Muquim Ahmed	Tara Miah
Director Administration	Vice Chairman
M A Matin	Alhaj Manik Miah
Public Relations Adviser	Chief Adviser
Alhaj S B Chowdhry	S C H Jennings FCA
Ayub Ali	
	International Co-Ordinator
	Faruk Haider
Chairman Editorial Board	Chief Editor
K S Matin	Ghulam Quader

Editor
Mohib Chowdhury
Associate Editor
Syed Faruk
Executive Editor
Syed Nahas Pasha

Assistant Editor	Photo Journalist
Misbah Islam Zamal	Shah Ahmed Sadeque
Advertising and Circulation	Staff Reporter
Shahab uddin Chanchal	Dewan R H Faisal
Correspondent	Rehan Uddin Dulal (Italy)
Md Zahirul Haque (Dhaka)	Partha P Majumdar (France)
Ragib H Chowdhry (Sylhet)	Ataur R Shamim (U S A)

NOTUN DIN

সম্পাদকীয়

বাংলাদেশের রাজনীতিকদের সংলাপ

বাংলাদেশের বর্তমান রাজনৈতিক অচলাবস্থা ও সংকট দূর করার লক্ষ্যে কমন ওয়েলথ–এর মহাসচিবের মধ্যস্থতায় বিরোধী দলগুলো আর সরকার পক্ষের মধ্যে সংলাপ চলছে ।এটা বেশ আশার কথা।

আগামী ১৯৯৬ সালে সাধারণ নির্বাচন পরিচালনার জন্যে একটা তত্ত্বাবধায়ক সরকার গঠনের ব্যাপারে বিরোধীপক্ষের দাবী সরকার মেনে নিতে চাইছেনা। বরং তারা বলছে যে নির্বাচন কমিশনকে আরো শক্তিশালী করা যেতে পারে,যাতে নির্বাচনগুলোতে অনিয়ম কিম্বা কারচুপি ঠেকানো যায়।

কিন্তু বিশেষ করে আওয়ামী লীগ বেশী করে সোচ্চার যে বিএনপি–র অধীনে কোন নির্বাচনই নিরপেক্ষ হতে পারেনা। কাজেই সংবিধান সংশোধন করে তত্ত্বাবধায়ক সরকারের ব্যবস্থা করতেই হবে।

ঢাকায় সরকারী ও বিরোধীপক্ষের নেতারা প্রাথমিক আলাপ আলোচনার পর্যায়ে আছেন। কিন্তু আলোচনা কি হচ্ছে সেসবের কোনপক্ষই কিছু প্রকাশ না করার নীতি বজায় রেখেছে।অথচ একইসংগে বিরোধীপক্ষের তরফ থেকে সরকারবিরোধী আন্দোলনও চলছে। আওয়ামী লীগের নেত্রী শেখ হাসিনা বিভিন্ন জনসমাবেশে একনাগাড়ে বলে চলেছেন যে বিএনপি সরকার অদক্ষ

দুর্নীতিপরায়ণ,কাজেই তাদের সরে যেতে হবে। তিনি অবশ্য সুস্পষ্ট করে বলছেন না যে তারা এখনই তত্ত্বাবধায়ক সরকারের চাপ কিনা । তবে এটা বলে যাচ্ছেন যে তত্ত্বাবধায়ক সরকারের দাবী মেনে না নিলে তারা রাস্তায় রাস্তায় আন্দোলন চালিয়েই যাবেন।

অন্যদিকে সরকার প্রধান বেগম খালেদা জিয়াও বিভিন্ন সমাবেশে প্রকাশ্য বিবৃতি দিচ্ছেন যে তারা তত্ত্বাবধায়ক সরকারের দাবী মানতে পারেন না। আর তিনি এমনও বলছেন যে প্রয়োজন হলে বিএনপিও শেষ পর্যন্ত রাজপথে নামতে পারে।

যেসময়ে দেশের রাজনৈতিক সংকট অবসানের লক্ষ্যে আলোচনা চলছে সেসময়ে দুই নেত্রীর এধরনের বক্তব্য–বিবৃতি জনগনের জন্যে বেশ বিভ্রান্তিকর । তারা এধরনের কথাবার্তা এইমুহূর্তে বলা থেকে বিরত থাকলেই বোধহয় দেশের জন্যে মংগলকর হতে পারে । কারন তারা একদিকে সমঝোতার জন্যে দলের অন্যান্য নেতাদের দিয়ে সংলাপ চালাচ্ছেন আবার নিজেরা নিজেদের পুরনো অবস্থানেই অটল থাকার বক্তব্যে দিচ্ছেন ।

প্রত্যেকদিন সংলাপের বৈঠকের পরেসেসংগে কোনরকম কথাবার্তা যখন প্রকাশ না করারই সিদ্ধান্ত তারা নিয়েছেন সেক্ষেত্র জনসমাবেশে গিয়ে বিবৃতি দেবার কি প্রয়োজন ? এতে করে তারা নিজেদেরকেই খাটো করছেন ।দেশের লোক এধরনের রাজনৈতিক সার্কাস দেখে হয়তো মজাই পাছে কিন্তু চূড়ান্তপর্যায়ে এতে ভালো ফল আসবেনা বলেই আমাদের ধারনা। দেশের মংগলের জন্যে যদি তারা সত্যি যদি ভাবেন তাহলে দুইপক্ষকেই কিছু ছাড় দিতে হবে এবং আলোচনা চলাকালীন নেতারের পরস্পরবিরোধী কথাবার্তা বন্ধ রাখার মতো সংযমশীল হতে হবে । আর প্রকৃত গনতান্ত্রিক প্রক্রিয়া প্রতিষ্ঠার খাতিরেই এটা তাদের কর্তব্য।

The paper was published from Wickham House, East London at the outset, but the remarkable Mohib Choudhury was obliged to move the young publication from Wickham House to his Sherland Road office because of the debt incurred during the time at its original headquarters. The newspaper was struggling; it could no longer bear the expenses of the editorial board or the publishing costs. Abdul Guffar Choudhury amicably resigned.

At Shirland Road, Maida Vale, Mohib Choudhury tried his best to continue publishing the newspaper, but in 1990 more difficulties arose due to printing and logistical disruptions. Advertising was difficult to obtain: most relevant Bangladeshi businesses were based in the East End of London while this paper was based in West London.

Notun Din desperately needed to move to East London so that it could be where all the action was. Mohib was assured by Tower Hamlets' Bengali councillors that they could help with advertising from the local authority if Notun Din were based in their borough.

In 1990 Mohib convinced me to buy a 50 per cent of the share in Din Publishers Ltd, trading as Notun Din. No cash was to be paid for the stake because the paper was a losing concern, but the underlying condition was that I would have to bear the printing cost proportionately and provide office space for the staff.

My businesses were growing. I thought that supporting a journal with few hundred pounds of expenses weekly at that time was of little consequence to my growing enterprises.

Moreover, I would be supporting my community through the newspaper. Sylto Distribution Co Ltd occupied a vast freehold building and had ample office space to spare. We allocated a 1,000 square foot space on the first floor of our 7 Chicksand Street offices, at no cost, to Notun Din.

Syed Nahas Pasha, the Executive Editor; Syed Faruk, the Associate Editor; and Sanaul Haque Chowdhury, the Advertising Manager, were given permanent desks with few more desks made available for the part-time journalists. Working desks were also provided for participating directors, but they could also use the boardroom for meetings.

Notun Din found a new lease of life and it flourished amid the densely populated Tower Hamlets borough where so many Bangladeshis lived and worked and were eager for news from their community.

The Notun Din group gave my son a gift for the help I extended in rescuing the group from bankruptcy. They presented him with a solid gold chain on his first birthday at the London Hilton in 1992.

Under Mohib Choudhury's stewardship, Notun Din's popularity in the community grew, circulation increased and at one point the newspaper became profitable. Young journalists coming from Bangladesh would find employment with Notun Din. They found a home with the paper.

But again, good things do come to an end. After five years of success, the fire came. Our Chicksand Street headquarters were destroyed. Notun Din's offices, all its equipment, was burned to ashes. Janomot came to the rescue, as I mentioned earlier.

The paper's owners and staff — based nearby — were truly benevolent at that time of great distress. So both The Asian Post and Notun Din were, for some weeks, produced from Janomot's offices.

But a new headquarter was needed, and as mentioned, Habib Bank provided us with a repossessed property at Fournier Street, next to Brick Lane Mosque. Instantly Notun Din, Asian Post and other related businesses were quickly shifted into these premises. Not everyone was happy, however. Khurram Matin, the then influential director of Notun Din, did not approve of the arrangement.

Believing that I was doomed and unable to help the paper, he had made prior arrangements with Tower Hamlets Council and had accepted a unit at the Micro Business Centre at Greatorex Street. This move ultimately proved fatal to my partnership with Notun Din. A year after the fire this acclaimed newspaper went under.

London Bangla Press Club

In 1993, the owners of the Bengali-language newspapers Notun Din, Janomot and Surma, got together at Milfa House, Chicksand Street to form the London Bangla Press Club (LBPC). Mohib Choudhury played a leading role in getting the editors and owners of these Bengali news weeklies together and he was elected as the club's first president, with Nazrul Islam Bason as general secretary Nobab Uddin as Treasurer

For a number of years, this ad hoc committee continued to meet before finally becoming a fully-fledged organisation. In 2005, the LBPC started to raise funds for the press club to buy a freehold property as its headquarters. Initiated by Mohib Choudhury, Syed Nahas Pasha, Emadul Haque Choudhury, Monsur Uddin, Belal Ahmed, Nobab Uddin, and many other journalists, the campaign raised a considerable amount of money and in 2021, they were able to buy a freehold property. The press club turned out to be a powerful organisation in the Bengali community in UK. I was made a lifetime member. Till today, I enjoy good relationship with LBPC.

Muquim Ahmed, receiving an award in recognition for his contribution towards social work.

From left to Right: Taysir Mahmud General Secretary, H E Muna Tasneem High Commissioner for the People's Republic of Bangladesh, Muquim Ahmed, Emdadul Hoque Choudhury **President and Saleh Ahmed Treasurer.**

LBPC Complex Opening Ceremony, in Sylhet, Bangladesh - 2024

Bangla Mirror

I cannot help but write about the Bangla Mirror, an English-language paper established by Abdul Karim Goni and a few others in 2002. I enjoyed a good relationship with AK Goni who, at one time worked, for Notun Din. Quite frequently I would write a column in the Bangla Mirror about issues affecting the community.

Goni and his son, the barrister Shadat Karim, founded the British Bangladeshi Who's Who in 2008, an annual journal promoting success stories from the British Bangladeshi community. I was fortunate enough to be featured annually.

Whenever I was in difficulties,
I would follow this advice:

"One must look to the future with hope, as well as reflect on the past for lessons, discard the frills to embrace the present."

Chapter Seventeen
Sylto PLC

Having started Sylto Distribution Company in 1978, it became a limited company in July 1982, later becoming a Public Limited Company in September 1993. Initially it traded from 48 Brick Lane where Glamour International existed. Sylto Distribution Company took over from Glamour and expanded its operation further afield in London. Its exponential growth required a bigger property and so it moved into 7 Chicksand Street & 11/12 Heneage Street. Both of these streets branched off from Brick Lane. I personally owned this 20,000 square foot warehouse at the edge of the great City of London.

Sylto Distribution Company quickly became a successful wholesaler and distributor of electrical, household and fancy goods, and of Japanese products imported by the Japanese companies in the UK. We were a distributor for JVC, Casio, Sony, Hitachi, Panasonic, TDK, Maxell, Seiko, Citizen and other major brands. We were regarded as one of the leading 20 distributors of Panasonic products, and I was invited to Japan in October 1988.

The warehouse was crammed with stock. We imported 200 different models of watches under the brand name Harper. Table fans, standing fans, audio cassettes, video cassettes, 30 varieties of headphones were all imported under the brand HARPER. We stored radios, clocks, calculators, telephone answering machine, cassette players, video tapes and cameras. We sourced much of our own-branded merchandise and products from Hong Kong.

I would travel to the Far East four times a year, visiting different factories, sourcing these products. Beside importing own-brand merchandise, Sylto also imported goods such as umbrellas, toys of all sorts, electrical and telephone accessories and seasonal fancy goods from Taiwan as well as from Hong Kong. We predominantly acquired products from the Japanese companies based in the UK. Sylto Plc was also the national distributor for 3M Scotch, BASF, Phillips, GEC and Kelvinator products.

Sylto was doing so well that it hired three reps and three drivers to market and deliver stock all around the United Kingdom. The company was ahead of its time with regard to marketing and operations. This was the advent of the computer age and Sylto Plc took full advantage of this new world at that time. In 1989, we were the first firm of our kind to use the Kalamazoo computerised account operating system.

Reception 1982

Warehouse of Sylto Plc 1996

Chartered accountant Clive Jennings ran the accounts department with two staff under him. We had a warehouse manager, warehouse pickup staff and four salesmen on the cash-and-carry floor to service the market traders, as well as the said sales reps and the drivers who took charge of nationwide distribution. In all, a formidable team of fifteen staff.

The Berlin Wall came down in 1989, so East European countries were opening their borders. Containers loaded with home appliances, fancy goods and TVs headed for Poland and Hungary. It was vital we maintain our presence not only in the new Europe, but also at home. Sylto exhibited in trade shows at Earls Court and Olympia in London. We attended the major event for bulk/wholesale international trade at NEC Birmingham. We picked up regular buyers from Spain, Malta and Italy.

Because of the British government's unique position in Hong Kong (then a British Colony), we were importing products which were duty free or had quota sanction. If Spain was importing the same products, for example, they had to pay duty in their own ports. With our new Spanish connection, we imported products into London then shipped them to Spain by road without custom duty because of the European Union.

Sylto Plc, over a period of 18 years, grew from being a small retail shop at 48 Brick Lane to being a national wholesale distributor and importer of household appliances and electrical goods. But we did face financial challenges as one after another of our bankers were either dissolved or stopped trading. However, the business overcame most of these difficulties. We rolled on. We ran a cash-and-carry business that supplied market traders and London-based independent shops. We expanded from Britain to Europe. Banking disasters and businesses around us going bankrupt did not stop us growing. But sometimes, even the boldest businesses face a challenge they cannot recover from.

The fire at its premises at Chicksand Street in October 1994 delivered the lethal blow to Sylto Plc from which it could not survive because of the insurer going bust. I was forced to put the business into a Compulsory Voluntary Arrangement (CVA), which allowed the firm to settle debts by paying only a proportion of the amount owed to creditors or to come to another arrangement over payment. The CVA concluded on 20 February 2017.

During this period of anxiety, upheavel and its implications compounding I suffered a great fall. The tightrope walker had slipped. However, I gathered all my energy and strength, and harnessed my steady nerves. I clung on to the rock and climbed again. My family helped me reinvent myself – to be the man I was again — focused and resilient.

Though wounded and hurt, my boldness to hope did not desert me despite all the disasters. I have faith in myself. I never get tired of trying. Where there is a will, there is a way. I shrugged my difficulties.

Sylto Products

Sylto Products

So from a retail shop at 48 Brick Lane, selling watches, torches, cassette players to my countrymen in the 1970s, the business transformed into a nationwide distribution company in the 1980s and then into a public limited company in the 1990s which was delivering worldwide. But this journey over three decades has taught me that nothing is certain in life or in business. No matter how hard you work, and whatever success you achieve, it has to find its own resolution.

Hard fact of life!

Sylto Catalogue

"I did suffer a great fall. The tightrope walker had slipped. However, I gathered all my energy and strength, and harnessed my steady nerves.
I clung on to the rock and climbed again.
My family helped me reinvent myself –
to be the man I was again — focused and resilient."

- Muquim Ahmed

Chapter Eighteen
Institutional Failures

Background to my startups:

In 1975, I was fortunate to start business with £3,000 borrowed from BCCI's sole UK branch in Mark Lane, London. Moin provided the guarantee.

BCCI was founded by the banker Agha Hasan Abedi, who had set up the United Bank of Pakistan in 1959. A decade after opening, BCCI had over 400 branches in 78 countries and assets in excess of $20 billion, making it the seventh largest private bank in the world. With the phenomenal growth of the bank, I also became richer. Most of my ventures were financed by BCCI. When I started importing products with my own brand from the Far East, BCCI was facilitating this whole operation.

In the early 1980s BCCI gave Sylto Distribution Co a credit facility of £2 million, and a further limit of £500,000 of letter-of-credit facilities, where the bank guarantees that a buyer's payment to a seller will be honoured on time. Sylto Distribution Co Ltd later became Sylto Plc and the business was turning over £8 million a year. But dark clouds were gathering, none of which were to do with our business.

In the late 1980s, BCCI came under the scrutiny of financial regulators and intelligence agencies. There were concerns that it was poorly regulated. Investigations revealed that it was involved in massive money laundering and other financial crimes and had illegally gained the controlling interest in the US bank, First American.

BCCI became the focus of a massive regulatory battle. In July 1991, regulators in seven countries raided its branch offices. BCCI was put into compulsory liquidation. Because of this, many legitimate businesses, unaware of these practices at the bank, were hit hard, and I along with many more lost deposits and extended facilities from the bank.

Many of those involved in the criminality were never brought to justice, despite charges being laid against a number of individuals in America and the UK. Abedi was under indictment in the US and UK for crimes related to BCCI, but Pakistan refused to extradite him because they claimed the charges were politically motivated. He had been ill since suffering a stroke in the 1980s and died in 1995.

But I have to say that it was only because of BCCI in the 1970s and 1980s that many ethnic businesses like mine were able to grow. We flourished because of the ease of banking facilities and the favourable credit terms that were offered despite difficult trading positions and at that time a 15 per cent interest rate. However, BCCI's collapse left us in a precarious situation, but fortunately I was able to transfer my business to Habib Bank. So when one door closes, another opens. Fortune was still smiling on me despite the perilous situation I had just gone through.

London and Provincial Factors (L&PF)

L&PF was one of the very first invoice-factoring company in the United Kingdom. Invoice factoring is a way to stop late payments from customers affecting your business. A company can raise money by selling a percentage of the value of an unpaid invoice to a factor, in this case L&PF. It helps a company release much-needed cash. So when an invoice is issued, or raised, a copy is sent to the factor — L&PF, for example — who then credit the company with anything between 70-80 per cent of that invoice. The rest of the invoice is paid to the company when the customer pays the factor, with a fee included.

Sylto Plc was growing fast. We needed more finance in place. Goods had to be cleared from customs. VAT had to be paid. To fund much of this, we looked to invoice factoring and were introduced to L&PF in 1991. We would receive 80 per cent of every invoice factored within three days. Batches of invoices would be sent at the beginning and end of the week with payment coming twice in the week. This went on for few years. It helped Sylto Plc grow. The firm was in profit and was increasing its customer base. Things were going well.

But then L&PF went bust.

Accountancy firm Grant Thornton was appointed as receiver and demanded that we pay the entire book debt which we had with L&PF within a fortnight. Our costumers became difficult. Because they normally dealt with L&PF, using the factoring service, many refused to pay Sylto Plc what they owed. It left us in a precarious position.

Grant Thornton proved difficult to deal with throughout the process, but eventually we bought the book debt back from them for £200,000. The outstanding debt in the market at the time of the fire was over £1.2million. We paid a little over of 16.5 per cent of the total debt. But we still had issues with customers refusing to pay us due to the fact that we could not provide proof of delivery. The fire at our warehouse destroyed the folders where proof of delivery notes were kept. Eventually we had to threaten court action with whatever proof we had to get our money. Ultimately most of them were forced to settle up because of our threat of impending court action. It was a tough time. But as Churchill said: 'Opportunity can be found in turbulence. Never let a good crisis go to waste.'

And Sylto Plc made a profit out of it by buying the book debt from Grant Thornton for a heavily discounted price.

Habib Bank Ltd (closing operation in London)

Founded in 1941 before the partition of India, Habib Bank became the first commercial bank in Pakistan. In 1974 the government of Pakistan nationalised the Bank, but Habib Bank retained its status as the largest bank in the country. However, in 2003 Pervez Musharraf's government privatised Habib Bank, and sold 49 per cent of it to the Aga Khan Fund for Economic Development, a Swiss international development finance institution. During this upheaval Sylto Plc fell victim to these drastic changes, and as a result of Habib Bank Ltd closing all its operation in the United Kingdom, Sylto Plc's position became precarious again.

Habib had of course rescued Sylto Plc from the BCCI disaster in 1987, and from then until 2003 played a vital role in shaping most of my enterprises, providing combined loan facilities of more than £3 million. But the closure meant I had to immediately pay off much of that debt to them immediately.

A few years later, in 2008, banking failures became more prolific and rampant. Financial institutions were getting into serious problems.

Lehman Brothers - the American banking giant collapsed. Washington Mutual, with $307 billion in assets, soon followed. The domino effect had a chilling effect around the world. And here in the UK, Bradford & Bingley and Northern Rock, with billions of pounds of assets, just melted away.

A recession gripped the world. Governments were perplexed and considered what they should do. In Britain, then Prime Minister Gordon Brown chose to recapitalise the banks, bailing out big names like Lloyds and RBS. He increased the deposit guarantee scheme to £85,000 which made sure people's savings up to that amount were safe if their bank collapsed.

I have faced much adversity in business. But with this dilemma I still remained a positive person and thought this will pass. Having this positive dimension has helped me to propel myself out of much more direct dire situations, and while many institutions I was associated with failed, I survived.

Burned in 1994, bombed in 1999 in Brick Lane, and squeezed by banking failures in 2003, I almost collapsed. There were days that I thought that life was not worth living. I was physically and morally at my lowest ebb, I used to have nightmares and wake up sweating profusely. I had to change my wet pyjamas for dry ones.

But I am resilient and persistent and thought I must not give up. I have to carry on regardless of all my difficulties. And I did.

"My sense of purpose and my commitment was paramount in my life. My constructive outlook, and incisive thinking, helped me navigate the oceans of difficulties I faced. I believe that I am an idealistic man with a realistic dream. I reinvented myself, started again with the business of my progenitors – the restaurant trade."

- Muquim Ahmed

Chapter Nineteen

Innovating in the food industry

Café Naz — The first modern chain of Indian restaurants

I was knocked down completely by the fire at my premises at Sylto Plc. Everything burned to ashes, the structure and the buildings, all gone. I was totally devasted. But as we say, and as I learned as a boxer in my younger years, we must get up when we've been knocked down. Life must go on regardless. I was looking for a prospect, something I could quickly start and from which I could generate an income. The eureka moment was: Indian restaurants.

I started doing some research. Indian food became popular with the British public in the 1970s, even overtaking Chinese cuisine in the 1980s. Those from the Indian subcontinent — whether from Bangladesh, Sri Lanka or from Pakistan — were regarded as Indians by the indigenous British and consequently, the restaurants that popped up all around the country were commonly regarded as Indian, despite having names such as Bay of Bengal, Dhaka Tandoori, Akash or Jalsha Ghor – all Bangladeshi references. In the strictest sense, they were all provincial Sylheti-owned restaurants. They were, however, providing varied Indian dishes.

The Bangladeshis quietly enjoyed the success that came with the growing popularity of the food and like any enterprise, the business evolves and transforms to the need of the consumer. Clever Bengalis created Chicken Tikka Masala, for example, which became the most popular dish in Britain — superseding even fish and chips, the staple food of the Isles.

British so-called Indian chefs were apparently exporting this British cooking phenomenon back to India/Bangladesh/Pakistan.

Cafe Naz Wine Bottles

In those good old days, opening a restaurant was easy and you would be sure of success. All other familiar industries — tailoring, repetitive factory work, janitorial and manual labour — were abandoned, and people jumped on this newly-created bandwagon, almost as if this trade was the natural abode for Bangladeshis. Therefore, I became enchanted by the idea of opening a restaurant. In those days it was impossible not to be successful. Though it was hard to find an empty shop in the high street or to obtain a A3 licence for restaurants. Bangladeshis worked hard and persevered and always found somewhere to open a restaurant. There was a time when virtually every high street had one of these restaurants.

Evidently a Bengali living in the United Kingdom, when finding a town, however remote, that had a decent population and a high street, would invariably open a restaurant that would turn out to be an instant hit. Because of the success of these restaurants, Bangladeshis were building mansions in the villages of Sylhet. Their wealth was visible, their success never-ending.

In the 1990s, the restaurant business was at its peak. I avoided it in the earlier days because it was widespread, and the hours were long and unsociable; it was intensely labour-oriented. But eventually, I realized this was good business to generate a decent profit. This time I had to avail the chance and turn to the industry that had proven so successful for my community, and I did so to revitalise my zeal for enterprise.

In all honesty, I had to turn to this easy-go-lucky trade to help maintain my lifestyle and my sanity.

The fire at Chicksand Street had caused many problems, and it was this event that ultimately forced me to enter my compatriots' restaurant trade. It seems that there is not one household of Bangladeshi origin in the UK that did not have at least one member working in the industry. So it was not difficult for me to put together a team and open a restaurant at my old cinema site in Brick Lane.

The development of the restaurant trade or evolution of the Indian curry in those days was clear and simple. The concept that a single man, living abroad without his family, was forced to do his own cooking. Soon, he must have realised that this food was exotic to the palate of the British. He opened restaurants, selling this supposedly exquisite cuisine. Success follows. And so, more men opened restaurants; it became a trend — a machine to print money.

Cafe Naz Dessert

Soon, the curry became a necessity for the British, a taste they so much enjoyed. The Indian hors d'oeuvre — the curry and rice and the dessert.

All nations from the Indian sub-continent soon participated in this phenomenon, including supply and delivery of the ingredients and so on. The Bangladeshi restaurant owners would not need to leave their businesses but would get all their provisions delivered to their door. Predominantly all these wholesalers were Indian, with the exception of a few Bangladeshi companies. The best known was Gandhi Oriental Foods.

It was customary in those days for the supplier to phone the restaurant at the beginning of the week for the order to be delivered by the middle of the week.

Everything from spirits, beer, soft drinks to all the spices would be supplied. Vegetable and meat supplies would come from other sources. So, with everything supplied to our door, we had nothing to worry about apart from cooking and serving customers, an easy and convenient business in those days.

The restauranteur did not need to do much advertising either. Our place of business was in the high street, visible to the potential customers. The restaurant trade was as if it were embedded in our genes; a compelling success story for us, the Bangladeshis of Britain.

At the beginning of the 1990s, the trade was becoming more sophisticated and colourful, and, serendipitously, that is when I entered the fray. I still maintain that I had no choice but to open a restaurant. This was not my first choice, every Bangladeshi was doing it and by then, resourceful Indians and Pakistanis were also entering the industry.

Of course, there were one or two Michelin-star Indian restaurants that existed long before for the most prestigious clientele.

I had been involved in a modest way before then. In 1981 I invested in two Indian restaurants, one in Cambridge and the other in Canterbury. And later, I formed partnerships at Monsoon Palace, 368 Walworth Road with Chef Musabbir and Tandoori Palace, 275 Old Brompton Road with Kais Choudhury and Mohib Choudhury. These were simple investments with no participation on my part. Every week I would get the profit while running my many other enterprises in the East End of London.

In those days the norm was that profit and loss accounts were balanced weekly; wages, grocery, meat, vegetable and beer were all paid weekly, The VAT, rent and rates and other recurring expenses were deducted proportionately, and the residue was apparently the profit; a simple way of maintaining the finances of a running restaurant. If there was a partnership, which is how most Indian restaurant run, then the division of profit was invariably done in this way.

After the fire, I became completely absorbed by and focused on the restaurant business. While continuing the wholesale trade from 16/18 Brick Lane and awaiting the insurance claim of Sylto Plc to materialise, I started my first Café Naz Indian restaurant in the foyer of my old cinema building facing Brick Lane. I did not go looking for premises in the high streets; obviously it would have been difficult considering my circumstances at the time. But the foyer sufficed brilliantly.

Despite all the upheaval and commotion in my business life at the time, I tried to maintain my ingenuity and inventiveness.

I wanted to bring a new concept to Indian restaurants. A high-class café-style, open-kitchen Indian eatery.

I founded the Café Naz chain on the principle that its food presentation should have a unique style. It should have consistency in flavour, quick-service reliability, and service intimacy in a superb, modern environment.

Authenticity was of paramount importance to bring the true flavour of the regional Indian dishes to customers. The dishes were to have a distinctive taste, indicative of the true aroma of the dish, whichever region of India it originated from.

For the brand to be exclusive it had to have clear and well-grounded values in service, ambience and value for money, and the food had to be delivered with panache to meet the diner's expectations.

The brand also had to have an essential identity, which should be pursued with pride and vigour and communicated to the customers, delivering the same taste, same palate, colour, and texture consistently every time.

With this philosophy in place, and my business ethics at the forefront, the Café Naz group of restaurants was established. The first opened in 1996 at 46/48 Brick Lane. It was soon a roaring success, and thereafter branches were opened in other parts of the country.

By the year 2000, I had opened ten branches, all with the same theme, same menu and same ambience: two in Brick Lane, one in Middlesex Street, Old Brompton Road, Brockley, Horsham, Chelmsford, two in Cambridge, and another in Cardiff. But I do recall one incident that, despite my success, reminded me that still for some people my face was not welcome in the UK. I was visiting the Cambridge restaurant and my parking space was occupied, so I parked outside a nearby house.

As I did so, a man opened a window and shouted, "You can't park there, go back to the jungle where you came from." I was really upset,

I felt so sad. And, instead of getting angry, I apologised and moved my car. I wish I could say that he later came into the restaurant and saw that I was the owner, but he didn't.

The restaurants became successful not only because of the demand for Indian cuisine but probably because of my farsightedness in adopting varied regional dishes for the menu, matching this with the service provided by a team of professionals who were brought in from the five-star hotels in Bombay, Dhaka and Calcutta. Team spirit was of paramount importance.

The ambience was created to reflect an affluent contemporary design, with glass frontage and a fabulous glass staircase that was something for the eyes to behold. Initially, people came to Brick Lane's Café Naz to view the glass staircase only. It was indeed a spectacle.

Interior; Cafe Naz, Brick Lane

With regards to staff, on one flight alone 17 Indian personnel, consisting of chefs, cooks and managers, were flown in from India to man roles in the ten restaurants dotted around the country. Steve Gomes was the corporate chef and Salim Salique the corporate manager. All were highly trained professionals from international five-star hotels.

Café Naz rose, of course, from the ashes of Sylto Plc in 1996, but that was almost destroyed too, by the Brick Lane bombing in April 1999 which I depicted in my opening chapter of this book. After the bombing we quickly renovated the site and reopened.

I organised an Asian Food Festival to break away from the misery of the attack's aftermath. I invited the executive chef of five-star Sheraton in Dhaka, Robert Gomes, to orchestrate the festival.

Cafe Naz, Brick Lane - First Floor Bar 1996

A planned cultural programme was added to the food festival. Restaurants were decorated with artefacts from Bangladesh. Artists from India were invited to perform in the evenings. The renowned Kathak dancers from India, Moni Dipa and Ashim Battacharia, performed.

The festival highlighted the varied cuisine from all around India. Chef Gomes grabbed the headlines on the Evening Standard food pages, the critics singing his praises. The unique display of different dishes from different regions attracted a varied clientele from all around London.

The 50 Best — ON THE HOOF — SERIOUS POWER LUNCHES — HIPPEST HANGOUTS — CHEAP & CHEERFUL

23 TOM'S

Very Notting Hill, Tom's is the foodiest scion of Conran. His deli, café and shop does a brisk takeaway trade, with staff weighing out dishes like seafood salad, pasta salad with boccocini, tomatoes and celery or sundried tomato, olives and pine nuts; or shiitake mushroom and rocket. A top-selling sandwich is roast beef with roast tomato, rocket and shaved Parmesan; then there are savoury tarts such as leek, parsley, ham and mushroom, all cooked on the premises. The cakes and pastries are from Patisserie Valerie.
Where and when: 226 Westbourne Grove, W11 (020-7221 8818) Mon-Fri 8am-10pm, Sat 8am-6pm, Sun 10am-4pm. ● Notting Hill Gate
How much: Salads from £1.95 to £19.95 for a kilo of seafood salad. Sandwiches £2-£3.50. Savoury tart £2.95.

24 THE SEQUEL

This is Max Clifford's Clapham hideaway, where he meets editors and others for secret newsbreaking lunches – except it only opens for lunch at weekends. "I love the food, and the whole feel of the place; I suppose they'd call it Pacific Rim." The globally surfing food – ostrich fillet, spinach, chickpea mash and paw paw tamarind chutney (all together) is surprisingly good; and they show old movies on a giant screen. "I'll have to move on," laments Clifford, now that his secret is out. Over the road, sister restaurant The Rapscallion opens for lunch.
Where and when: 75 Venn Street, SW4 (020-7622 4222) Mon-Fri 5-11pm, Sat 11am-4pm, 6-11.30pm, Sun 11.30am-5.30pm, 6.30-10.30pm. ● Clapham Common
How much: Three courses around £25, excluding wine.

25 CAFÉ NAZ

Tracey Emin's lunchtime local is this relatively glitzy restaurant in Brick Lane, East London's curry corridor. The Naz has the edge with its black-and-glass front, chrome-and-glass interior, and food and prices that distinguish it over its rivals. On weekdays until 5pm there's a help-yourself buffet for an all-in price, with a bigger helping of fish on Fridays. The evening menu also offers a greater array of Bangladeshi specialities than your average curry house.
Where and when: 46 Brick Lane, E1 (020-7247 0234) Mon-Fri 12pm-12am, Sat 6pm-12am, Sun 12-3pm, 6pm-12am. ● Aldgate East
How much: Weekday buffet lunch £7.95, evening meal £10-£15.

INDEPENDENT 6 - 12 May 2000

At the height of Café Naz's popularity,
The Independent newspaper listed it as 25th in London's top 50 restaurants — and
number one among Indian restaurants. Independent, 2000

After the appearance of Café Naz on ITV's Dinner Date show, Café Naz became the epitome of an Indian restaurant in London.

According to The Independent, artist Tracey Emin's lunch-time local 'is this relatively glitzy restaurant in Brick Lane, East London's curry corridor. The Naz has the edge with its black-and-glass front, chrome-and-glass interior and food and prices that distinguish it over the rivals.'

Evening Standard food critic Fay Maschler wrote on 8 June 1999, 'The sweetly obliging waiters at Café Naz brought, at lengthy intervals, items of varying exquisite taste. Best of the first courses tried were prawn poori in which the shellfish had retained some personality and a dish of aloo chat hot enough to give a person pause.'

Food critic Charles Campion would walk around London's restaurant scene and write about the food he sampled. Part of his piece on Café Naz, which appeared in Evening Standard, is shown below:

Article in Evening Standard 2000

With the advent of Café Naz, the restaurant scene completely changed. I branded everything from napkins, coasters, table mats, chocolates, hot towels, still and sparkling water bottles, dinner plates to saucers, cutlery and serving bowls. Café Naz wine was also branded. The logo was designed by someone who worked for Saatchi & Saatchi in South Africa.

Café Naz's appearance was contemporary and upmarket but yet reasonable in price. Queen Mary University, when giving me their fellowship in 2009, wrote: 'The iconic Café Naz — the first of the modern Bangladeshi restaurants.'

As with all success stories, things will level out. The restaurant trade was slowly changing. The trade was over supplied, besieged by staff shortages, immigration raids, tax avoidance and so on. Because the market had expanded exponentially, there were too many restaurants, too few personnel to man them, and too few customers. Government legislation was tough on new immigrants, and on top of that, the shine was obviously coming off the trade. People were more concerned about their eating habits and invariably thought Indian cuisine was too rich, and hence not good for one's health. All these issues hammered the trade badly; restaurants were closing at an alarming rate.

Everything has a life cycle, that is the nature of existence. Business as well. The Bangladeshis had a good run for more than 60 years. For the trade to survive and prosper, even in tortoise fashion, slowly — it must adapt and change.

After a run of 20 years, Café Naz started to wrap up its operations. The last venue to close was the Cambridge site on 15 October 2015. The lease was sold to a Chinese operator, "Me and I," I was really sad.

But what goes around comes around. We took over the Chinese food fad in the early 70s they are now taking over Indian restaurants in 2020s.

"Despite all the upheaval and commotion in my businesses at the time, I tried to maintain my ingenuity and inventiveness."

- *Muquim Ahmed*

Cafe Naz Express

- a coffee shop serving ready meals, a first of its kind

I wanted to redefine the traditional idea of a coffee shop by including Indian ready-meals served with tea and coffee at a convenient time for the customer — an all-day lunch; snacks or appetisers at various hours, similar to a Spanish Tapas bar where you would be presented with small portions of larger dishes.

The mission was to sell cooked food not prepared on the premises therefore not requiring the A3 licence. I bent the rules by cooking the food at 46/48 Brick Lane and selling it at 16/18 Brick Lane.

Tower Hamlets council could not take me to court because the hot meals sold there were not cooked on the premises. The freehold of 16/18 Brick Lane was owned by the council therefore the lease could be revoked if the lease terms were violated. But there was no kitchen or cooking facility at 16/18 Brick Lane. So Café Naz Express became the first coffee shop in the country to sell Indian ready-meals not cooked on the premises.

Many shops in and around Tower Hamlets started copying Café Naz Express. Hot Indian food could be sold from coffee shops, along with hot panini and ciabatta. One of the most famous examples of those who followed our lead is the Amar Gaon at 50 Brick Lane, which opened in 2005.

Cafe Naz promoted in London Underground 1999

Cafe Naz, Cardiff Bay 2000

Cafe Naz, Middlesex Street, London E1 7AA

Cafe Naz, Middlesex Street

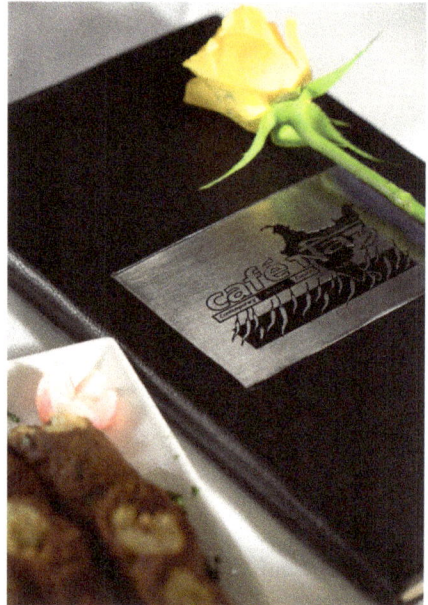

Cafe Naz, Menu

Rayners Bakery

After the success of the Café Naz chain, it was a natural progression for me to move into the mass preparation of cooked meals, or ready meals.

In 2002, I bought a vacant 12,000 square foot warehouse at Caxton Street North, Canning Town to produce ready meals. It had a mezzanine floor and housed several offices, with a large reception area.

Asian House, Caxton Street North, Canning Town

The former glass manufacturing warehouse's unique position — in a designated regeneration area — enabled me to qualify for a grant from the London Development Agency (LDA) and it was also, fortunately, exempt from stamp duty.

Life was evolving, the city was moving fast, people wanted readily available cooked food. I saw a gap in the market. A sense of urgency overwhelmed me. I wanted to venture into this evolving market. I started setting up a ready-meal factory at the Caxton Street North site.

We bought equipment and employed a general manager, someone with a background in food production.

We applied to the LDA for a business development grant. They carried out several site visits. They had to consider all aspects of the project, and how it could benefit the community. There was fierce competition for LDA grants in London. It was easier to obtain funding of this kind if you were based in the North, the Midlands or in Wales. The North-South divide was apparent even in those days.

Finally, however, Asian Foods Ltd's application was accepted by the LDA and we were to receive a grant of up to £140,000, based on the number of jobs the enterprise would create.

The jobs were not created, in fact the factory was not built, so the grant was not granted.

But as we were preparing the site, with everything in full swing, a developer offered me £2.3m for the site. Obviously, this was a very lucrative offer and not to be refused since I had only paid £725,000.

So the deal was done, and I set about finding another site — a bigger and better one. I lost the grant because it could not be transferred to another location. However, after several months' searching for a site, our general manager, Paul Jones, found a 13,000 square foot industrial bakery in South London. Beside producing exquisite bespoke bread, bagels, donuts and savoury products, the factory also produced cooked pies. There was also some spare space inside the factory's top floor — 3000 square feet, which could be utilised to produce the targeted 2,000 ready-meals a day.

A deal was struck with the owners. The property was bought as a going concern. A contract was signed by the vendor that he would stay along with eighteen full time staff for three months to help with the transition.

Rayners Bakery, 12000 sq. ft. warehouse

It was further agreed that owner Paul Rayner would not take any remuneration for the three month transition period. This was to enable us to get the handle on the operation.

Paul was a born baker, whose great grandfather made Queen Victoria's birthday cake. A portrait of the enormous cake and his ancestor hung on the office wall at the bakery. Paul did not need to work the full three months. By the second month, I had learned the intricacies of the trade. All hands were on deck, with all 18 staff members retained.

Production was under the control of master baker, Chris Brown, by then 52, He had started his career at this factory floor as a 16-year-old apprentice.

The business was already making a healthy profit. My initial thought was that lady luck has struck again; I have added another jewel to my crown. It had a superb distribution network, delivering to more than 200 independent shops, and was the main supplier to Benjys, the coffee and snacks shops found in London, with more than 130 branches. Several local schools as well as Ikea and the Ford Motor Company were Rayners' customers. Distribution was organised by Lee Anne with the help of a part time assistant. The ordering system was quite complex; it was done through a computer programme designed specifically for the bakery trade.

General manager Paul Jones was more involved with the development of the ready meal project for which he was initially employed. Paul came to sell me an industrial oven which is how we met. But he also undertook the responsibility of managing and running the bakery operation.

Rayner's Bakery was a fully automated bakery, Rondo complex special savoury machine, the mighty ovens, prover rooms, rolling machines, doughnut machines created a real sense of industrial environment. The machines described above were huge, juggernaut industrial size machines. A few of the production lines were over 100 metres long.

We chose Shahnaz as the brand name for our ready meals. It has connections, of course, to the Café Naz name. Shah means king and Naz means delicacy in the Indian language. Preparation was in full swing. Paul Jones put all his efforts into gearing up the production.

An industrial kitchen was set up on the first floor. There were enormous industrial cooking pots, and 21 burners; huge cookers, were also installed. Paul was pro-active and managed to get bulk orders from Compass, a catering giant and the world's largest supplier of cooked food. They supplied the US military around the world and provided catering services for major events.

We were lucky to get into this niche market because Paul knew one of their managers. They used Asian Foods Ltd for all their Indian food requirements.

For a couple of years, the business went from success to success. The Shahnaz brand also supplied the bakery's existing customer base.

We exhibited our products — from the Rayners and Shahnaz brands — at ExCel London where we picked up more customers.

It had been going so well; distribution was at full speed. Orders were coming in and they were dispatched quickly and efficiently. The income from Benjys alone paid for all the staff.
Rayners Bakery production would start at 5am and finish 2pm.

The packaging team would take over then and finish off by 11pm. This second shift team would also organise the four delivery vans.

One van was assigned for Benjys delivery alone; the chain required several deliveries a day. The other three vans would deliver all night so that when schools and coffee shops opened in the morning, they had their bakery products fresh, ready to distribute and sell.

Eventually, the bakery faced a challenge when Benjys — the major customer — applied for voluntary administration. The chain was bought by James Caan of Dragon's Den fame, who paid several millions to the administrator for the chain.

I was devastated by this upheaval as I had over several hundred thousand pounds outstanding from Benjys at the time. My whole operation depended on Benjys. The automatic packaging machine for Benjys' products was a new line we had recently bought, specifically for Benjys. Almost half of my factory's production was for Benjys. I made an appointment to see my contact at Benjys in Cannon Street immediately. The best I was offered was 20p to the pound; there was no alternative. We had to wait for our money.

Meantime I was still supplying and Benjys was still operating in the city, but on cash up front. After several month of cash trading, Benjys requested a 45-day credit term. After much persuasion, I agreed to extend a new credit line, but in hindsight this was a big mistake; within a year Benjys folded completely.

This blow was too big for Rayners Bakery to bear, and the firm, sadly, ceased to operate.

And when misfortune comes, it comes in waves. Asian Foods Ltd also got hit with problems when Compass — our main customer — cut operations in France and the UK. They stopped taking their ready meals from us, which proved to be the end of my ready-meal operation.

A lesson I learned: Sometime, no matter how positive and industrious one can be, if the tide is against you, no matter how hard you swim, you will find yourself sinking deep into the ocean.

Yet I console myself.

I take inspiration from my guru, Sir Adamjee Haji Dawood who flourished inspite of nationalisation of his huge enterprises in four countries – Burma, India, Pakistan and Bangladesh.

And, of course, I was educated in the school which bears his name Dawood Public School.

Neither Rayners nor Shahnaz could survive.

"A lesson I learned:
Sometime, no matter how positive and industrious
one can be, if the tide is against you, no matter
how hard you swim, you will find yourself sinking
deep into the ocean."

- Muquim Ahmed

"I like to believe that I am an inquisitive,
industrious individual, always trying to see the
positive in difficult situations. Even during this
miserable time, I retained my sense of urbanity
and wit, my wisdom and intellect, and held myself
together to make a continued success of my other
enterprises."

- Muquim Ahmed

Chapter Twenty

Quantum Securities Limited

I came into the property business serendipitously. I had no thoughts or intentions in that direction. It was sheer luck, an opportunity from heaven. I mentioned that I bought the Caxton Street warehouse for £725,000 to build a ready-meal factory, and it was sold for almost within 18 months, in December 2007, for £2.3 million. The sale coincided with a loan of £3.8 million (and subsequently another £4 million) from Lloyds Bank. Fortune knocked on my door; I welcomed the opportunity with open arms. Lady Luck, this time spectacularly, was on my side.

It was 2008, the right time, the right moment to invest in property. I wasted no time. Using the revolving credit facility from Lloyds, I bought a string of properties from the Allsop Auctions on 20 May 2008. My friend who is also my manager, Paul Jones, and I spent a lot of time evaluating the properties before we bid for them, of course. All the properties that we listed had tenants and leases in place.

This was, of course, the year when Lehman Brothers went bust, thus precipitating the financial crash and recession. The big four clearing banks were clinging on to their cash and refusing to lend overnight funds to one another. Northern Rock had queues outside half-a-mile long of customers waiting to withdraw their money as panic gripped the financial sector. The interest rate dropped from five per cent in June 2008 to one per cent in January 2009.

With an unprecedented financial crisis looming, I thought I had to act quickly and use the Lloyds Bank loans. Lloyds, on the back of the properties which Quantum Securities Limited (a company I started in 1996) had already owned and the sale of Caxton Street North for £2.3m, provided me with an opportunity to buy more properties worth millions of pounds. This was the beginning of my property business.

I was on the verge of closing my restaurant operations due to staff shortage, immigration raids, HACCP (Hazard Analysis and Critical Control Points, which manages food safety) and so on. Indian restaurants had started fading and falling out of fashion. The health-conscious British public avoided curry and rice. It seemed to be the right moment to jump ship, and thereafter, property became my focus.

Speculate to accumulate became the theme. I marched onward with the facilities made available by Lloyds, and the backing of Richard Hughes, the bank's relationship director. I switched my position from trading to producing staple-curry rice and bread to real estate. From that day, I kept adding to my property portfolio.

A shrewd property operator will buy where the properties are run down, the area is derelict; preferably a slum that is neglected and in squalor. This was Brick Lane in the early 1970s. Muslim bought a number of freehold properties at the end of Brick Lane for only few thousand pounds but sold them for a small profit within a year after renovating them.

But to benefit from the rise in property prices, one should hold on to them and not sell so quickly. My view is that one should hang on and re-mortgage the portfolio after a time and borrow more when needed and buy when the interest rates are low.

Before the 2008 recession, it was easy to borrow; banking rules were not so tight. The Bank of England did not have such stringent lending criteria as they now have. But during the recession, the loan-to-value ratio went so badly into negative territory that foreclosures were rampant. RBS and NatWest, especially, were remarkably active in carrying out what appeared to be willy-nilly foreclosures. The Times newspaper highlighted the matter, and then-Business Secretary Vince Cable of the Tory-Liberal Democrat coalition government, came to the rescue of these struggling businesses.

One should probably enter a market in decline just when it is bouncing back. That may be hard to evaluate. But I was successful: the properties I bought in 2008 had doubled in value by 2018; the properties I bought in the 1970s and early 1980s have gone up five-to-six times in value. Mount Mascal Farm, bought in 1981 for £130,000, is now worth millions. So it is profoundly important to invest into your own homes and properties. Minimally, one should invest in a house. Historically, it has been demonstrated over and over that house prices have always exceeded generational expectation in value.

The Bengali community has done very well thanks to Margaret Thatcher's right-to-buy policy. Hundreds and thousands of my compatriots bought their homes from their local council. They became homeowners. And some of these clever people living in the East End of London sold their flats and moved to leafy suburbs in search of a better quality of life for themselves and for their children. I read once that statistically we Bengalis own more homes than the Pakistanis or the Indians. Bengalis have become affluent. We have realised that house price, historically, rise, so understandably that is a smart investment.

We know that if we decorate our home, and carry out home improvements, adding an extension perhaps, it will add value to the property. Noor Miah, a friend of mine, demolished his old home and built a ten-bedroom house, which is worth millions. So did Mimbor Ali, a second-generation immigrant. He built a beautiful, detached house with eight bedrooms in place of his old home. Many august Bengali fellows like Iqbal Ahmed, Shelim Hussain, Ashfaqul Bari and others have exponentially grown in their achievements and in their success.

So we should take inspiration from our fellow immigrants and say to ourselves: If he or she can do it, so can I. We are all members of a diaspora; we all have that instinct to better ourselves, enhance our position in the world, achieve our dreams and improve the quality of our life and the community in which we live.

This is one way to encourage our compatriots, and another way to do this is through leadership. I believe that leadership is about actively raising people up to your level, not just showing them how you got there. I always persevered and I will not give up till I succeed.

And one way I had to help my community thrive and prosper was through my involvement with the British Bangladesh Chamber of Commerce, an organisation of which I was president for three terms.

As president of the London region of the BBCCI, I wrote an article for the organisation's newsletter in 1998.

An excerpt below:

'Many a sage over time immemorial has been noted to say: Set your aim high, high enough to reach, but yet not too far beyond to lose sight.

You can set yourself a life goal to strive for, or you can set series of smaller goals throughout your life.

When you achieve your goal, you feel a sense of fulfilment. Fatigue and tiredness will seem to disappear. Sigh of satisfaction overwhelms your inner self.'

Be it in business, education, research, politics or social work, ambition can take various forms. If you do not have ambition, you cannot be motivated to achieve, you are then merely living from day to day. Life becomes monotonous, less enjoyable and less meaningful. However, if you have a goal, you develop strength in the process of trying to achieve it.

Life is what you make out of it!

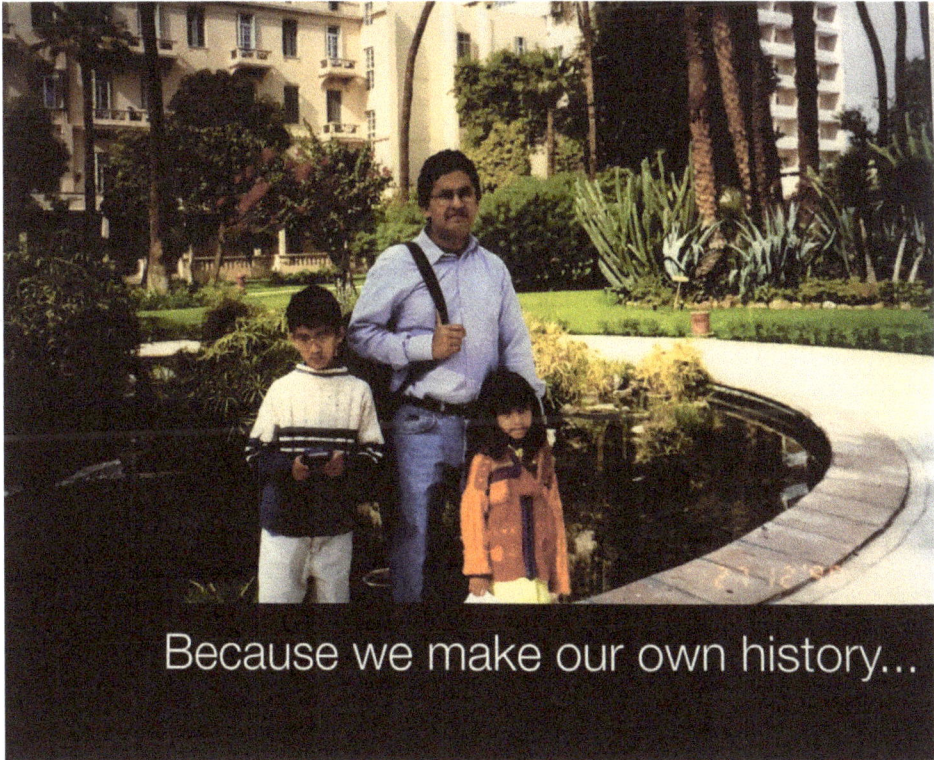

Because we make our own history...

My son Miraj and daughter Monique 2001

"When you achieve your goal,
you feel a sense of fulfilment.
Fatigue and tiredness will seem to disappear.
Sigh of satisfaction overwhelms your inner self."

- Muquim Ahmed

Chapter Twenty One
British Bangladesh Chamber of Commerce

*'Social mobility is not just a moral imperative
but an economic emancipation'*

—*DAVID CAMERON*

Kudos to Abdur Rahim and Dr. Kabir Choudhury for contemplating, and establishing, the British Bangladesh Chambers of Commerce and predicting that one day this organisation would become a major force in the social and business growth of the UK's Bangladeshi community. At one point, the UK Government provided a grant of £500,000 to help develop Bangladeshi businesses, and the Bangladesh government advanced the substantial sum of Tk 4,500,000 (Bangladesh currency) to promote trade between the countries, which is the objective of the British Bangladesh Chamber of Commerce & Industries.

The challenge facing the Bangladeshi community was to establish itself as a progressive, contributing force in the British economy through which wealth and prosperity could be created for the individuals, and hence the nation. Without enterprise and entrepreneurship, a community cannot grow and prosper. Therefore it is of paramount importance to have a platform for the business community to encourage talent and initiative and to promote businesses in the United Kingdom and British businesses in Bangladesh.

With these fundamental principles in mind, Abdur Rahim and Dr. Kabir Choudhury founded the Bangladesh-British Chamber of Commerce (BBCC) in December 1991.

A few weeks later, on 16 January 1992, we celebrated my son Miraj's first birthday at the Park Lane Hilton.

Around 200 people attended this function as this was our first child after 15 years of marriage, we celebrated his birth with much pomp and grandeur. All dignitaries of our community, and our relatives from America and Canada, also came to the event.

Mr. Rahim and Dr. Choudhury, both of whom are stalwarts of our community, decided to visit me at my home on the pretext of personally giving their blessing to my son. I was delighted to have them as my guests, naturally. After the pleasantries — and the heartiest of good wishes for my son — we sat down for dinner. Mr. Rahim began to explain that he and Dr Kabir had registered the BBCC as an entity the previous month. He said: 'Dr. Kabir is the director general, and I am the chairman, and both of us desire that you join us as president of the London region.'

Dr. Choudhury said: 'Muquim Bhai, you are a young entrepreneur; you have established quite a number of enterprises. You have been very successful in a very short spell of time. It would inspire others in our community to join the Bangladesh-British Chamber of Commerce if you were to agree to join us as the London regional president.'

I thought for a moment and realised that in this foreign land we all need to work together, inspire one another by deeds and association to further our aim and objective.

I agreed to participate because I thought this could be our forum, to promote business and social activities. From there on in, Mr. Rahim and Dr. Choudhury started recruiting, with my help and co-operation, other successful entrepreneurs from across the country.

In 1993, Ahmed-ud-Samad was appointed President of the BBCC for Bath; Iqbal Ahmed for Manchester; Matab Miah for Newcastle-upon-Tyne; Wali Tasser Uddin for Scotland.

The seeds were sown for the BBCC to become a formidable organisation. It became a body like any other trade and commerce organisation, a group that not only facilitated trade and commerce between Britain and Bangladesh, but it also became a forum to share experience and knowledge with associates and members, and to encourage aspiration so as to accelerate growth and progression in the community.

For a couple of years, from 1996 to 1998, Mr. Rahim's office in the West End was used as a base for the BBCC. Later in 1998 the organisation moved to a small office at the Greatorex Business Centre in Greatorex Street. Occasionally, Café Naz my restaurant at Brick Lane was used as a meeting place, and invariably complimentary lunch would be provided.

When Mr. Rahim died suddenly in 1999, a gloom befell the chamber. He was an engaging personality. He used to own three Indian restaurants. He would also do voluntary work. He helped people any way he could. He was at the time President of the Bangladesh Catering Association (BCA) as well. His died on stage during an event, suffering a massive heart attack. His death was a great loss; the community was shattered.

I wrote in a newsletter issue 2 april 1998, that Rahim was a relaxed, easily engageable character. He is attributed to be the engineer and architect of the modern BCA [Bangladesh Caterer's Association]. 'I am certain in my mind that before long he will play even a greater role in establishing the chamber. Men like him are few and far in between.'

Rahim's stature and dignity was larger than life. His epitaph is that his rapport, his positive attitude and discourse, his ever so indomitable personality, will remain among us always and inspire us to live and let live with compassion, care and industry.

There had been other personnel changes. Dr. Choudhury, a versatile, witty and an erudite personality, had left for Bangladesh, creating another void in the chamber, but Wali Tasser Uddin fortunately took on the role of director general. By then the organisation was renamed the British Bangladesh Chamber of Commerce and had moved into a bigger office at the Greatorex Business Centre. As our community grew, and ethnic businesses here in the United Kingdom expanded, the organisation was growing too.

Rahim's unexpected loss caused a vacuum in the BBCC. The organisation was without a leader for over a year. But after much persuasion from colleagues, I agreed to take the reins, and took over as Chairman in February 2000.

There were hundreds and thousands of businesses owned by British Bangladeshis by then. The BBCC's membership grew at a rapid pace.

With this exponential growth, BBCC's involvement became more extensive and complex. It was time for us to look seriously for an executive who could help and manage the day-to-day running of the chamber.

EXPO Bangladesh 2005 - The first single country Trade Fair

I worked diligently and relentlessly in making sure the BBCC became successful in obtaining the support of The Bangladesh Government to stage the Expo Bangladesh 2005. My tenure as Chairman was extended by a year by the board so I could help facilitate and implement the

Expo. The Bangladesh High Commissioner to the UK and Ireland, His Excellency AH Mofazzal Karim, supported the Expo. We held regular meetings at the High Commission to manage and organise the first ever one-country trade fair here in the United Kingdom.

Mr. Karim's dynamic personality — and the inspiration shown by Peter Fowler, the ex-British High Commissioner — made it possible to stage the Expo Bangladesh 2005.

A budget of a £250,000 was allocated. The Bangladesh government granted £35,000. Oil and gas explorer Cairn Energy sponsored the event for another £30,000, and the rest of the money came from the exhibitors and the directors of the BBCC. London's Barbican Centre was to be the venue at a cost of £72,000 for the three-day show. It was the first ever one country trade show to be held internationally by Bangladesh. Expo Bangladesh 2005 was held from 15-to-17 September 2005.

Muquim Ahmed, Ken Livingstone, Minister Altaf Hossain & others

There were over 60 exhibitors from Bangladesh and 15 from here in the United Kingdom. The event was a success, generating orders of more than £14 million and it raised Bangladesh's profile internationally.

Beximco, Shinepukur, Apex Footwear Ltd, Patwari Group, Moushumi Fashion all of whom managed to get large orders.

Ethical Fashion Shows, Fashion Parades and information workshops dominated the three day exhibitions where over 10,000 visitors - commercial and fashion enthusiast paraded the whole of the Exhibition Centre. Probably the intensity of the forthcoming supremacy in the shirt and apparel trade in the world market was more strengthened then. Bangladesh is regarded as a reckoning force in the readymade garment industry internationally.

Altaf Hussain Choudhury, Minister, Ministry of Commerce, Mirza Fakhrul Islam Alamgir, State Minister for Agriculture, Enam Ahmed Choudhury, Chairman Privatisation Commission and I presided over various workshops intended to make foreign companies aware of the many facilities extended by the Government to invest in Bangladesh - concessions like the tax holidays, loan facilities, cash incentive , duty free import of raw materials and importation of manufacturing machineries in the Bangladesh Export Processing Zone (BEPZA).

All the BBCCI directors worked diligently and made the Expo 2005 a roaring success. Every director contributed financially to materialise this mammoth event which luckily produced dividend.

The executive committee worked relentlessly.
Sayed Choudhury had the special task of press and publicity which he handled efficiently and effectively. Liaison with the different media was of paramount importance for the success of this exposition. Choudhury's Media Mohol Ltd was chosen as the BBCCI's media partner.

Bajloor Rashid, a formidable organiser with minute attention to detail, managed the stalls with the allocation of space and their position, he exceedingly 'well managed' the seminars and the work shops' functionality.

Bangladesh High Commissioner, His Excellency Mofazzul Karim and his team organised meetings at the High Commission initially to manage the nitty gritty of the event, subsequently it was all left to the executives under my leadership. Mr. Shahab Uddin Patwari, the commercial Councillor and Press Minister Fazal M Kamal played vital roles in the whole process.

The Bangladesh Export Promotion Bureau (EPB), Bangladesh Board of Investment, Commonwealth Business Council, Confederation of British Industries, Department of Trade and Industries UK, Federation of Bangladesh Chamber of Commerce and Industries all of these national organisations paved the way for the success of Expo Bangladesh 2005.

Progression of BBCC

An executive body, separate from the BBCC board, was elected on the 17 November 2005 with Wali Tasser Uddin as the President and Abssar Waess as the Director General. Things developed further. During the presidency of Shahagir Bakth Faruk between 2008 and 2009, the organisation received a grant of £500,000 from the UK Government to develop and promote micro businesses in London. The grant was possible because of the phenomenal growth of the BBCC during my time as President. Our group's aspirations knew no bounds. We enthusiastically promoted our mission to grow and expand extensively.

Miraculously, I understand that Rafique Hyder - the person who should had been the President in default, when Enam Ali bounced his election fee cheque of £5000 has now become the President of BBCCI. The Truth must always prevail!

Cultural Growth

Expo Bangladesh 2005

EXPO 2005
BANGLADESH
15-17 September 2005

Expo Bangladesh 2005 is the UK's first single-country exhibition of Bangladeshi products. Organised by the Bangladesh British Chamber of Commerce (BBCC-UK) and Bangladesh Export Promotions Bureau (EPB), Expo 2005 will be an important, exciting and innovative showcase for Bangladeshi products, manufacturers and talents.

Expo Bangladesh 2005 is for
• Trade buyers large and small
• Chambers of Commerce representatives
• Companies looking for new products and partners
• Organisations and manufacturers looking for raw materials, ready made items and services

• Organisations with an interest in the development of Bangladesh's export trade
• People with an interest in products and developments in modern Bangladesh.
Partner Organisations:
The main organising bodies are co-ordinators Bangladesh High Commission, London and Bangladesh Export Promotion Bureau (EPB).
Other partners include:
Bangladesh Board of Investment
British Chambers of Commerce
Chittagong Chamber of Commerce and Industry
Commonwealth Business Council
Confederation of British Industries
Department of Trade and Industries of UK
Dhaka Chamber of Commerce and Industries
Edinburgh Chamber of Commerce
Federation of Bangladesh Chambers of Commerce and Industries
France-Bangladesh Chamber of Commerce
German-Bangladesh Chamber of Commerce
London Chamber of Commerce and Industries
Oldham Metropolitan Borough Council
Scottish Chambers of Commerce
Sylhet Chamber of Commerce and Industry
British High Commission, Bangladesh
University of East London
The bobNetwork
Council of Foreign Chambers of Commerce
Exhibitors
There will be over 90 stands, presenting traditional Bangladeshi products such as food and fashion as well as newer industries and services at the cutting edge of modern developments. They represent large national companies and small independent traders.

• Fashion
Ethnic Dress

Ready Made Garments
Dyeing and Fabrics
Home Textiles
Handloom Weaving
Footwear
Leather Goods
Jewellery
Hair Bonding
• Ceramic Table Ware
Furniture
Handicrafts
Bathroom Fittings
Household Plastic Ware
Jute Products
• Herbal Medicines
Pharmaceuticals
• Food
Beverages
• Hotels
Travel
Tourism
• Outdoor Ceramics
Horticulture
• Information Technology
Information
Real Estate
• Media
Print
Design

Events

Ethical Fashion Showcase
Saturday 17th September
Organised by the Ethical Fashion Forum in association with Expo Bangladesh 2005, this dynamic showcase will feature outfits by well known and emerging designers and businesses, with the emphasis on quality and fair trade.
Seminars
Programme covering a range of exciting and stimulating topics, with speakers representing government, business and senior academics.
Celebrity Chef Competition with Tommy Miah
Saturday 17 September
The best Bangladeshi cuisine using Bangladeshi products including traditional spices and ingredients combined with innovative cooking styles and presentation.
Expo Bangladesh 2005
Barbican Exhibition Hall 1
Golden Lane, London EC2
15 - 17 September
Thurs & Fri 10am - 8pm
Sat 10am - 5pm
£5 / £10 family / students free

Bangladesh - A Lot To Offer

"We are proud to have the largest Bangladeshi community of any city in Europe... I wish Expo Bangladesh 2005 every success."

- Ken Livingstone, Mayor of London

How to get to the Barbican
Underground
The nearest Underground station is Barbican, on the Circle, Metropolitan and Hammersmith & City lines. To reach the Barbican Exhibition Hall 1 exit the station and cross Aldersgate Street in front of you. Walk through the road tunnel (Beech Street), take second left in the tunnel into Golden Lane.

Other Underground stations nearby are Moorgate, St. Paul's, Bank, Liverpool Street and Mansion House.

Train
The nearest rail stations are Liverpool Street, Farringdon and Blackfriars. City Thameslink services serve Barbican, Moorgate and Cannon Street.

Bus
Route 153 stops outside the Barbican on Silk Street. Starting from outside Liverpool Street Station, it runs to the Barbican. Angel and Finsbury Park. Other services running near the Barbican are listed below:

8, 11, 25, 35, 42, 43, 47, 48, 55, 56, 76, 78, 100, 133, 141, 149, 172, 214, 242, 271, 344 (7 days a week), 4, 243 (Mon-Sat), 21, 23, 25, 501, 505, 521 (Mon-Fri)

Underground Stations
B Barbican
O Old Street
M Moorgate
S St Pauls
K Bank

Bangladesh is a young, friendly nation, rich in natural resources including water, natural gas and high quality coal. Like Japan and other Asian tigers, Bangladesh's economic growth (averaging over 5% since the return to parliamentary democracy at the start of the 1990s) is led by private sector exports.
• The UK is Bangladesh's 3rd largest export partner, with a total of £480m in 2004
• Leading the exports is the massive garment industry with over 2 billion metres of fabric annually going through 1500 factories, heading for H&M, Sainsbury's, Tesco's and other major high street stores. Bangladesh ceramics are also establishing a reputation for quality with trading partners including prestigious names like Royal Doulton. These traditional industries are being joined by a wide range of trades and services, from pharmaceuticals to ICT.
Expo Bangladesh 2005 is an exciting, innovative showcase for Bangladeshi manufacturers, services and talents. It is a pioneering initiative of the Bangladesh British Chamber of Commerce to promote trade and investment between the UK and Bangladesh. "Trade not aid" is a current world focus - and a real focus here! There will be stands representing up to 100 companies from Bangladesh, UK-based organisations with an interest in Bangladesh's export trade, and non-resident Bangladeshi business in the UK. Exhibits include ready made garments, ceramics, leather, food, handicrafts and furniture, plastics, metal, pharmaceuticals, fashion, ICT, print & design, media and travel. There will be a number of associations and charitable organisations, including Fair Trade and Women Entrepreneurs Association of Bangladesh, and a series of seminars on trade and related subjects. Over 8,000 people are expected to attend. On Saturday 17 September there will be several live presentations, including a dynamic catwalk showcase by Ethical Fashion Forum UK presenting outfits by well known and emerging designers and businesses, with the emphasis on quality and fair trade. And a Celebrity Chef Competition with top Edinburgh-based Bengali chef (and restaurateur, hotelier, writer and businessman) Tommy Miah.

EXPO BANGLADESH 2005
15-17 September 2005
Barbican Exhibition Hall 1,
Golden Lane, London EC2
Tel (information - public and buyers):
0207 247 5525
www.expobangladesh2005.com

News Letter

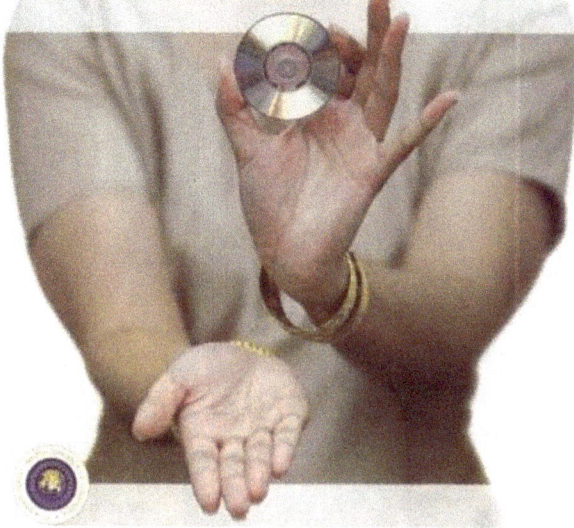

Workshop Chaired by Muquim Ahmed

*Muquim Ahmed, Ahmed Ud Samad and Muhaimin standing with
the Prime Minister Sheikh Hasina 2014*

British Bangladesh Chamber of Commerce

Executive Committee

Muquim Ahmed	: President
M R Chowdhury (Matab)	: Director General
Mohib Choudhury	: Director of Finance
M M Noor	: Senior Vice President
Nazmul Islam Nuru	: Vice President
Sayedur Rahman Ranu JP	: Deputy Director General
Monir Ahmed	: Director, Membership
Sayed Chowdhury	: Director, Press & Publicity
Jamal Uddin Mokoddus	: London Regional President
Aziz Ur Rahman	: Midlands Regional President
Mahtab Miah	: North East Regional President

Directors

Abdul Hamid Chowdhury
Abdul Malik
Abdul Muhaimin Miah
Abssar M Waess
Ahmed Us Samad Chowdhury JP
Ali Md. Zakaria
Anawar Babul Miah
Azad Ali
Bajloor Rashid MBE
Bashir Ahmed
Enam Ali MBE
Iqbal Ahmed OBE
M A Quyyum
M A Rouf JP

Board of Directors BBCCI - 2014

BCA (Bangladesh Caterers Association)

Shirajul Islam alias Israil Miah and Bashir Ahmed (my uncle) became the founding president and Secretary General of the Bangladesh Caterer's Association (BCA) in 1960. The organisation was established to represent the catering industry, the restaurants and takeaways, the staff, managers and the owners. During its 60 years of existence, it has become a powerful advocate for, at one time, 20,000 Indian restaurants, employing hundreds of thousands of staff. I was the Senior Vice President of BCA during the presidency of Abdur Rahim.

When the restaurant trade began, nobody was trained or knew how to present the cuisine. It was with, curiosity, and intuition that propelled them to cook meals that were already common in so many of our homes. These are our predecessors, who were inventive and creative.

They launched the restaurant trade which become a phenomenon; a curry revolution that rocked the British Isles.

Incidentally, Bashir Mamu married Taru Miah's daughter Maya Khala. Taru was the Chairman of Sylhet Municipality now equivalent to mayor. The wedding took place in my parents' home Mubarak Monzil in Sylhet.

Mrs. Thatcher said,
"If you have never turned a wrong to right
You have been a coward in the fight"

Chapter Twenty Two
Misapprehension

S ome people are mistaken, and many are overtly ignorant. And someone's ignorance nearly led to my death.

Bangla TV had arranged for a cultural programme with dinner at my 350-seater Café Naz Restaurant in Middlesex Street on 28 October 2007. It was Ramadan and the television station had invited religious leaders from different parts of London, as well as dignitaries from our community. Since it was the month of Ramadan, some of the guests objected to the music and songs being played on the stage that evening. Like a few other community leaders, I was invited to speak.

Anticipating a conflict between those present and the TV company over the music, I tried to diffuse and pacify the situation by simply saying that Allah created the Azan – the call to prayer made by the Moazzam. The Azan is the sweetest of all rhythms. Nobody has ever created such sweet melody. Allah created the Universe; the Earth goes around the sun and the moon comes around the Earth. Night follows the day. There is a majestic rhythm in all Allah's creation.

But my attempts at reconciliation were misunderstood. Adul Gafur Khalisader, an influential community member, was totally out of his depth. He was seated among the Brick Lane Mosque's small group and shouted ominously: 'Muquim, do not compare Azan with music'. He had misunderstood what I meant. He had taken my words out of context.

Gafur Khalisader was clearly furious. He shouted at me, accusing me of making comments against Islam. The situation became acrimonious, and Gafur even became violent; it almost came to blows. There was confusion and the organisers had to call the whole thing off. Gafur and his misguided friends left the hall but muttered threats that 'They will sort the kafir (non believer) out.'

The next day, some miscreants attacked me in front of Café Naz, my restaurant in Brick Lane as I was putting the shutters down. Normally my manager closed up at 3pm after lunch but unfortunately that day I was entertaining a friend, so I let all my staff go home leaving us inside the restaurant. In addition, I had let my driver go along with my friend Mira to my other shop Café Naz Express and had asked them to wait for me there.

As I was holding on to the keys for the shutters to go down. Three men approached me. One greeted me, 'Assala Mualikum' — peace be upon you. I said: 'Walikum As Salaam.' Simultaneously, another tasered me from behind. I lost control of my senses. CCTV shows me struggling to stay upright, but I fell flat on the pavement.

The trio then mercilessly kicked me around the head and body and left me bleeding, unconscious, on the pavement.

Before passers-by realised what was happening, the perpetrators fled the scene. A crowd gathered and someone called the police. An ambulance rushed me to Royal London Hospital at Whitechapel.

I nearly lost my life. It took several hours before I regained consciousness. I was lucky. While I recovered in hospital, hundreds visited me. The East End Bengali community was angered by this hideous attack, which happened in daylight. Many were worried for their own safety.

An urgent meeting was called at the community centre. Community leaders demanded that police should take immediate action. They condemned the barbarous attack on me. They said: 'He is a stalwart and respected member of the community, a gentleman and a generous social activist.'

The senior police officer and detective present in the meeting assured everyone that they would act quickly and bring the perpetrators to justice. Some offered to help identify the culprits. And indeed, that very day, later that evening, two men were arrested and taken into custody. All Bengali media carried this story on their front pages. News of the attack was reported on local TV bulletins. Everyone condemned this barbaric attack.

The lesson to learn from this unfortunate saga is that religion is a sentimental, subliminal, highly inflammable private topic and it must be handled very carefully and delicately.

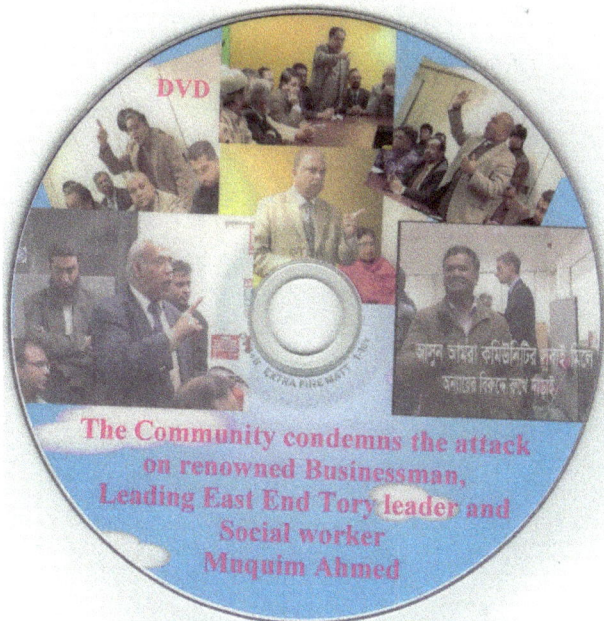

DVD of Community Meeting

"If one has determination and the will to succeed, then success is inevitable; perseverance and ingenuity will always prevail.
It is not about the way of life,
it is about attitude to life,
it is a battle between the pessimism
of the intellect and the optimism of the will.
The spirit of the age is for rebalancing
that imbalance in society."

- Muquim Ahmed

Chapter Twenty Three
Queen Mary University — Honorary Fellowship

In 2005, the Director of Development at Queen Mary University, Bernie McDermott invited me for tea at the university coffee shop overlooking the Mile End Road. After tea he give me a tour of the campus. I was delighted by the opportunity. Subsequently later another day as arranged, I met Bernie at the university's London Hospital site. I was overwhelmed by the extensive underground laboratories which housed medical science department's research and development project. We encountered a scientist, deeply absorbed with his microscope, who gave us a detailed explanation of the human micro-cell structure. I will never forget that experience.

Bernie took me all around the university campus, a huge place extending to the lake behind the numerous buildings, where 16,900 students studied.

I was told that the university was looking to make me a Director on the board. They wanted local representation on their executive committee. No mention of the Honorary Fellowship was made. I met the principal, Professor Adrian Smith FRS, for tea several times and we discussed various prospects of the university. I was not keen on becoming a director of their board; it would have taken lot of my time and it was a serious business.

However, on 20 December 2007, the principal wrote to me, informing me that the Academic Board of Queen Mary had decided to elect me as the Honorary Fellow of the College because of my achievements in business and my outstanding contribution to the communities of

East London. Professor Nigel Relph was my mentor and he presented me at the ceremony. Miraj was there and my brother and sister's sons Minhaz and Mitu. I was totally overwhelmed and bewildered as I was paraded into the great hall, much as they do to newly-elected peers in the House of Lords.

Receiving my fellowship in July 2009, I said: 'I feel deeply honoured to receive such an accolade; this recognition by Queen Mary University proves beyond doubt that the college acknowledges that ordinary people like me in the community — who strive hard to achieve in the field of business and other social enterprises — are also indispensable.'

Colette Bowe, Chairman of Council, Professor Nigel Relph,
Wendy Appleby, Secretary to the Council - 2009

If one has determination and the will to succeed, then success is inevitable; perseverance and ingenuity will always prevail. It is not about the way of life, it is about attitude to life, it is a battle between the pessimism of the intellect and the optimism of the will. The spirit of the age is for rebalancing that imbalance in society.

The fact that the university continuously encourages members of the local community to study there shows how committed it is to improve the life of those who live in the area around the campus. Bangladeshis lag behind the general population in terms of economics, education, enterprise and initiative. But the intake of students born locally to Bangladeshi parents is growing, not only because of their ethnicity but also because these students are achieving success with A and A* grades.

After the departure of Professor Adrian Smith FRS, Professor Simon Gaskell became principal in October 2009. His arrival marked Queen Mary's membership of the prestigious Russell Group, an association of public research universities in the United Kingdom. Queen Mary has 3800 staff and an annual turnover of £300 million. It is one of the biggest constituent colleges of the University of London. The Whitechapel campus is one of the two sites that accommodates the School of Medicine and Dentistry, and includes the Blizzard Institute, the Institute for Health Sciences Education, the Institute of Dentistry and the cell Science Education Centre.

In March 2016, I was thrilled to be asked to speak at BPP University's Business School at St Mary Axe, London by the institution's Entrepreneurs Society. I was an ideal candidate to address the students: an immigrant who came to the UK as a student, an entrepreneur who built successful businesses and faced many adverse situations. Here is an edited version of my speech:

Ladies and gentlemen, I am delighted to be here today. I feel really honoured and have a good feeling that I should talk about my success. Of course, success is relative; the perception of success could vary from one person to another.

QUEEN MARY AND WESTFIELD COLLEGE
UNIVERSITY OF LONDON

This is to certify that

Muquim Uddin Ahmed

was elected an

HONORARY FELLOW OF THE COLLEGE

on

22nd November 2007

Colette Bowe
CHAIRMAN OF COUNCIL

Philip Ogden
PRINCIPAL

DATE OF ADMISSION: *15th July 2009*

Wendy Appleby
SECRETARY TO THE COUNCIL

Certificate of Q M

I came to England in 1974 to study engineering at Southeast London College, now known as Lewisham College.

While studying I got increasingly involved in my family business of importing fridges and colour televisions into Bangladesh. I was organising shipments from Philips in Holland, coloured televisions from Japan, fridge/freezers from Italy and Bedford trucks from the UK. The market in Bangladesh was ripe in the 70s; every urban household wanted a fridge and a colour TV.

Participation in the family business was the turning point in my life. Business was intense — too busy, too much happening. I lost sight of my education and thought that I could get my degree later while the opportunity for making this money might not come again. I started missing my classes; I could not sit for my final exam.

I made a lot of money and became the first Bangladesh millionaire by the age of 25. I was immensely motivated, ruthlessly determined to look at the brighter side of life. I aspired to achieve even more.

There was truth in the old adage 'The more you earn, the more you yearn.'

Entrepreneurs successfully sets up businesses. I have set up many types of businesses: electronic, home appliances, watches, radios, TVs, video and audio products. These products were manufactured under the brand name Harper in Hong Kong. In the 70s and 80s I was involved in shipping, travel, home remittance, cinemas, stage shows, amusement arcades, garments, restaurants, an industrial bakery, properties and so on, and was also the national distributor for TDK, Sony, JVC, National Panasonic for the Japanese companies here in the United Kingdom.

I have seen success in most of my business ventures, however, Café Naz restaurants gave me the most thrill and fame. It was an institution and in a lot of ways set a benchmark for the Indian restaurant. It received country wide acclamation.

Let me now illustrate how, and what, made me who I am today.
I am a restless, resilient and incisive person. If opportunity knocks on my door, I open it wide open. My moral compass is overly sensitive; I must do the right thing at the right time. No scruples, but resource, courage and determination.

When opportunities meet determination, the sky become the limit.

The old proverb says, 'If you are born poor, it is not your fault, but if you die poor then it is your fault.' So, my dear friends, rise and shine in knowledge, intellect, wisdom and wealth. Ambition, motivation and a sense of desire to succeed are essential for an entrepreneur. Set your aim high. High enough to reach but not too far to lose sight.

Remember, a positive attitude turns adversity into advantage almost all the time. Your own motivation, ambition and talent will shape your path of success.

In 1994, I lost almost everything in a devastating fire in one of the factories in my building. I had to borrow money from relatives and sell my Rolls Royce to raise £150,000 with which I reinvented myself. I rose again from the ashes.

Brave and strong, fierce and bold
Focused and resilient will never fold.

To come to the gist of what will make you a successful entrepreneur, one must adhere to the following, which I applied to myself.

How to get started when you have nothing:
1. *Identify what you want to do.*
2. *Believe in the objective you want to achieve.*
3. *Plan for the objective.*
4. *Financial requirement is always an important element.*
5. *Borrow from family/friends.*
6. *Budget carefully.*
7. *Be persistent and do not give up halfway.*
8. *Fruition of all your hard work will come at the end so perseverance is a must.*

How to maintain success:
1. *Be focused.*
2. *Be diligent.*
3. *Be informed.*
4. *Be relentless in your efforts.*
5. *Work with a rhythm and enjoy work.*
6. *Plan ahead.*

Ladies and gentlemen, it's all about self-confidence: you can do it, you can shine because you are special! Faith is the motivator.

But remember Freud:

"The capacity to defer the gratification of instinct is the basis of all civilisations."

"A country needs a stable, predictable
tax system to encourage investment.
In addition, the enforcement of property law,
which allows the bank to lend money and foreclose
the property, if necessary, is of paramount
importance for financial institutions to be able to
transact business and for a country to grow."

Chapter Twenty Four
Political Affiliation

B ritain's greatness was not achieved by chance, but by choice. For hundreds of years, Britain has always looked beyond its shores. Its liberal, progressive outlook helped it to become, at one point, the mightiest of all nations. Of many things, we are also an increasingly egalitarian society — where many from different ethnic backgrounds have worked astonishingly hard and have scaled the ladder of success into the highest offices in the land and now the office of Prime Minister.

A country needs a stable, predictable tax system to encourage investment. In addition, the enforcement of property law, which allows the bank to lend money and foreclose the property, if necessary, is of paramount importance for financial institutions to be able to transact business and for a country to grow.

The fortune of a country is measured by, among other things, its industrial performance, trade and commerce, which ultimately forms the basis of the gross domestic products (GDP) ratio. When Margaret Thatcher became the Prime Minister in 1979, she was confronted with a debt that was at crippling 44 per cent of GDP. By the time she was unfortunately ousted, it was below 27 per cent. In other words, the country became richer.

I have firm conviction of Baroness Thatcher's philosophy - uphold enterprise and initiative for progress and prosperity; surely excessive taxation stifles enterprise. Meritocracy is the order of the day.

Francis Maude, Chairman of Conservative Party, Faruk Bakth, Anne Main MP,
Muquim Ahmed 2006

The rule of law is paramount in Conservative thinking; it is indispensable. The secure ownership of property, the freedom to do business with confidence, the right to personal liberty and the ability to live without anarchy and intimidation is fundamental of our democracy.

Free-market capitalism is hard-wired into Tory DNA. Enterprise, initiative, fiscal prudence, and good economic management —are the attributes of Conservative philosophy — and are intricately woven into the Party's fabric.

Benjamin Disraeli, twice Prime Minister in the 19th century, said: 'The Conservative Party should be the party of change but change that goes along with the customs and manners and tradition and sentiments of the people rather than change according to some grand plan.'

Liz Truss did not follow this mantra, her 'grand plan' failed miserably, and she became the shortest reigning Prime Minister presiding for just seven weeks.

And Disraeli's 21st century successor David Cameron said: 'The Conservative Party only succeeds if it is a party of the future — modernisation isn't an event. It is a process.'

Conservatives concede to the principle of wealth creation, job creation, enterprise, initiative and fair taxation to encourage growth and prosperity. Rishi Sunak became the UK's first Prime Minister of Indian origin and produced a pragmatic and finely tuned budget in autumn 2022, which calmed the markets' nerves. Pound Sterling was forced down to its lowest ever - a £1 - $1.03 because of Liz Truss's orthodox economic plan. In the next leadership contest I didn't get to vote for Rishi Sunak as the process didn't call for party member votes, but I was delighted to see him ascend and was also thrilled to be invited to meet him at a drinks reception on the12th December 2022 at the Army Museum at Chelsea.

Meritocracy has been firmly embraced. The class system has completely been shattered. It is not where you come from, or what is the colour of your skin, but what is your conviction and where you are going. It is the politics of aspiration; to achieve for yourself and for the nation. Technology and inventions are created by few but enjoyed by millions. I have seen immense changes since I arrived in the UK in 1974. I have experienced racism, but I feel it is decreasing. When it comes to class, I don't feel I have experienced classism. I feel there are only the upper class and the rest of us, the commoners. And that too has changed. The now Duke of Sussex married Meghan Markle, a divorcee and of African American origin.

CONSERVATIVES

Win for Britain

Change to Win

Conservative Campaign
Headquarters
25 Victoria Street
London SW1H 0DL

tel: 020 7222 9000
fax: 020 7222 1135
www.conservatives.com

Muquim Ahmed Esq
Chairman Quantum Securities
Quantum House (Concorde)
Caxton Street
London E161JL

25th April 2006

Dear Muquim,

Just a note to say many thanks for the meeting on Tuesday with the Bengali media and candidates in Tower Hamlets. It really was an excellent opportunity you created for the Party and for myself and I am grateful for all your efforts for the Conservative cause.

It occurs to me that you might like to fix an appointment for a coffee and a chat with me sometime after May 4th. If you think this would be useful then please contact my office through Eric Ollerenshaw. It would be good to see how we can build on your efforts among the Bengali community and the wider Asian community and business world.

Yours sincerely,

The Rt Hon Francis Maude MP
Chairman of the Conservative Party

HRH Prince of Wales is married to a commoner, Kate Middleton, as is King Charles with his second wife.

'I want us to go on being the open, liberal, tolerant party,' said Cameron. Tolerance is the omnipresent facet of British way of life. He added: 'Social mobility is not just a moral imperative but an economic endeavour.' He also said in a speech during his visit to India that he had a number of Secretaries of State in his Cabinet who are of Indian origin but the day is not far when an Indian will become the Prime Minister of United Kingdom.

His prediction came true on the 25th October 2022 when Rishi Sunak became the Prime Minister of the United Kingdom.

Most people detest being able to live more comfortably on subsidies than on the proceeds of work. Certainly this is an affront to common sense and basic fairness. A fair society is not one in which money should simply be given to compensate for the predicament of a few. Welfare should be the engine of mobility not only a safety net or only a means for subsistence.

'A challenge to us all to follow our conscience to ask not what my entitlements are but what are my responsibilities,' said Cameron. 'A political party should be asking all the time: Am I properly in touch with, and reflecting on, the society and the country.'

Tony Blair wrote in his memoir, 'A Journey' - 'I want us to be the nation, proud of being today, a land of many cultures and faith, breaking new ground against prejudice of any sort, paying more attention to merit than to class, and being at ease with an open society and global economy; a society of equal opportunity and compassion.' Albeit he is now out of power, Boris Johnson pulverised the opposition in the 2019 election and has welded in place an iron-clad majority, which would not easily rust. Before the election in 2019, on 1 November I wrote an article titled Why I Support Boris on the request of Dinah Glover, Chairman of Bethnal Green & Bow Conservative association, for a local newspaper:

Boris Johnson comes across to me as an enigmatic, persuasive person. He is an intellectual with many facets. A highly intelligent and incisive, constructive thinker. It is only Boris in our Conservative Party who can get us out of this impasse. He has the charisma and the aptitude to unify the Conservatives and the nation.

Boris has a proven track records as London's two-term, successful Mayor. His astute relentless persuasion of the Brexit issue makes him the perfect candidate to negotiate Brexit in the interim and deliver a victory for the Conservatives in the upcoming General Election.

We at the centre right must make sure that Jeremy Corbyn is devoid of going into Number 10 otherwise the great work and philosophy Margaret Thatcher — induced and infused amongst us — that society should uphold enterprise and initiative for progress and prosperity will be in vain. We should resist the extreme left taking over our world and the person who can do this is Boris.

We must be careful of Nigel Farage; we do not want to be the Brexit Party only. Boris will take Nigel's shine away because Boris is 'Brexit' and a true Conservative at the core.

The letter box hijab metaphor is not impairing our ability to support Boris. He is a journalist, a prolific, imaginative writer with twist and turn of the custom and manner of the society we live in. But he is also tough, serious, articulate, and conciliatory. He should make an excellent Prime Minister representing everyone.

Muquim Ahmed, Entrepreneur and a political activist of Bangladeshi origin.

(2022 update – But alas! Boris's chauvinistic, rule breaking attitude cost him his premiership.)

Politically and Socially, a Tory

I have lived and worked in Tower Hamlets for more than 40 years. I am generally regarded as a leading British Bangladeshi entrepreneur and a community activist. I have achieved success in a range of businesses. I appeared in The Sunday Times Rich List in 2005, and I am regarded as the first Bangladeshi millionaire.

I have always worked to make a difference to the lives of communities in East End of London by inspiring and empowering local people. I have tried to help the Bengali community integrate into mainstream British society through my work with individual and community organisations.

I was the Chairman of the British Bangladesh Chamber of Commerce, based in Tower Hamlets, for three terms. As Chairman, I organised successful seminars and trade exhibitions at local and national level, including the first ever single-country trade fair held under my leadership in the Barbican Centre, London in 2005.

I have been a leading supporter, fundraiser and campaigner for the Conservative Party in London for over 40 years. I joined the Conservative Party because I believe that it is the party of aspiration, liberty, enterprise, initiative, innovation and personal responsibility.

I have been a stalwart of the party, and I have campaigned for it in eight General Elections, and local elections, in Tower Hamlets. I have previously been Vice Chairman of the Bethnal Green and Bow Conservative Association.

Campaigning with Michael Howard former leader of the Party at Clacton 2015

Recently I was made the Honorary Vice Chairman. I bid to become the Conservative Candidate for Executive Mayor for Tower Hamlets in 2010. The day I made my campaign public, I made a speech which outlined my beliefs and my philosophy:

I was an applicant for the Candidacy of the Mayoral Election, October 2010.

And this is what I said for my campaign and the speech I delivered at the selection process at the Britannia Hotel, Marsh Wall, E14:

'I have worked and lived in Tower Hamlet for the last 35 years. I am well versed with the advantages and disadvantages of living in this borough.

Please allow me to say a few words about myself.

I came to England when I was 19; I have worked hard, long hours, seven days, diligently and effectively, and have managed to improve the quality of my life and the life of my family.

Now, I want to help improve the quality of life of my fellow beings and go along with the traditions and sentiments of the people.

Charles Darwin said: The survival of the species depends on not how strong they are but on how quickly they can adapt.

I have adapted to the way of life in this country, and I consider myself lucky to be in the Asian Rich List.

I am astute and determined, assiduous and resilient in my disposition. I have immense energy for organisation. Give me the chance and see what I can do for you and for the community.

We have deep-rooted social and economic problems in Tower Hamlets. Drug manifestation, law and order breaches, lack of safety in our neighbourhood.

I was beaten unconscious by the Jihadis just because I said in a speech that God loves music.

We have limited job opportunities in this borough, we have crowded housing problems, schooling and social deprivation are some of the problems inundated within the fabric of Tower Hamlets.

Why should you support me?

I think from my past records I can safely say that I can achieve the goal we all so desire. I can assure you that I can start the process of turning this borough blue 'quicker' and make it affluent and progressive. But of course, with your help!

We are at the fringe of the mighty City; we have Canary Wharf, the hub of economic activities in the country and the world, and yet we are so behind in progression.

We are nationally branded as a deprived inner-city borough.

Let us change this conception.

Let us all work hard and empower the community and pull it out of the clutches of Labour, a party of deprivation who believes that you should remain stagnant where you are in the class struggle. These people do not strive for economic or intellectual emancipation but wants you to remain in poverty and deprivation through funnily unconscious choice!

We, the Conservatives, will have to create the environment conducive to the creation of jobs and opportunities, to enhance the facilities for education and training so that in progression and in the future, we do not have to have this black hole in the middle of our city.

Again, I ask myself why me?
Because I am passionate, and I believe in the wellbeing of this community. Because I care, I listen and emulate.

Because I am able and determined to bring about this change if I am given that chance.

Disraeli said: The Conservative Party should be the party of change but change that goes along with the customs and manners and traditions and sentiments of people.

Empower me and I can perform, I can contribute, I want to be a part of the society which is able and progressive.

John F Kennedy said: If society cannot look after the many who are poor it cannot save the few who are rich.'

Let us smash poverty and deprivation, let us smash inequality, let us create wealth, knowledge, prosperity, and tranquillity, let us create harmony. Conservatism is at its best when it is protean and supple.

I want to appeal to all the members present here today; we do not want to be second, third, or fourth in Tower Hamlets.

Trust me, have faith in me, take courage and give me the chance and I will win this Mayoral election for you.'

I am the co-founder of the successful Conservative Friends of Bangladesh (CFOB). I was the leading supporter of, and participant in, the Conservative Party's Project Maja, social action programme bringing together leading politicians and activists, which visited Bangladesh in 2011. I have always been in the forefront, providing support in monetary terms and through participation. CFOB has honoured me with the patronage of the organisation.

I have organised successful networking and fundraising events for senior figures in the Conservative Party, including Michael Portillo, Jeffrey Archer, Steve Norris, Francis Maude, Andrew Feldman, Damian Green, Sayeeda Warsi and Dr Liam Fox. Michael Heseltine and William Hague have both visited Café Naz in Brick Lane. I hosted a huge introductory party for Boris Johnson at my 350-seater restaurant at Middlesex Street when he was campaigning to be Mayor of London. I told him, *'Boris, if you don't look after the Bengalis, we'll not vote for you. Promise to look after us and we'll vote for you.'*
'I will do that,' he said. Afterwards I dropped him to where he needed to go.

I saw him a month afterwards at a mosque and he didn't recognise me until someone pointed me out. *'Boris!'* The man said. *'Muquim gave you a lift in his Bentley last week!'*

He got up and came over and shook my hand. He's a spontaneous man of charm and grace,

I have faced many challenges and much adversity in my life, but I have always shown determination, courage and resilience.

In 1999, my family and I narrowly escaped with our lives when David Copeland's nail bomb exploded outside Café Naz in Brick Lane. When the restaurant re-opened, 17 members of House of Lords visited to show support to the community.

In 2007, I was elected as an Honorary Fellow by Queen Mary College, University of London, in recognition of my achievements in business and my outstanding contribution to the communities of East London.

Indeed, I was politically and socially very active in the East End of London. Participating and arranging political meetings for the stalwarts of our party for the last several decades.

Sir Iain Duncan Smith, Muquim Ahmed & Rt. Hon. Dominic Grieve Attorney General -
2014

Conservative Friends of Bangladesh (CFoB)

Anne Main, MP for St Albans, took the initiative to establish CFOB. She believed that Bengalis are natural Conservatives, but they must be shepherded into the fold. Anne was the first President, Shahagir Bakth Faruk and I became the founding Vice Presidents.

It was serendipity that I became the co-founder of Conservative Friends of Bangladesh (CFOB). The organisation was launched at Conservative Party Conference in Bournemouth in 2006 where then party leader, William Hague, was the guest of honour.

Anne Main MP, Bangladesh High Commissioner Mr S U Ahmed, William Haig, Muquim Ahmed, Bournemouth 2006

The purpose of this organisation was to build on the fortunes of the Conservative Party within the Bangladeshi community, who are devoid of conservatism here in the United Kingdom, and at the same time build a bridge with Bangladesh as a whole.

Anne started facilitating and attending meetings, award ceremonies and seminars to convey the conservative philosophy into the community. She organised all the social action trips to Bangladesh. The first took place in 2011, named the Maja Project. CFOB was fortunate to have Baroness Warsi, the party's Co-chairman between 2010 and 2012, to head the delegation. Other prominent members of the delegation included Nicky Morgan (later Education Secretary), Tobias Elwood (later Defence Minister), Paul Scully (later Small Business Minister), Eric Ollerenshaw MP, Kamal Syed MEP, later made a peer at the house of Lords, Suella Braverman who later became Home Secretary on 25th October 2022 and few other MPs and constituency workers were also member of the delegation. It was a roaring success. The Prime Minister at the time David Cameron invited all the delegates to 10 Downing Street for tea to commemorate the success.

Subsequently this social trip to Bangladesh was renamed Shapla after the national flower of Bangladesh. It was left to the Chairman Mehfuz Ahmed to organize, every second year, a group of dedicated Conservatives to make the journey to Bangladesh and carry on with the social works, and to distribute different essentials donated by British companies and Conservative donors. As well as carrying on with teaching, enhancing extracurricular activities in schools, and cataract eye operations etc and other essential social works were the theme of the trip.

In 2017, MPs Paul Scully, Anne Main and Will Quince led the way, becoming the first Parliamentarians to visit the Rohingya refugee camps through CFOB. When they returned to the UK, they called a debate on the refugee crisis in Bangladesh. British Bangladeshis are proud that their MPs have spearheaded this effort to show the party's compassion and Department for International Development's (DFID's) effectiveness.

It is claimed that Bangladeshis are natural Conservatives and that they have come to this country to improve the quality of their life through work, enterprise and initiative. People who have started from nothing make the most compelling Conservatives of all. Conservative believe in the creation of wealth and sharing the proceeds of growth through fair taxation. We believe in creating an environment where enterprises can flourish, where jobs and wealth are created, due taxes are paid from the proceeds of the gain. Raising the tax burden on business, or otherwise increasing its costs, is the surest way of stifling enterprise and growth. Britain has become, under the Conservatives, a progressively more tax efficient, competitive, and business friendly economy.

Public representation and achievement are what the community needs most. The Prime Minister's Race Disparity Audit showed that just 7.2 per cent of British Bangladeshis achieve three A grades at A-Level compared to 15.3 per cent of Indian and 24.8 per cent of Chinese students and 30 per cent of Bangladeshi households are overcrowded compared to 7 per cent of Indian and Chinese households. In light of this, community leaders, national leaders and institutions should do much more to elevate and enhance the position of this relatively deprived community. The good thing is that we Bangladeshis are disciplined to save and set an example: Indeed 40 per cent of Bangladeshis own our own home compared to 38 per cent of Chinese and 37 per cent of other Asians.

We Bangladeshis have achieved fairly well in politics, but it is within the Labour Party. Labour has made deep inroads into this new, growing community of 900,000 people. In the December 2019 General Election, four members of the community were elected to Parliament. All were from the Labour Party of course. It is indeed alarming that, from the Conservative Party, there is not a single representative, either in the House of Commons or in the House of Lords.

Interestingly by 2020, however, the Conservatives had Chancellor Rishi Sunak (now Prime Minister), Home Secretary Priti Patel, Health Secretary Sajid Javid, Business Secretary Alok Sharma and Attorney General Suella Braverman (now 2022 Home Secretary) from the Indian sub-continent on the Front Bench. A remarkable feat by the ethnic minority. Again, in total serendipity in 2022 it seem to me, as if magically by a divine behest Rishi Sunak became the Prime Minister of the United Kingdom. How remarkable!

But there are serious gaps in Bangladeshi representation in the Conservative party. Although it is accepted that those of us of Bangladeshi origin lags behind drastically in Conservative politics, elsewhere in the social hierarchy, we are consistently at the forefront.

British Bangladeshis are in the House of Lords, they are Queen's Counsel, in the British Foreign Service and many are judges and doctors. This community will have to work that much harder to attain success in Conservative politics.

The party leadership will have to encourage and welcome the British Bangladeshis to come and join, and contribute, to the Conservative doctrine. The fortune and influence of Conservatives are enhanced by the greater participation of all different communities. To leave a community behind is to give in to the socialists.
True Conservatism is about social mobility. Social justice is to be the prime objective. 'We are the warriors of the dispossessed' said former Prime Minister Theresa May.

We show compassion, and we care for those at the bottom while motivating and supporting the aspirations of those at the top.

Board of CFoB 2024

David Cameron, Muquim Ahmed and Stuart Rose

CFoB Lifetime Achievement Award
Mehfuz Ahmed-Chairman, myself, Andrea Leadsom Leader House of the Common and
Abdus Hamid Vice Chairman

Chapter Twenty Five
Second Chance

The end of my 30-year marriage in 2005 came as a terrible shock. I accept that sacrifice and compromise are essential for any marriage to work.

I begged Rashmi my then wife, to reconcile and said I would accept any terms; even though her assurance to Vasant a common friend that she would never divorce me. Vasant made a prophecy at a consolation dinner after the fire where Satish our mutual friend and his wife were also present. Vasant's prophecy was that after the Chicksand Street fire which forced me down to my knees – almost to the point of no return that I would have a heart attack, go bankrupt or have a divorce. Vasant was right, the mental pressure on me was most intense and acute. I lost everything in the fire. Totally frustrated, crippled and a broken man.

Till today I remember Rashmi's exact words. She said, "I can assure you Vasant that I cannot foretell the bankruptcy or his heart condition, but I will never divorce Muquim. Our union is for life".

Mentally and physically, I was at the lowest ebb of my life. I could not concentrate and sometimes took my frustration out on Rashmi without realizing the effect on her. She in turn would retaliate and eventually filed for divorce. Instead of reasoning and finding a solution, I too became emotional and accepted her decision, albeit regretfully.

Later, I realised the implication the divorce would have on the family. But it was too late. She was adamant to go all the way.

This caused more problems – double whammy! I was paying two sets of solicitor's fees, businesses were failing. Life became difficult. I lost my focus. I had nowhere to live. I moved into my office in Canning Town, a small room which became my bedroom. I lived there for two years before I could empty one of the flats I owned and move in.

Being alone was difficult. All sort of thoughts come to your mind. Maybe I should just give up. Life is not worth living. Then I realised:

'Death might relief a pain
But love cannot relieve in vain.'

I had loved her with all my heart. But again, nature lives within us. A day could be lovely and bright another day could be rainy and dull and another stormy and violent. So, life and relations can mirror the majestic phenomenon of nature. One day happy, another unhappy, angry and upset, high mood or low mood. You must forgive, forget and march on. If I had understood human nature and more so women's psychology; perhaps I would not have that divorce.

But alas! She remained adamant and saw the benefit to herself and filed for divorce.

I never thought I would marry again.

But then I met Farzana at a Chamber of Commerce event. She comes from an illustrious family; her father was one of the personal physicians to Col. Gaddafi. She was born in Libya.

Her maternal grandfather was the Chief Justice of Bangladesh who later became the Head of Caretaker Interim Government (equivalent to Prime Minister). Her Paternal Grandfather was a lawyer and also a MLA (Member of Legislative Assembly) in East Pakistan from 1962 – 1969. We became friendly and slowly developed a relationship. Eventually we began to live together, and then four years later we were married. We have lots in common, she enjoys public life and business and is extremely hard working. We manage our property portfolio together and make sure we enjoy life too. We enjoy our new home. We have plans to make it exactly as we want it to be. We share a passion for gardening and are currently having ours landscaped. We have a flight of 72 stairs with a waterfall cascading from the top of the hill. A Stunning rhododendron canopy and a panoramic view over the surrounding hills. All kinds of fruits and vegetables are grown as part of a kitchen garden.

It is a joint venture that we really enjoy and grounds us amidst our business concerns. She's very kind and giving. I love having guests and entertaining and so does she. I really feel that she is my soulmate.

Farzana and I, 29th Dec 2015

Life today is good for me. I am semi-retired, and keep in touch with my family, including my sister Rokiya in Bangladesh where she lives alone – her children are in the UK and we see them regularly. Moin and his wife are both passed now but I keep in touch with their children who live in Canada. Muslim is no longer with us either, of course, but I am in touch with Sokina and their children who live in Spain, New York and the UK. I am happy. I have been fortunate and I am content.

Yasmin, Minhas and Matt 1976

Monique 1999

Miraj 1998

Chapter Twenty Six
Origin

I was always proud to be a Bangladeshi but then one day I was caught up in a practicality issue. 1987 I was invited by BASF the German chemical company to visit their headquarters and factories in Germany. I did not need a visa for Germany with my Bangladeshi Passport but one of their factories was on the border of France, for which I did need a visa since we would land in France than travel in a coach back into Germany to the premises. But I hadn't understood this entirely. The other five national distributors for BASF, that I was travelling with were allowed to go but I was detained. I felt humiliated and inferior.

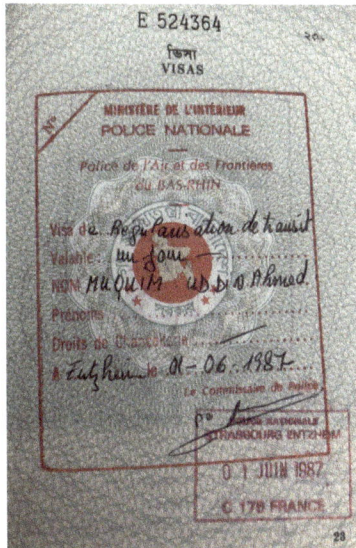

French Visa

Fortunately, BASF is such a powerful company that it was quickly sorted but it was not lost on me how different it would have been if I'd had a British passport. With one of those, you just wave it and keep walking! So that's when I applied for British citizenship. I could already vote because I was a member of the Commonwealth and on the electoral role. I voted for the first time in 1979, for you know who.

That said, I was born and bred in Bangladesh. I lived there for 19 years. During my formative years I absorbed Bangladeshi culture, the deference, the custom and manner, moral peripheries, respect for the elders and obedience to parents, bound by family tradition and social boundaries too. A vase is shaped by an artisan and here I was shaped and nurtured to be a Bangladeshi boy reflecting my motherland Bangladesh.

My origin is Bangladeshi before I am British. All aspects of the society, culture and customs were induced into my character before I came to this country. I have lived here 48 years (2022) and still I am a 'Bangladeshi origin British' – in fact and in reality. After the independence from Pakistan in March 1971, Bangladesh has progressed tremendously in leaps and bounds far ahead of Pakistan which was at one time, a rich and powerful country but now lags far behind Bangladesh in prosperity and progression. Henry Kissinger the then US Secretary of State famously called Bangladesh a bottomless basket economy destined to fail but here we are just the opposite his doom and gloom prophesy.

George Harrison and Ravi Shankar organised an international concert to raise money for UNICEF's relief work in Bangladesh in 1971. A good gesture for us in hapless circunstances. Now after 50 years of progression we are a middle income country. GDP growth in Bangladesh is ahead of Pakistan by far and beyond India as well. (Bloomberg research Mihir Sharma, 1 June 2021):

The Bangladesh economy is progressing so rapidly as pointed out by a Pakistani economist. Pakistan could be seeking aid from Bangladesh in 2030. The famous Boston Consulting Group (BCG) has predicted in a report in November 2022 that Bangladesh is on course to become a trillion dollar economy by 2040.

Bangladesh is one nation and the only nation in the Indian sub-continent that has an independent country of its own. Pakistan has number of nations; Punjabi, Sindhi, Baluchi, Pathan, Mahajir and others. India has too many to mention and Sri Lanka has Tamil and Signalise. Bengalese outnumber any nation in the sub-continent by far when taken together the population of Bengalis in India and Bangladesh.

There are world renown Bengalis like Rabindranath Tagore – the Noble Laurate for literature, Swami Vivekananda – spiritual leader who showed a beacon of light to a nation that had lost faith in its ability under British rule and inspired self-confidence among Indians that they are second to none. His ringing words and masterful oratory galvanised the slumbering nation. Amartya Sen who was awarded the 1998 Noble Prize in Economic Science, Netaji Shubas Chandra Bose - the nationalist hero who delivered the independency for India, Noble Laurate Dr. Muhammed Yunus who founded the Grameen Bank, the concept now followed by major financial institutions around the world promoting the concepts of microcredit and microfinance. They are international figures who are world class and renowned for their contribution to humanity.

It is a known fact that Bangladesh has superseded its competitors in the world market in the manufacturing of shirts and apparel in quality and value for money. The work force in Bangladesh is productive and efficient – we can safely say that our weaver's gene pre-British Raj has ultimately caught up with the world even after the British Raj cut off our thumbs so that we could not weave the muslin which was in so much demand by the ladies of the great British Empire. Bangladesh has truly established itself as the textile and readymade garments' hub of the world. An emerging nation – truly the Royal Bengal tiger.

*"We can do what Pichai and Obama and Rishi
have done if we have the will and tenacity.
We can excel in our own environment,
in our own world, however small or minute that
world may be. We are all performers,
and we can perform; have faith.
Whatever you are doing, just do your best."*

- Muquim Ahmed

Chapter Twenty Seven
Leadership

There's an old adage that says that a ship without a radar is lost in the wilderness of the ocean; it does not know which direction it needs to go.

A leader is someone who harnesses the energy of all his/her followers and propels everyone in the direction that they all want to go. A mutual, endless progression, a search for that enhanced quality of life, both physical and intellectual, all together on a quest for a common goal.

If the oar men in a boat is rowing individually in all directions, the boat will be unsteady and will not know which direction to go. All the oarsmen are directed by the coxswain, who steers the boat, coordinates the power and the rhythm of the rowing in a specific direction. The boat, therefore, gathers speed and reaches its destination quickly and efficiently because of a collective response to leadership.

It is always true, historically, that a good, robust leader can change the fate of an entire nation. And in any business or corporation, there is always a managing director or a chief executive. His or her reflection, their energy, is relentlessly transferred through all the workers in the company. They all move in one direction to achieve a goal.

Sundar Pichai, the South Indian genius, became CEO of Google because of his dedication and excellence. He is a born leader and has created a meritocracy out of the ordinary. Barack Obama became the leader of the free world. He shattered the race barrier. Rishi

Sunak became the Chancellor in 2020 and on 25 October 2022, (as if magically and expeditiously) became the Prime Minister of Great Britain; an unprecedented, unimaginable position in the annals of the British Raj (politics) - the highest office in the country. He came into politics in 2015 – the former seat of William Hague. He did not waste time. I met him when he first became the member of parliament at a small Conservative dinner at Dinah Glover's house, in Bethnal Green. She was the Conservative Chair of Bethnal Green and Bow at the time. It was 7th June 2018. Rishi was cordial and very amiable. He asked me whether I knew Kuti of Southampton (because I said that I was from Bangladesh), I replied, "Of course I know Kuti Bhai, he is a friend of mine."

Rishi retorted, "I worked for him in his restaurant at Southampton." I was stunned and bewildered at his modesty. A smart guy, member of Parliament admitting that he worked for a fellow friend made me feel what an extraordinary human being he is. I was full of awe and admiration for him. No vanity, full of determination and courage.

When Rishi became the Chancellor in 2020, I rang Kuti.
"Kuti bhai, Your one time employee Rishi Sunak has become the Chancellor of Great Britain, you must be very proud of your association with him." He said, "Muquim Bhai my heart has filled with immense honour, I am so proud of him and befittingly we all should celebrate his achievement."

A few weeks later, Kuti Bhai rang me and said, "Muquim Bhai, please speak to my GP." And that general practitioner Dr.Yashvir Sunak is Rishi's father.

We can do what Pichai Obama and Rishi have done if we have the will and tenacity. We can excel in our own environment, in our own world, however small or minute that world may be. We are all performers, and

we can perform; have faith. Whatever you are doing, just do your best.
I operated 10 restaurants at the same time, and I could not cook a
single grain of rice or balance a bottle of beer on a tray. I was the
producer of various electronic goods without having a single factory
of my own. I was only a manager — a leader — who got the job done.

Honour and dignity lie where you are, whatever you are doing,
wherever you are going. It should be meaningful and satisfactory to
you and to others and the community you live in.

Sometimes leadership can be cultivated and harnessed, but mostly it
is an inborn instinct.

Here are some principles which I followed and encourage others to
follow:

- Faith — in yourself
- Motivation – to move on and attain
- Rhythm – space and action
- Continuity – keep on the pursuit regardless
- Enjoyment – must feel good; sense of pride and fulfilment

The capacity to be persistent and endure, to have faith and belief,
will surely steer you to your destination. I am adamant that one can
acquire these qualities. It is all in the mind; it is about will and physical
determination. It is all about self-confidence — one can do it; faith is
the motivator.

Identify what you are good at, what you enjoy doing. If you can
find the rhythm, then tiredness will elude you. Of course, reward is
an important factor for all of us. At the end of the labour, when the
mother is handed the baby, the fatigue and pain disappear. I do get
down sometimes, of course, but I am very good at reassuring myself

and telling myself that things will be okay. I learned this at Dawood Public School. I would tell myself, I can do it, I can do it. I would convince myself. For example, I think I was quite ugly when I was younger but I would tell myself I was handsome and I think I've become quite distinguished looking.

Motivation is an important factor. Gratification, as I said earlier, will drive you to move on and achieve. Sometimes, however, there will be failure. This is when your tenacity and endurance should kick in and drive you onwards. Ambition and motivation and the desire to succeed should thrust you to your destination.

When setting up your goal in life, aim high. If you are, for instance, travelling to Manchester (200 miles) and you have reached Birmingham (100 miles), you will not get tired; fatigue will only set in when you reach your destination. Therefore, it is essential to aim high but not too high that you cannot reach. Success is a relative term. One might have more than the other. It is contentment that defines a success of a man. To misquote Gandhi nothing is enough for the man to whom enough is too little.

To retain success and sustain, it is an art in itself. Find the rhythm and then continuity will follow automatically. Be focused, diligent and plan your enterprises in a structured way.

Service industry, trading, jobs and products will have a limited shelf life but assets — properties and shares — will always increase and have added value.

However you make your money, put it into property. As pointed out by entrepreneurs who built on the wealth of the past and progressively became aristocrats. The modern world to my mind is made of meritocrats.

But again, as Welsh poet WH Davies wrote in Leisure:

> *'What is this life if, full of care*
> *We have no time to stand and stare...?*
> *A poor life this if, full of care*
> *We have no time to stand and stare.'*

Then of course, some are born great, some have greatness thrust upon them, some acquire greatness, and others forever are trying to be great.

I was born to a comparably rich, well-off family. I had a privileged education. After arriving in the United Kingdom, fortune smiled on me. I was in the right time at the right place. There is an old proverb that says: If you are born poor, it is not your fault, but if you die poor then it is your fault.

There was no stone left unturned, not a breath missed; I had fierce determination and resolve to succeed. I had successes after successes, but sometimes strife would engulf me too. There are no roses without thorns. Businesses have ups and downs. Mine were no exception. I had my fair share of misery and failures. It is the will and the tenacity to weather these storms and arrive at your preferred destination no matter how difficult the path is, it is the iron wheel of determination, that will propel you.

Change is inevitable; it is a continuous process. The human race is forever trying to improve, adapt and change.

To improve is to change, so to be perfect is to change often; therefore, we keep on evolving. We humans are indomitable and certainly supreme in all of creation. We have conquered the Black Death, leprosy, chicken pox, the Spanish Flu, many other epidemics and pandemics; we have also beaten the hell out of Covid-19 — within a matter of time. Our inquisitive, inventive, capable minds found the solution. The conundrum then was how quickly we could come out of this unfortunate situation unscathed physically and financially.

Neither The Great Depression of 1930 nor The Great Famine of 1845 could hold us back. Covid-19 had not dampen our zeal to progress either. Humans and humanity will excel and march on together regardless of the consequences.

We have vaccines: Pfizer Biontech, Moderna, Oxford AstraZeneca, Johnson & Johnson and more. These have helped to end the horror of death and misery, and the world has completely bounced back. The human race is resilient, formidable and momentous.

Then again, unexpected things are changing rapidly. Life is shifting at a rapid pace and time has become of the essence — as if there were no tomorrow. We want everything here and now: texts, emails, tweets all replied to immediately.

Science is progressing at a phenomenal speed in all directions, giving us more possibilities but making us more detached from each other, I would argue.

Lord Sacks, the former Chief Rabbi, wrote: 'Children have been the victims of our self-serving beliefs that you can have partnerships without the responsibility of marriage, children without the responsibility of parenthood, social order without the responsibility of citizenship, liberty without the responsibility of morality, a self -esteem without the responsibility of hard work and achievement.'

Individualism, and a self-centred, lackadaisical lifestyle is the choice of the many in urban areas, but rural areas are still compassionate and caring because they have to rely on each other more, not reflecting Sacks' dictum.

Our historical legacy of social structure is changing. Aristocracy and class structure have become prosaic, nostalgic ideas. We are more meritocratic. Colour and creed do not form the basis of our denouncement. We are who we are.

Honour and dignity lie in deeds and disbursement; not where you come from or the colour of your skin but how you have evolved to that perfection.

Prime Minister Rishi Sunak and Muquim Ahmed, 15th April 2024
at Syon House

WHAT THE PRESS SAY

'In the 1990s Muquim Ahmed was one of the first to see the potentials of Brick Lane as an entertainments district at the heart of Bangladeshi community in Tower Hamlets and launched his first restaurants — the iconic Café Naz. The first of the 'modern' Bangladeshi restaurants'—
Queen Mary University Journal, when awarding the Fellowship in 2009

'He is also becoming a leading restaurant owner through his expanding Café Naz chain, which has six sites in Britain' -
Carlsberg Curry List and Restaurant Magazine 2002

'In 2005, Muquim Ahmed bought the century-old Marshalls & Rayner's Bakery at South Wimbledon. The bakery was his steppingstone to ready meals wholesale transmission from the restaurant trade. The bakery comprised of 13000 square foot usable space with a dedicated floor for producing ready meals' —
Curry Life

'With the distribution of confectioneries, savouries, pastries and ready meals into schools, hospitals and national multiples from the factory, Muquim Ahmed had successfully built up quite a sizeable business empire' —
Curry Life

'Everyone in London's East End Bangladeshi community knows Muquim Ahmed. He is their youngest and most successful entrepreneur; a millionaire' —
Dr Sean Carey, Honorary Senior Research Fellow in the School of Social Science, University of Manchester, April 1985

'Muquim, I think the three of us made an excellent and formidable team
– winning the debate at the Cambridge Union' —
**Philip Cole, Author of the Philosophies of Exclusion; Principal
Lecturer Applied Philosophy, Middlesex University.**

'Twenty pounds, a suitcase of clothes and a fierce determination to
succeed — that's all Muquim Ahmed had to start on the road to riches'—
The East London Advertiser, 1985

'The recipe of his success is a simple motto: if you have the will to be rich,
you will become rich. Faith and unwavering determination will guide
you to your destination'— The East London Advertiser, 1985
'[Muquim has] a virile confidence, a quick and lively mind, the ability to
lead from the front with an equable temperament' —
The Asian Times, 1993

'The award-winning curry connoisseurs Café Naz offered the best Naz-
E-Shahi (chicken tikka) in town' —
The Evening Standard (Olive)

'Apparently William Hague and Jack Straw have been, so, perhaps you
should too. The most romantic restaurant for that first date' —
Fay Maschler on Cafe Naz in the Evening Standard

Featured in **George Monbiot's** 1999 documentary **Growth of a City**
which highlighted the social and economic progress and regeneration
that was taking place in the East End of London.

Acclaimed by **Estate Gazette**, issue October 2005 and October 2007 as
'King of Brick Lane' and 'Curry King' by the East London Advertiser
edition of 1 November 2007.

Featured in the hour-long documentary **Property King** as a successful property tycoon describing how I succeeded into the road to success. The documentary has been uploaded to YouTube.

Featured on a **BBC Panorama** edition with **Eddie George**, the governor of the Bank of England, depicting the demise of BCCI.

Appeared in Tariq Ali's **Bandung File** in 1987, which featured the ghetto community that occupied the inner city, and the emergence of the Bengali community.

The Café Naz chain was featured on **ITV's Dinner Date** in 1999. The appearance made the restaurant popular overnight. From that Sunday onward, business went sky high.

"It is a remarkable success story of a man whose inchoate personality before his journey to England blossomed in the multi-racial, multi-cultural schooling at the American convent – Our Lady Fatima Cambridge School and Dawood Public High School in the then East Pakistan now Bangladesh. That helped him to become a man of ideas and ideology – imbibed in him the western liberalism with its secular disposition. He encompasses in his character a true reflection of both cultures that bridge the gulf between the east and the west. His personality reflects a blend of diverse cultures that a modern society symbolizes. There is nothing more that can exemplify his spectrum of values and beliefs than the practices he pursues in his personal life.

His father late Haji Mubarak ud-Din Ahmed was a skilled and successful entrepreneur, his late brother Moin ud-Din Ahmed enhanced their family fortunes. Muquim ud-Din Ahmed's enterprising ability and skill are all instinctively inherited from the family tree.

All these transformed him into an amiable, ebullient, and intelligent person, poise distinctively to become the first Bangladeshi origin millionaire in the United Kingdom" -
Ridoya Bangladesh 2000

Sunday Times February 19, 2006

The restaurant's owner, Muquim Ahmed, is thought to be the first Brick Lane millionaire. He arrived in east London in the early 1970s, aged 19, to study engineering with the intention of returning to join the family business.

He ended up staying when his father asked him to export goods from Britain and Netherlands to Bangladesh. Soon he was importing electronics and then he turned to property and restaurants.

"The nail- bomb was obviously a disaster, " said Ahmed, who along with his wife and daughter, was barely 40ft from the explosion.

"But behind every disaster is often a success. I was very fortunate that nobody was killed, but the bomb also raised our profile and we managed to reopen within three weeks and enjoyed really good business."

His property portfolio now has some 50 buildings and there are six Cafe Naz branches around the country. Ahmed believes immigrants and ethnic minorities are driven by a work ethic that can be lacking in the existing population.

"Immigrants work harder because we feel we have do that much more to earn our keep," he said. "We have an urge that many people don't have."

HOWEVER, experts warn that we should not view immigrants enterprises through rose-tinted spectacles.

"Ethnic entrepreneurs should not be viewed solely as stories of extraordinary success," said Patrick McGovern of the London School of Economics. "Small family -run businesses have been criticised for offering poor wages and conditions, with family members working long for little or no direct payment. A large proportion of ethnic-minority businesses fall into this category."

HARD-SLOG

Millionaire!

Muquim Ahmed has spent the past 40 years building a burgeoning business empire - which has seen the millionaire businessman dubbed as the King of Brick Lane. Here he tells Curry Life how he has risen through the ranks – putting his success down to tenacity and being in the 'right place at the right time'.

"I am a restless person, I need to be doing something all of the time," Muquim Ahmed tells me, not five minutes into our meeting. We're gathered (socially-distanced style) at Ahmed's offices at Canary Wharf in east London on a dreary, rainy day.

Pre-Covid, the area would be buzzing but the offices are eerily silent and empty. Reassuringly though, the biggest presence is from the cleaning crew. Such an atmosphere, however, does little to dampen Ahmed's enthusiasm; he is clearly a person who is constantly on the go, no matter the situation.

In the last 40 years, he has built a business empire spanning a myriad of industries - from electronics, to hospitality, from travel to finance, from wholesale distribution to catering, among others. He is currently chairman of Quantum Securities, a substantial property portfolio business, worth millions, established decades ago consisting of both residential and commercial properties.

Ahmed attributes his success to tenacity and endurance and the belief that when setting up your goal in life, you need to aim high. His current position at Quantum Securities is also in recognition of his vision of the long-term. As he puts it, 'the service industry, trading and jobs have a limited shelf life, but assets, property and shares will always have a greater continued growth value for generations.

Ahmed is also an avid gardener, which presumably helps him to unwind from his business interests. He is a proud owner of a stately garden. Yet he is perhaps best known for being dubbed 'the first Bangladeshi millionaire' and the 'unofficial king of Brick Lane', credited with helping to transform the area in London's East End into a vibrant hub in the 1990s.

Various press reports documenting his rise have referenced his 'fierce determination to succeed', his 'boy wonder' personality and his hunger for business. He has appeared in the Estates Gazette and Asian Rich list which highlighted his achievements as a self-made millionaire and how he has raised the profile of the Bangladeshi community. He appeared in the Sunday Times Rich List, the definitive list of the richest people in the country. Presently, research shows in the Companies House that his fixed assets supersede by millions within his peer group.

At Cafe Naz in Brick Lane

From entrepreneur to restauranteur

Even with 40-plus years of business under his belt, Ahmed is still as passionate about business now as he was then, with the firm mantra that you have to believe in yourself if you want to achieve something.

Like many before him, Ahmed arrived in the UK from Bangladesh in 1974 to finish his engineering studies. As he explains, there was - and still is - a belief in his home country that if you don't go abroad and study, it can become difficult to get a good job back home.

"The high earning, doctors, the lawyers [in Bangladesh], they were all educated abroad; my parents wanted me to be someone important in the community so they sent me to England to complete my studies," says Ahmed.

His studies, however, were soon abandoned in favour of several business opportunities, such as exporting electrical goods from the UK to his native Bangladesh, and acquiring the lease first and later the freehold of Naz Cinema in Brick Lane. Ahmed admits being in the right place at the right time. He imported movies from Bangladesh and showed them on the big screen at the cinema, gaining a loyal following among the Brick Lane locals.

Ahmed was also quick to spot how to make a thriving business better, reflecting his determination to go further. Noting that there was a huge demand for electrical goods, he looked at how to improve margins, recognising the Far East's potential. This led to his move into wholesaling, sourcing products mostly from Hong Kong factories. These included watches, radios, clocks and cassette players, all

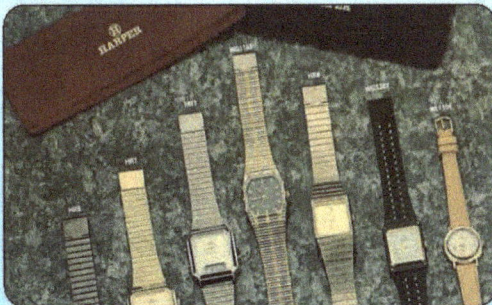
Harper, his own brand of watches

under the brand name of Harper (chosen because Harper sounded more English and branding was for UK customers) and other electrical accessories. His Sylto Cash and Carry attracted customers from far and wide and established itself as a national distributor for popular Japanese brands such as TDK, JVC, Panasonic and Casio. In the late 1980s he was also instrumental in raising the profile of the community by helping out Notun Din and later - the weekly Asian Post English newspaper.

Survival instinct and being a role model

Ahmed is also a survivor - in more than one sense of the word. In October 1994, his warehouse at Chicksand Street, just off Brick Lane, burnt down to the ground, with his Christmas trade - one of the most lucrative times of the year, literally going up in flames. The accidental fire destroyed the entire Sylto business, as well as the offices housing his media and other companies, incurring losses of over £4m.

Undeterred, Ahmed turned to what he had left - the cinema, where the concept for the Cafe Naz chain of restaurants took hold, having opened the first such restaurant in the former cinema's foyer. He opened another nine restaurants, with same theme and name, all around the country within five years of opening the first. Once again, Ahmed was looking to capitalise on a growing demand in the UK - this time for Indian food and the popularity of dishes such as chicken tikka masala. Cafe Naz quickly built a following among diners and restaurant critics for its take on contemporary Indian cuisine, providing authentic-tasting dishes highlighting the flavours of regional Indian cuisine. Ahmed brought in top chefs from five-star hotels in India and Bangladesh, with the restaurant not only showcasing authentic cuisine but Indian culture too. Chefs shared recipes with customers while the restaurant provided Indian-themed entertainment, as well as organise a number of food festivals.

In April 1999, Ahmed narrowly escaped death during the 'Brick Lane bombing', an attack targeted at London's Bangladeshi community. There had been two similar nail bomb attacks in the run up to the one on Brick Lane, targeting Brixton's black population and the LGBT community in Soho. Just moments before the bomb exploded, in the trunk of a car parked outside Cafe Naz. Ahmed had been at the restaurant. It was destroyed by the bomb, with Ahmed putting his narrow escape down to sheer luck - he was seating by the window which took the brunt of the force of the blast as the front and back house was preparing for the lunch trade when his wife Rashmi called and he crossed the road to meet her and their five

Naz Cinema in 1970's

After Brick Lane bombing

Fire in main warehouse. 1994

1985

Muquim Ahmed with his wife Farzana Ahmed

Above: Muquim Ahmed (far right) with his Brother Moin Uddin Ahmed and his wife Nurun Nessa Khanam. Front row his mother Haji Umarjan Bibi and nephew and niece Tipu and Rubi. (1970)

Left: Father Haji Mubarak Ahmed

Right: Monique Ahmed (daughter) and Miraj M Ahmed (son).

ar old daughter Monique just as the blast went off.

how did Ahmed bounce back from such life-changing events such his warehouse being destroyed and the bombing? Following the vastating warehouse fire, he was lucky enough to be able to rrow money from his family and his brother-in-law to get himself ck into business, but crucially, his success has been about spotting opportunity and running with it, as well as knowing when it's the ght time to move on. Muquim's former wife Rashmi Ahmed also ayed an important role to support him to meet new challenges in siness. After fire he did not try to rebuild Sylto for example, oving on to Cafe Naz. By 2000, a year after the bombing, there ere 10 such restaurants under the 'Naz' brand, across various cations such as London, Cambridge, Horsham, Cardiff and helmsford. After 20 years of successfully running the chain of Café az, he decided to exit from Restaurant trade recognising he had ken that opportunity as far as he could. He is still involved in a ndful of restaurants through Quantum Securities, but this time as eir landlord.

here were several reasons to get out of the restaurant industry," he ys. "There was personal stress, gross profit margins became lower, e suffered from staff shortages and the European HACCP & laws.

Residence: Mount Mascal Farm

With Prime Minister Boris Johnson

With Former Prime Minister David Cameron

With Former Prime Minister John Major

It became harder to ensure the chefs are properly trained and you can't be everywhere - sometimes too much can be just that."

Ahmed had also established a bakery and a food manufacturing business alongside running Cafe Naz. With several of his restaurants preparing thousands of meals every week, moving into the industrial production of ready meals seemed like a natural progression - and one which again filled demand at the time for ready-cooked meals. The warehouse Ahmed purchased for his ready meal production facility turned out to be a lucrative move - he sold it for more than three times the purchase price, which led him to where he is today - property investment under Quantum Securities.

So what would Ahmed say to the younger generation? His advice is simple: identify what you are good at and what you enjoy doing, Believe in yourself and do your best and give it your best shot. If you have 'it', don't give up and if you are not successful, keep on trying.

"It's essential to aim high, but not too high that you cannot reach," he says. "To retain success is an art in itself. Be focused, diligent and plan your enterprises in a structured way. Ambition and motivation and a desire to succeed should propel you to your destination."

And if the warehouse fire taught him anything, Ahmed says it's that no matter how hard you try, accidents can happen. "Consolation and encouragement does go a long way, and you can feel incapacitated and debilitated. You've got to pick yourself up again; it's difficult, but life must go on."

Political point

A firm remainer during the Brexit process, Ahmed feared that if the UK left the European Union, the country would suffer from a number of issues, labour shortages for example being his main concern. He has since changed his mind however, and says that leaving the EU is a better position for the UK to be in.

Only time will tell whether or not this is the case, but one thing is certain: as a businessman, Ahmed is proud to give his support to a Conservative government and has campaigned for the party over the years in a number of general and local elections. He was the co-founder of Conservative Friends of Bangladesh, an organisation that aims to develop relationships between the Conservative party and the British Banglasdeshi community. Currently he is serving as the Patron of CFOB.

"When you are faced with a situation like Brexit,

Receiving honorary fellowship at the Queen Mary University

With Former Chairman of the Conservative Party Francis Maude

everyone looks after their own interests," he says. "I am convinced now that we will be more successful on our own. I believe in meritocracy - in a socialist-type state, there is no incentive for the individual to thrive." Unsurprisingly, we touch on immigration - a subject very close to Ahmed's heart, who says the current situation is 'far,'far better now than some 40 years ago' when he first arrived. Without immigrants, he says, he would not have been able to run his businesses. "Immigrants come here with nothing - just their hopes and aspirations, they make a life for themselves here by working hard," he says. "If you have the ability and determination you can achieve anything; you can be anywhere if you have this belief in yourself."

Community action

Working with and for the local community is another of Ahmed's passions. He is adamant about having worked hard to make a difference to the lives of those in London's East End, and helping the Bengali community integrate into mainstream British society.

Ahmed was previously the chairman of the British Bangladesh Chamber of Commerce (serving three terms), and played a prominent role, overseeing a number of seminars and trade exhibitions, including The Expo Bangladesh 2005, held at London's Barbican Centre, the first ever one-country trade show held internationally by Bangladesh. This helped to raise the profile of the Bangladeshi on an international front. His take is very much that leadership is about actively lifting people up to your level, not just showing people how you got there.

"Our community is a new community, we have been here not even 60 years and we have achieved glowing heights. In the field of politics, we have four member of Parliament, we are in the House of Lords, Queen's Councillors, Judge, Doctors, Scientist and City High flyers, High Commissioner/Ambassadors in the British foreign service. We are a young and vibrant community and are certain to achieve many more distinctive heights in the years to come.

Leading BBCCI trade delegation to Bangladesh

Lifetime Achievement award to Muquim Ahmed by former leader of the house Andrea Leadsom. On left Mehfuz Ahmed and on right Abdus Hamid.

Appendix

Board of Intermediate and Secondary Education, Jessore, East Pakistan

Serial No. 8098

Secondary School Certificate Examination

I Certify that *Muqim Uddin Ahmed*, son/daughter of *Mubarak ahmed* of *Dawood Public High School* bearing Roll *Jess* No. *22*, duly passed the Secondary School Certificate Examination (in *Science* Group) held in the month of *April* 19 70 and was placed in the *First* Division

The date of his/her birth is *First September* Nineteen hundred and *Fifty four*

The *24th June* 1970
Written by *Rahiman*

RESULT OF THE EXAMINATION

OF HIGHER SECONDARY CERTIFICATE

BOARD OF INTERMEDIATE AND SECONDARY EDUCATION

COMILLA.

Name: Muquim ud-Din Ahmed

Father's name: Haji Mubarak Ahmed

Institution: Government College, Sylhet.

Roll. Syl. no. 36828

Branch: Science

Compalsory Subjects	Full Marks	Marks Obtained	Combination Subjects	Full Marks	Marks Obtained
Beng I	50	28	Mathematics I	50	45
Beng II	50	28	Maths II	50	33
	100	56		100	78
Eng. I	50	33	Physics I	50	41
Eng. II	50	24	Physics II	50	35
	100	57		100	76
			Chemistry I	50	46
			Chemistry II	50	40
				100	86

TOTAL MARKS: 378

PERCENTAGE : 75'6%

Division : 1st

Date: 5-5-73

Written by: Sd/Illegible

Compaired by: Sd/ illegible

Optional		
Biology I	50	37
Biology II	50	28
	100	65 = 25

attested

Tt Sarm
17. 4. 74

Sd/ Principal,

Dr. Harun-ur- Rashid

Serial No . . . .

GOVERNMENT COLLEGE, SYLHET

I have pleasure in certifying that *Muquim uddin Ahmed*

. . . . is/was a student of this College in the

XI & XII Science Class during the Sessions 1970 -1972

He/She appeared/passed the . . . . . . *H.S.C. (Science group)*

Examination from this College in the year . . *1972* . . . . in . *First* . . . . .

Division with *Eng. Beng. Phy. Chem & Math, and* as his/her subject . *Bio (opt)*

His/Her conduct in the College . . . . *was* . . . . . . Satisfactory. To the best of my knowledge he/she is of good character. He/She is not known to have taken part in any activity subversive of the State or of discipline during the period of his/her study in the College.

vice Principal,
Govt. College, Sylhet
Principal.

Dated . . . . *15 . 9 . 73*

Department of Physics.
Government College, Sylhet.

This is to certify that Muquim ud-Din Ahmed S/O Haji Mubarak Ahmed is a bonafide student of Government College, Sylhet. He is now in B.Sc. 2nd year doing Honours in Physics with Mathematics and Statistics as his subsidiary subjects. To the best of my knowledge he is of good character.

17/4/74

(Dr. T. Hoque Ph.D)

Head of the Department

Head of the department of Physics,
Govt. College, Sylhet.

Inner London Education Authority

South East London College
for Technical, General and Commercial Education

Principal K. J. Dean MSc, PhD, FInstP, CEng, FIEE, FIERE
Lewisham Way, London SE4 1UT Telephone 01-692 7296

25.8.77

CRM/Refunds/63722R
/ June 1977

Mr Muquim Ud Din Ahmed
48 Brick Lane
London E1

Dear Mr Ahmed

I am writing with reference to your letter of 20 April, 1977 which has been referred to me by Mr McNeillis.

I am sorry to hear that you are at present unable to continue your studies owing to ill-health. I am pleased to say that Mr McNeillis has agreed to your returning to the College in September, 1977 subject to the payment of the fee beforehand. The fee is £440 but, taking into account the circumstances of your case, it has been decided to reduce the fee by £193. Perhaps you would be good enough, therefore, to send me a cheque for £247 by return. (Cheque to be made payable to ILEA, SELTEC). If you wish to have a letter for the Home Office you should call at the College office and pay the fee in full in cash. Please bring this letter with you.

For your information, I have advised the Home Office that you are technically not a student at the college owing to ill-health. I have also advised them that a place will be reserved for you at the college subject to the early payment of the fee of £247. Obviously, they will require confirmation that the £247 has been paid in full before any further visas are issued.

A copy of this letter has been given to Mr McNeillis.

Yours sincerely

C R Moule
Office Manager

Telephone Number:
01-601
    4355/AFJN/GES
Any reply to this letter
should be addressed to
The Chief of
Exchange Control
quoting the reference

BANK OF ENGLAND
(Exchange Control)
New Change
London
EC4M 9AA

A/1249 EC 65/C.6

4rc   May 1977.

The Manager,
National Westminster Bank Limited,
Exchange Control Department,
Overseas Branch,
53, Threadneedle Street,   COPY
London,
EC2P 2JN.

Dear Sir,

Muquim Ud-Din Ahmed - Collection Services
(your 130, Whitechapel High Street branch)

     I refer to your letter (EXC/27785/COR) of the 20th April and to the Bank of England's reply of the 22nd April and confirm that the undertaking completed by Mr.M.U.Ahmed has now been received direct from your above-named branch.

     Subject to the undermentioned terms and conditions, permission under the Exchange Control Act 1947 is given for Mr.Muquim Ud-Din Ahmed to act as a "collector" in connection with the Notice EC 76, paragraph 21. The Bank of England would normally require a declaration on a Form DE from each donor, but, provided that the aforementioned terms and conditions are fulfilled, this requirement is dispensed with. Permission under the Act is therefore given for your bank to maintain a Resident "Collection Account" in the name of H.M.Ahmed-M.U.Ahmed Collection Account which will enable Mr.M.U.Ahmed to collect sums from United Kingdom residents for transfer to non-resident dependants.

     The above-mentioned terms and conditions are as follows:-

1. If your bank has reason to believe that credits have been made to your customer's Account, other than those specifically authorised in this authority, the Bank of England must be notified immediately with full details. (In these circumstances such credits are not available for payment to any person other than your above-named customer until the specific permission of the Bank of England has been obtained.)

2. Transfers from the Account are made only to an Account, designated External, held by your 130, Whitechapel High Street branch in the name ofMr.Haji Moinuddin Ahmed.

3. Cheques, or other instruments effecting payment to the above-named External Account should be marked by your bank, "eligible for credit to External Account", quoting the reference and date of this letter. Sterling Transfer Forms will not be required.

4. A return is submitted by your bank, to the Bank of England, by the seventh day of each month showing the total sum credited to the "Collection Account" during the previous month together with the amount paid to the named External Account and the balance remaining. Nil returns are required.

5. The Bank is informed should your customer decide not to proceed with, or to discontinue, these arrangements.

6. The Account may be credited with interest on the balance and debited with bank charges; in no circumstances may the Account be overdrawn.

7. Your bank is provided with an undertaking, in the terms of the attached pro forma, on an annual basis; it should be signed by your customer, authenticated and returned by your bank to the Bank of England at the end of December each year to cover the following year.

It is noted that your customer's application contained the undertaking required by the Bank for the current year; the arrangements detailed above may therefore become effective.

In the event of any of these terms and conditions not being fulfilled, or at any time on notification, the Bank reserve the right to require any balance on the Account to be repaid to your above-named customer and to cancel the arrangements by which the Forms DE are not required.

I enclose a copy of this letter for the information of Mr.M.U.Ahmed.

Yours faithfully,

Bank of England,
Exchange Control.

café Naz

Contemporary

46 / 48 Brick Lane London E1 6RF   (020) 7247 0234   (020) 7247 8505

18th June 2004

ON APPEAL

O/A 32 18/04

VR 25/5/2004

RECEIVED
CORRESPONDENCE UNIT

0 1 AUG 2004

Ms Amanda Cooper
First Secretary
Immigration Section
British High Commission
PO Box 6079.
United Nations Road
Baridhara
Dhaka – 1212

Ref: Applications for Entry Clearance to take up Sector Based Work
Permit Employment:
(1) Sufianur Rahman Chowdhury (Case Reference: 274668)
(2) Siraj Uddin Ahmed   (Case Reference: 276716)   *1465/2004*
(3) MD Nazrul Islam   (Case Reference : 276750)   *1529/2004*
(4) MD Hipjur Rahman   (Case Reference : 277613)   *1401/2004*

Dear Madam

The Café Naz chain of restaurants and Food Processing Warehouse
applied for and obtained 9 Work Permits under the Sector Based Scheme
to employ Kitchen Porter/Assistants at our chain of restaurants.
Unfortunately, to the present date, only two to of our applicants have
been granted visas to take up their employment.

I would like to address you firstly of our present frustration in having our
applicant's visas refused and secondly I would like request you to kindly
reconsider their permission to enter the United Kingdom to take up their
employment.

As you are aware, the Government has formulated the Sector Based Work
Permit Scheme to help relieve the pressure we presently have in our
restaurant industry of inadequate numbers of unskilled labour.
In fact, in my view, there is satisfaction for everybody in the operation of
the scheme.
1) The Government receives employment tax

2) Employers succeed in getting their jobs done and thereby provide the service to the public.
3) The employer makes a profit from running the restaurant and hence pays further corporation Tax.
4) The overseas worker, who is granted permission to take up sector-based employment, receives one hundred times his local wages in a comparable job.
5) The overseas worker also has the opportunity to receive international work experience in a high level-working environment giving him or her an excellent start in advancement of his/her career.

In other words UK Govt. is helping to elevate poverty in the Third World countries.

The SBS work permit is sufficiently strict to prevent abuse of the system by the stipulation that the SBS employment is only for a one year period and that the employee will have to return after the completion of the year. (May return after 2 month break in between).

I wish to appeal to you, on behalf of all Bangladeshi employers to consider the SBS Work Permits major benefit to the restaurant catering trade and not withhold entry visa for reasons that these people will not return home.

Under the present scheme, employers are only entitled to employ the worker for a period of twelve months. No employer will run the risk of facing criminal prosecution if they continue to employ the person after the twelve months or another person without lawful permission to work. There is a clear directive from the Govt. which stipulates that the employer will be fined £5000 and will risk imprisonment if they employ illegal immigrants (Section 8 of the Asylum & Immigration Act 1996).

Historically, the United Kingdom has successfully allowed controlled and managed migration in the 1950's and is now embarking on the same path after 50 years to fulfil the vacancies that we have in various industries. According to Govt. Data some £2.5 Billion is generated by the Work Permit Scheme. Barbara Roche MP in a TV interview said that controlled immigration enhances our society and certainly attracts inward investment because of diverse nature of people. Lord Andrew Green said in the same interview that London will grow and boom with legal managed migration.

Please allow me to introduce myself; I embark on this exercise to establish my credibility and **not to create undue influence.**

My name is Muquim Ahmed. I am the present Chairman of the Bangladesh British Chamber of Commerce.

I knew quite well His Excellency David Walker. His predecessor His Excellency Peter Fowler (presently our Honourable President). I also know His Excellency Anwar Choudhury, his predecessor His Excellency Dr. David Carter.

Your predecessors Mr. Geoffrey Fairhurst & Mike Johnson, I had the pleasure of meeting them on several occasion.

I also have acquaintance with the Foreign Secretary Jack Straw, the Home Secretary David Blunkett and Michael O'Brian through our present positions in the Bangladesh British Chamber of Commerce.

Financially, I am regarded as one of the most successful entrepreneur in our community. In addition, I am the owner of eight restaurants of which six of them trade under the name of Café Naz.

I have been successful in obtaining staff of excellent repute, three of whom were previously employed at the five star Dhaka Sheraton and around 35 Chefs and Cooks from India who have worked in the Taj Group and other reputed five star hotel chains.

We presently require under the Sector Based Scheme, eighteen Kitchen Porters/Assistants. We have been granted 9 SBS Work Permits out of which you have issued only two visas both of whom are already working in our Cardiff and Brick Lane branches.

In reality, it will be a futile exercise for the applicants (refused an entry clearance visa) to appeal against the refusal because it will not be cost effective. We will require these people to pay the solicitors fee if we are to appeal on their behalf. The cost of an appeal can be £1000-£1500. The truth is that these Work Permit applicants are poor by definition and they will not have the means to incur such costs. The only people who will benefit from such appeals will be the lawyers and the waste of court time and our time.

We earnestly request you to grant entry clearance visas to all of my applicants who do not need any experience to come and work for us.

Infact I will further request you to give visas to those who <u>genuinely</u> have a job to come to. The Home Office has given ultimate power to your entry clearance officers, it is their discretion whether they should refuse or allow. The recent directive by the Govt. is to refuse a visa merely on the ground that they "might not return" is in reality a vague directive. It is understandable that these (SBS unskilled) people are poor and will not want to return. "<u>Every one of them will not want to return</u>". Who would? If you are getting 100 times your present wages. It is our Law that should force them to return. ***And return they must***. It is in the hand of our Govt. to uphold this Law and implement it vigorously.

It is not practical for the Govt. to issue Work Permit on one hand and than to stop it on the other merely because they will not return.

We appreciate some misappropriation will occur, middleman will profit from the situation, but it happens in most Third World Countries.

Specifically on my cases, I request you earnestly to grant entry clearance visas to all my applicants and bid them to withdraw their appeal.

I will be pleased to answer any questions you might have as clearly and transparently as I can.

If you require any further information or would like to talk to me, please do not hesitate contacting me at your earliest convenience on my Head Office number 020 7476 6969 or office fax 020 7476 8555 or Mob. 07958 494922.

Yours sincerely

Muquim Ahmed
Chairman & CEO

Cc Mr. Nick Bostin ECM

Issue 183, Friday, June 09, 2006

BANGLA MIRROR

THE FIRST ENGLISH WEEKLY FOR BRIT BANGLADESHIS

High Commission apologises to Mukim

By Alexandrina Galieli

The British High Commission in Dhaka has apologised to restaurateur Mukim Ahmed for an incident last year that created a furore in local community newspapers.

It is believed that the Cafe Naz owner applied to the HC for visas for potential employees under the sector-based scheme but the applications were refused on the grounds that the candidates were poor and may not return to Bangladesh.

Mr Ahmed then wrote to the HC, asking how a candidate's economical status in Bangladesh affected their ability to work in the UK. He also said that the visa clearance officer's decision based on the candidates' intention to remain in the UK was subjective.

The HC went on to claim it was Mr Ahmed who stated that Bangladeshis who enter the UK on SBS visas fail to return. The misinterpretation of Mr Ahmed's letter was widely publicised and made headlines for weeks with certain publications claiming he had brought the community a bad name.

However, after receiving a letter from Mr Ahmed's solicitor, entry clearance officers in Dhaka sent him a written apology, regretting the inconvenience the misinterpretation had caused.

Mr Ahmed said at a press conference on Monday that his image was tarnished by the High Commission's claims but he was now glad to accept the apology.

Mukim Ahmed

প্রেস কনফারেন্সে মুকিম

চেয়ে মুকিম আহমেদ সলিসিটরের মাধ্যমে একটি চিঠি পাঠান। বীঘদিন পর এই চিঠির জবাবে হাইকমিশনের কর্মকর্তা এর জন্য দুঃখ প্রকাশ করেন। গত ৫ জুন সন্ধ্যায় এক সংবাদ সম্মেলনে মুকিম আহমদ এ তথ্য উপস্থাপন করে বসেন, বুটেনের শত শত রেস্টুরেন্ট ব্যবসায়ীর মতো তাঁক সেক্টরের কারণে আমিও চরম ভুক্তভোগী। রেস্টুরেন্টের শ্রম সংকট নিরসনের জন্য ২০০৪ সালে আনিত ওয়ার্কার্সের জন্য আমি বেশ কিছু ওয়ার্ক পারমিটের আবেদন করি। এতে প্রথমে বিন্দুটী সফল হই। আবার সেই সময়ই আমার করা কয়েকটি আবেদন রিফিউজ করলে আমি হাইকমিশন বরাবরে একটি চিঠি লিখি। সেই চিঠির একটি অংশ সম্পূর্ণ অপ্রাসঙ্গিকভাবে ধরে সেবা হয় অন্যের ভিসা প্রত্যাখ্যানের চিঠিতে। এতে কমিউনিটিতে ভুল বোঝাবুঝির সৃষ্টি হয়। এরই প্রেক্ষিতে ২০০৪ সালের ১৪ মার্চ এক সংবাদ সম্মেলনের পর আমি হাইকমিশনের সলিসিটর নোটিশ পাঠাই। বীঘদিন পর হাইকমিশনের এন্ট্রি ক্লিয়ারেন্স কর্মকর্তা দুঃখ প্রকাশ করে তার বক্তব্য প্রত্যাহার করেন। এই চিঠিতে কোন চুদ বোঝাবুঝি হলো তার ব্যাখ্যা দিয়ে কর্মকর্তা উল্লেখ করেন এটা ব্যাপকভাবে ধীকৃত এসবিএস স্কিম কর্টিযুক্ত ছিল। এসবিএস স্কিমেও 'ইন্টেনশন টু লিভ' বিষয়টি সবসময়ই সক্রিয়ভীন ছিল। কর্মকর্তা আরো লিখেন, এই সময়ে মুকিম আহমদ পরিস্থিতি উপলব্ধি করে যে উদারতা দেখিয়েছেন সে বিষয়টি আমি মূল্যায়ন করি।

মুকিম আহমদ বলেন, আমার দেখা চিঠির অংশ অপ্রাসঙ্গিকভাবে তুলে ধরে যে চুদ বোঝাবুঝির সৃষ্টি হয়েছিল আজ তার অবসান হলো। তিনি বলেন, আহমেদের বিশাল করি ইতালীকে বিস্তৃত-জনক ওয়ার্ক পারমিটের

মুকিম আহমদের চিঠি নিয়ে সে সময়ে প্রকাশিত ইউরো বাংলার রিপোর্টে প্রেক্ষিতে আইনি পদক্ষেপ সংক্রান্ত এক প্রশ্নের জবাবে মুকিম আহমদ বলেন, আমি কমিউনিটিতে কখনো অসদল চাইনি তবে তখনকার ঘটনায় দুঃখ পেয়েছিলাম। আবেদ অনুভূতিকে দয়াতে পারিনি বলে একটি পদক্ষেপ নিয়েছিলাম নতা, তবে তা শেষ হয়েছে। পরিশেষে বৃটিশ বাঙালিদের ভিত্তি যে করি ইতালীর উপর দাঁড়িয়ে আছে তাকে রক্ষায় সবাইকে ঐক্যবদ্ধভাবে কাজ করার অনুরোধ জানান তিনি।

BRITISH BANGLADESH NATIONAL COUNCIL UK
16 CLAYMORE STREET
ABBEY HEY
MANCHESTER M18 8SP
Tel: 0161 370 4528 & 0161 225 1014 Mobile: 07766634218

PRESIDENT: GIAS-UDDIN-CHOUDHURY

Muquim Ahmed Esq.   15th March 2005
Cafe Naz
46/48 Brick Lane
LONDON
E1 6RF

Dear Mr. Muquim Ahmed

I thank you very much for your letter received by me yesterday, 14th March. I have read the contents of both letters, that of your communication to the British High Commissioner and that to myself. I have also read the articles appearing in the Euro Bangla weekly Bengali newspaper dated 7th - 13th March 2005. The front page articles containing your picture is concerning work permit applications that you have submitted to the British High Commissioner under the SBS for the recruitment of employees from Bangladesh to the UK.

I am very disappointed in relation to the unfortunate argument that has arisen by the actions of certain respectable members of the Bangladesh Caterers Association. The appearance of these so called allegations has really shocked me especially given that they relate to a letter which is now 9 months old. All of a sudden these allegations have appeared in only one Bengali paper and is worrying not only to myself but to the majority of decent peace loving Bangladesh respectable community in the UK and overseas.

It is patent that the article relies on a paragraph of your letter which has been taken completely out of context. I have analysed every paragraph and can find nothing that indicates that you have expressed anything other than your interpretation of the Government directive to which you have referred. In the following paragraph you qualified that you did not in fact accept the interpretation by stating that it was not practical for the Government to issue work permits on one hand and stop them merely on the basis that the potential employee would not return to Bangladesh on the conclusion of his work permit. I do however feel that this would have been slightly better expressed as follows:

It is not practical for the Government to issue work permits on the one hand only to then stop them on the mere allegation that the person to whom the work permit has been issued will not return to Bangladesh on expiry.

267

I note that in the article Mr. Anam Ali has raised objections to your writing on behalf of the Bangladesh British Chamber of Commerce. However there is no indication that you have written on their behalf and, in the event that you had, I can see no objections being raised to this as you are dealing with a topic which is relevant to all of its members. I believe that what Mr. Ali has raised objections to is the allegation that you support the Government in its directive which, had that particular paragraph not being taken out of context, would self evidentially have been qualified in your following paragraph. It seems to me that Mr. Ali has raised his objections in order that further clarification could be given and I support him in that respect.

I am however heartened to note that most of the Committee Members appear to be backing you and have, no doubt, realised that the articles have been written on the basis of what is, at best, a misunderstanding in the full letter not having been made available and which appears, in any event, to be based on hearsay.

For many years it has been the practice of the British Government to refuse entry clearance on the basis that the person to whom entry has been granted will not return to their country of origin. This practice has been exercised in relation to several nationalities, all of which are Third World Countries. I am well aware of this as I have assisted many people over the years and it is clear that this is a hidden policy of the British Government to enable to deny entry to persons who are entitled to claim it. Whilst it is accepted that many people do not return, and this is widely publicised, it is no reason to refuse entry clearance. I note that no figures have ever been given by the Government to substantiate this allegation. In those circumstances I feel that it would be prudent to debate the matter and question the Government in relation to its policies.

Mr. Mahmudur Rashid is right in saying that your application has been misused by the Entry Clearance Officers on behalf of the High Commissioner and the British Government. I fully agree and support this view. I find the majority of the members arguments and statements very interesting. This letter should have been laid to rest rather being brought into the public eye for no reason. I do not believe that the majority of the community would believe that there were reasonable grounds on which to lodge an argument on this unfounded and unnecessary allegation against yourself.

The British Government, The High Commissioners Entry Clearance Department have made errors in publicising your letter in the ethnic minority newspapers. It was a private and confidential application and was not destined for public domain but was personal to your business interests. In the circumstances:

1. The British High Commission should be asked to give explanation as to why your letter was made public knowledge;
2. You are entitled to know the identity or identities of the persons to whom they disclosed your letter.
3. On whose authority was your letter disclosed to the press.

The newspaper, Euro Bangla, should be asked on what basis they publicised your letter. It seems clear that they do not hold a copy of the entire letter or that they have been entirely selective. I feel that they should have consulted their lawyers before publishing this article. It is clearly wrong and I feel that you may have an action against the newspaper for libel. This has been confirmed by Mahmudur Rashid who stated in the Euro Bangla that it is a legal question of liability.

In relation to your introduction wherein you advise the Entry Clearance Office of your role as Chairman of the Bangladesh British Chamber of Commerce and list the various persons that you know well or are acquainted with, you have committed no crime. I do however feel that it was something of an error of judgement and could be seen as an effort to exert undue influence. I regret to say that in including this introduction there is a smack of "Do you know who I am?". I am not saying this intending to be in any way disrespectful but merely pointing out that it could be construed as a threat by the authorities with whom you were dealing. Nevertheless you in no way suggested that you were communicating on behalf of anyone other than yourself.

I trust that the above is of assistance to you and I thank you for inviting me to comment on the sorry episode that has unfolded. If you wish to discuss any of the matters raised please do not hesitate to contact me. If I can be of any further assistance to you, again, please do not hesitate to contact me.

Yours sincerely

Gias-Uddin-Choudhury - President
Former Parliamentary Candidate 1997/MEP 1999

Acclamations

BANGLADESH HIGH COMMISSION
28 QUEEN'S GATE, LONDON, S.W.7

22 July 1994

HIGH COMMISSIONER

Mr Mukim Ahmed
Chairman,Milfa Group of Companies
Milfa House
Chicksand Street
London E1 6RF

Dear Mr. Ahmed,

     I am delighted to learn that you have been
elected as Director of Bethnal Green City Challenge
in its recent election. I offer my sincere congratulations
on your success in this elections and hope that with
your participation the City Challenge Company will be
further strengthened with positive outcome for the
community. *With best wishes and kind regards,*

Yours sincerely,

(signature)

(Dr A F M Yusuf)

High Commission for the People's Republic of Bangladesh
28 Queen's Gate, London SW7 5JA
Phone : 0171-584 0081
Fax : 0171-225 2130
E-mail : bdesh.Lon@dial.pipex.com

Report on the Milfa Exchange Co. Ltd.
21 Brick Lane, London E1 6PU.

During a business discussion on 19April, 2000 at 10.30 a.m. in the High Commission of Bangladesh in London, Mr. Muquim Ahmed, Chairman and Mr. F A Khan, Director presented a short brief on the resume of activities of Milfa Exchange Co. Ltd. During brief, it revealed that the said company are seeking arrangements with Dhaka Bank Ltd., Dhaka, Bangladesh, for the home remittances to Bangladesh. Dhaka Bank Ltd., is interested to establish drawing arrangement of drafts and telegraphic transfers extending remittances services to the British Bangladeshi expatriates in UK and the beneficiaries in Bangladesh through account of the Company with the Bank.

Memorandum and Articles of Association of Milfa Exchange Co. Ltd., a private Company Limited by shares, incorporated on 28 September, 1999, Company Number: 3849753, says that the dealing in the exchange, buying & selling of foreign currencies, travellers cheques and so forth as one of the Company's objectives.

Mr. Muquim Ahmed is a successful and eminent businessman. He is the Regional President (London city) of The Bangladesh-British Chamber of Commerce, UK and associated with good number of British Bangladeshi welfare & socio-cultural activities and known as one of the Britain's richest Asians.

Mr. Farhat Ali Khan is a well-known personality in the business circle with banking as his career anchor.

I have visited the business premises of the Company which is located at 21 Brick Lane, Bangla Town, London. The Company Office is ideally situated to serve the Bangladeshi community by way of providing services, among others, for home remittances. It is found that the Company has recently commenced trading in the premises. All other people of the managerial hierarchy are found to be experienced and of professional competence.

AFM Y Choudhury 10.5.2000

(A F M Yeahyea Choudhury)
Economic Minister.

FROM THE HIGH COMMISSIONER

7 January 2001

Mr Muquim Ahmed
Chairman
BBCC

**British
High Commission
Dhaka**

United Nations Road
Baridhara, Dhaka

Postal Address: P.O. Box 6079, Dhaka-1212

Telephone: (880) (2) 8822705 (5 lines)
Facsimile: (880) (2) 8823437

Email: david.carter@dhaka.mail.fco.gov.uk

Dear Mr Muquim Ahmed,

**LUNCH AT SHERATON HOTEL HOSTED BY ALAN JOHNSON,
BRITISH TRADE MINISTER**

Alan Johnson, British Minister for Competitiveness will visit Bangladesh from 14-16 January to inaugurate the fourth British Trade and Education Fair taking place at the Sheraton Hotel. I enclose a note on Minister Johnson.

Mr Johnson will host a seated lunch for key figures at the Sheraton Hotel in the Top of the Park Suite on 14 January at 13.00. Mr Johnson would be very pleased if you could join him on this occasion. The Honourable Commerce Minister Mr Abu Jalil will be Chief Guest.

I should be grateful if your office would contact my Personal Assistant Ms Susan Farrent on extension 2202 here at the High Commission to confirm whether or not you will be able to attend.

I look forward to seeing you again.

Yours sincerely,

David Carter

272

HIGH COMMISSION FOR THE PEOPLE'S REPUBLIC OF BANGLADESH
28, Queen's Gate, London, SW7 5JA
Phone : 020-7584 0081
Fax : 020-7581 7477
E-mail : bdesh.Lon@dial.pipex.com

29 August 2002

My dear Muquim,

I write to convey my family's and my own heartfelt thanks and gratitude to you and bhabi for the dinner you so kindly hosted and the cultural function that you took pains to organise for us on Sunday last at your grand mansion.

The food was delicious and the performances by Mr. and Mrs. Bhattacharya in the matching ambience of your spacious and tastefully furnished living room were enchanting. My wife, daughters and I myself enjoyed the evening immensely in the company of you and your family and friends. And I must mention that my daughters were totally mesmerised by the incredibly beautiful doll you presented them. The evening vividly manifested how deeply you cared for me. We hope, we shall have an opportunity in the near future to reciprocate your and bhabi's kind hospitality to us.

We thank you and bhabi once again for your kind gestures of friendship and the trouble that you took for us.

With regards for you and bhabi and affection for our cute little niece, and nephew.

Yours sincerely,

(Muhammad Azizul Haque)
Deputy High Commissioner

Mr. Muquim Ahmed
Mount Mascal Farm
North Cray Road
Bexley, Kent
DA5 3NH

Queen Mary
University of London

Queen Mary, University of London
Mile End Road, London E1 4NS
Telephone 020 7882 5001
Facsimile 020 8981 2848

From the Principal
Professor Adrian Smith FRS
Email principal@qmul.ac.uk

20 December 2007

Mr Muquim Uddin Ahmed
Asian Foods Ltd
6-48 Brick Lane
London E1 6RF

PERSONAL

Dear Muquim

I have great pleasure in writing to let you know that the Council and the Academic Board of Queen Mary have jointly resolved to elect you to an Honorary Fellowship of the College.

The College Statutes provide that Honorary Fellows should be *persons of distinction or who have rendered significant service to the College or to the community*. We should be especially pleased to be able to recognise your achievements in business and your outstanding contribution to the communities of East London.

I should be grateful if you would let me know whether you are willing to accept this offer of an Honorary Fellowship of the College.

We hope to admit you to your Fellowship at one of the graduation ceremonies to be held in July of 2009. At the ceremony, there will be an opportunity for you to give a short address, should you wish to do so. It would be very helpful if you would let me know as soon as possible whether there are any weekday dates in July 2009 on which you would be unable to attend.

Yours sincerely

Patron: Her Majesty The Queen

Incorporated by Royal Charter as
Queen Mary & Westfield College,
University of London

High Commission for the Peopole's Republic of Bangladesh
28, Queen's Gate, London, SW7 5JA
Phone : 020-7584 0081
Fax : 020-7581 7477
E-mail : hdesh.Lon@dial.pipex.com

Dear Muquim Bhai,

31 January 2008

Assalamu alaikum.

I am writing this letter to inform you that on completion of my tour of duty, I am scheduled to leave London on 2nd week of February 2008 for taking over the assignment in the Ministry of Foreign Affairs, Dhaka.

I would like to place on record my sincere appreciation and gratitude for your all out support and co-operation in discharging my responsibilities smoothly. Hope my successor Mr. Md. Allama Siddiki will receive similar co-operation from you.

As you are aware that I also served in our Birmingham Mission during 2000-2004 as the Assistant High Commissioner. I thoroughly enjoyed your company on both the occasions.

I am grateful to you for the warm hospitality extended to me and my family. I would like to avail the opportunity to reciprocate your warm hospitality. We are looking forward to receive you in Bangladesh in the near future. My mailing address and contact telephone numbers are provided below:

Ashraf Uddin
Director-General
Ministry of Foreign Affairs, Dhaka
Tel: 008802-956-2115 (Office)
e-mail: auddin 2003@hotmail.com

Yours sincerely,

(Ashraf Uddin)
Deputy High Commissioner

Mr. Moquim Ahmed
Chairman
Bangladesh British Chamber of commerce
16-18 Brick Lane
London E1 6RF

The Lord Sheikh

House of Lords
Westminster
London SW1A 0PW
Tel: 020 7219 4542
Fax: 020 7219 8602
E-mail: sheikhm@parliament.uk
Website: www.lordsheikh.com

Mr Muquim Ahmed
Café Naz
46-48 Brick Lane
London
E1 6RF

18th August 2009

Dear Muquim Ahmed,

I was very pleased to learn that you have been presented with the Honourary Fellowship of Queen Mary University at a recent graduation ceremony.

I would like to congratulate you on receiving this prestigious accolade which rightly recognises your achievements and the commendable work that you have undertaken for the community and the development of London, particularly in regard to East London.

You are indeed a role model and your path to success can perhaps be emulated by others who are focused and would like to achieve success like you have.

I am sure that you will not rest on your laurels and will go ahead from strength to strength.

Kindest Regards

Yours sincerely

The Lord Sheikh

DEGREE DAY

Muquim Uddin Ahmed

15 July 2009, 11am

Presenter: Mr Nigel Relph,
Director of Corporate Affairs

Muquim Ahmed is one of the outstanding success stories in Asian business in the UK in the last twenty-five years and is one of the leading contributors to the regeneration of the Brick Lane area and to the increasing success and prominence of the Bangladeshi community in London more generally.

Following a degree in Physics in Bangladesh, Muquim Ahmed came to the United Kingdom in 1974 to study Production Engineering, but then moved into business, initially working with his family, then moving into electrical distribution and wholesaling and ultimately into property and the catering industry. At the age of 26 he became the first UK Bangladeshi millionaire and has been on the 'Asian Rich List' ever since. He made an early move into the travel business and then into music production, importing Bangladeshi artists and marketing them to the growing Bangladeshi population in the UK.

During the 1990s, he was one of the first to see the potential of the Brick Lane area as an entertainment district at the heart of the Bangladeshi community in Tower Hamlets and launched his first restaurant, the iconic Café Naz, the first of the 'modern' Bangladeshi restaurants. This has been followed by Café Naz branches in Cambridge, Cardiff, Horsham, Chelmsford and elsewhere. The chain continues to expand.

Muquim Ahmed has seen continued success across a range of businesses, including banking, travel, publishing and property development. As well as being a major force behind the development of Brick Lane and support for the Bangladeshi community, he has been extremely active in a wide range of community and charitable initiatives and projects. He has been Chairman of the Bangladesh British Chamber of Commerce for two consecutive terms (2000-2005). Under his leadership, the Chamber became a major force and delivered the much acclaimed Bangladesh Expo 2005.

Dr Julian Lew, QC

15 July 2009, 3pm

Presenter: Spyros Maniatis, Professor of Intellectual Property Law in the Centre for Commercial Law Studies

Dr Julian D M Lew QC is a barrister and international arbitrator, as well as a member of Chambers at 20 Essex Street, London.

He has been involved in international arbitration academically and practically for almost 40 years, as both counsel and arbitrator. The cases in which he has been involved include disputes arising from international transactions of all kinds, investments, corporate arrangements, joint ventures, infra-structure projects, distribution, agency, licensing and construction, and international trade finance. Many of the arbitrations in which he has been involved have had state and state entities as a party.

Dr Lew has advised and represented parties in arbitrations all around the world. He has been appointed as chairman and co-arbitrator in arbitrations of many different kinds and under all the different systems, including ICSID, ICC, LCIA, ICDR, Stockholm Arbitration Institute, WIPO, Swiss Arbitration Rules, and under the UNCITRAL Arbitration Rules.

Queen Mary University of London

Park Place
communications

4th floor
Denman House
20 Piccadilly
London W1J 0DG
Tel: +44 (0)20 7734 0499
Fax: +44 (0)20 7287 8054
Info@parkplacecommunications.com

23 May 2006

Muquim Ahmed
Chairman & CEO
Asian Foods Ltd
Quantum House
Caxton Street North
London E16 1JL

Dear Muquim Ahmed,

Thank you for your letter of 8th May and many congratulations on the success of your campaign in Tower Hamlets. You personally deserve a great deal of credit for how well we did and I quite agree that with your drive and enthusiasm we have the prospect of even more gains in the future.

If I can help in any way with your political ambitions you know you only have to call.

With all good wishes

STEVEN NORRIS

Conservatives

Private and Confidential

Mr Muquim Ahmed
48 Brick Lane
LONDON
E1 6RF

13th November 2006

Dear Muquim

I gather the dinner with David Cameron was a great evening and we are very grateful for your generous donation. Hopefully in the next few weeks and months we can persuade you to become a member of the Leader's Group and play an active role in it, in addition to all the excellent work you are doing for the Bangladesh community.

Membership of the Leader's Group is £50,000 p.a. and would hopefully take into account any donations made to date. It would be fantastic to have you on board if you feel so inclined.

Thank you for everything you have done so far.

With best wishes,

LORD MARLAND OF ODSTOCK
Chairman of the Treasurers

Conservatives

Mr Muquim Ahmed
Quantum Securities Ltd
30th Floor
40 Bank Street
Canary Wharf
London E14 5NR

Wednesday, 8th April 2015

Dear Muquim,

Thank you for your letter of 25 March.

It was wonderful to see you for the luncheon a few weeks ago. It was very kind of you to organise it, and I was delighted to meet some of the members of the Conservative Friends of Bangladesh and to hear their views.

I'm very thankful to you for raising these funds. With the General Election so close, my diary is extremely hectic and I don't think I'll be able to find the time to meet. I do hope you understand, and I would be very grateful if you could send the cheque in the post.

Thank you, again, for your outstanding and continuing support. You have been by our side from the very beginning and I really do appreciate everything you have done for us.

With warmest best wishes,

LORD FELDMAN OF ELSTREE
Chairman of the Conservative Party
and Chairman of the Party Board

Conservatives

Mr. Muquim Ahmed
Cafe Naz
46-48 Brick Lane
London E1 6RF

18ᵗʰ October 2011

Dear Muquim,

Re: Project Maja Bangladesh

As ever you were a pleasure to work with. Your positive energy, generosity and team spirit were a remarkable addition. Your support right from the word "go" was very important and I thank you for all that you did to make Project Maja a success.

The British Prime Minister recently said: 'Just because you can't do everything – does not mean you should not do something'. In the scheme of things, the 'something' we did was very small. But as a direct result of Project Maja, I understand Bangladeshi MPs are now looking at the model we employed, of working through charities, as a way of effecting change in their constituencies.

Thank you once again for making our visit so pleasant and for all that you did to make us feel so welcome.

Best Wishes,

Sayeeda Warsi

Rt Hon Baroness Warsi
Co-Chairman of the Conservative Party

Conservative Campaign Headquarters, 30 Millbank, London SW1P 4DP, Switchboard +44 (0)20 7222 9000, Fax +44 (0)20 7222 1135, www.conservatives.com

Index

A

Abdul Guffar Choudhury 140, Abdul Korim 72, Abdul Matin 129, 139, Abdul Montaqim 135, 137, 138 139, Abdul Motalib Choudhury 65, Abdur Rahim 189, 191, Abssar Waess 195, Adamjee Haji Dawood Bhawani Sir 34, 181, Adrian Smith FRS 156, Professor 207, 274, Advertiser 124, AFM Yeahyea Choudhury 271, Aga Hassan Abedi 153, Aga Khan 156, Ahmed us Samad 191, Alex Brown 62 Alison Thompson 115, 116, Altab Ali 66, 67, Amartya Sen 237, Aminur Rashid 27, Amiruddin 72, Anis ur Rahman Barrister 113, Andrew Green Sir 115, Anne Main MP 214, 225, Apsana Begum 11, 63, Asia Express 84, Ashfaqul Bari 185, Ashique Ali Barrister 74, Asian Foods Ltd 176, Asian Post 129, 136, 137, 138, 139, Asian Times 122, Aurthur Conan Doyle 45, Ayub Khan 34,

B

Baishaki Mela 67, Bajloor Rashid 195 ,Bangladesh Caterers Association 199, Bangla Mirror 144, Bank of Credit & Commerce (BCCI) 153, Barak Obama 239, 240, Benjys 179, 180, Benjamin Disraeli 214, Bernie McDermott 205, Blue Bird School 26, 27, Bongo Bandhu 42, Boris Johnson 218, 223, Brady Centre 139, Brick Lane Palace Theatre 64, Burma Haji 86,

C

Cafe' Naz 159, 160, 162, 164, 165, Charles Campion 170, Charles Darwin 221, Charles Dickens 31, Churchill Winston 3, Chris Day 5, Clive Jennings 147, Covid -19 243, 244

D

Dan Jones 64, David Arnold Cooper 133, David Cameron 49, 215, 224, 226 David Carter 272, David Copeland 19, 222, Dawood Public School 34, 35, 40, 41, Deshi Store 48, Dinah Glover 240, Disraeli 222, Durbin Shah 72,

E

Eastern Fancy Store 88, 106, Ehsan Enterprise 86, Emdad Talukder 14, Eric Ollerenshaw 226, Evening Standard 169, Expo Bangladesh 2005 192, 193

FG

Farzana Kamal Al-Siraj 5, 232, 233, Fay Mashcler 169, Fazlu Rahman 89, Francis Maude 214, G.D.Govinder 122, 135, General Musharaf 156, George Harrison 236, Ghandi Oriental Foods 163, Glamour International 52, 53, 88, 89 Granada 90, Grant Thornton 155, Great Depression 244, Great London Mosque 65, GU Choudhury 113,

HI

Habib Bank Ltd 138, 156, 157, Harper 149, 150, 151, Hassan Bawa 89, Himangshu Goswami 71, 93, Iqbal Ahmed 185, 194, 195, Israil Miah 199, ITV Dinner Date 169,

JK

Jalal Ahmed, General Manager Biman 84, James Caan 180, Janomot 138, 142, Jasim Bhai 52, 89, 97, Jill Khan 27, JL Nehru 117, Joe Biden 45, John F. Kennedy 221, John Major 1234, Jonata Travels 84, Jugo Bari 27, Dr. Julian Lew QC 277, Kabir Choudhury Dr. 189, 190,

Kais Choudhury 164, Kamal Syed Lord 226, Kamal Syed General Manager Biman 84, Kari Amir Uddin 72, 90, Kate Middleton 217, Ken Livingstone 193, Key Haynes 125, Khurram Matin 139, 142, Kuti Miah 71, 240,

L

Lehman Brothers 157, Lilly Khan 38, 41, Liz Truss 215, London & Provincial Factor 155, London Barbican Centre 193, London Bangla Press Club 142, London Development Agency 176, Lord Levison 15, Lord Sacks Jonathan Henry 244, Lutfur Rahman 11, 63

M

Manik Miah 139, Margaret Thatcher 42, 185 200, 213, 218, Marnie Summerfield Smith 5 , Matab Ahmed 48, Matab Miah 191, Mayfair Cinema 69, MC College 40, 42, Mehfuz Ahmed 226, 230, Michael Heseltine 42, 223, Michael Howard 220, Milan Babic 74, Milfa Air-Cargo 87, Milfa Travels 83, 84, Milfa Shipping 85, Milfa Sterling Exchange 94, Mimbor Ali 185, Minhas Ahmed 48, 206, Miraj Ahmed 99, 100, 101, 206, Mitu 102, 206, Modern Store 86, 87, Mofazzal Karim AH His Excellency 193, Mohammed Yunus Dr. 237, Mohib Choudhury 129, 141, 164, Moinuddin Ahmed 25, 45, 48, 53 88, 234, Monica Ali 64, Moni Dipa 168, Monique Ahmed 14, 15, 99, Monu Bhai Patel 69, Mount Mascal Farm 59, 61, 185, Mubarak Ahmed 25, 104, Mubarak Monzil 26, 46, 106, Muslim (Moslehuddin Ahmed) 46, 47, 51, 88,

N

NAFG Fidelity SA 133, Nahas Pasha Syed 5, 129, Natwest Bank 56, 57, Naz Cinema 69, 70, Nazrul Islam Bashon 142, Nelson Gomes 35, 36, 37, 40, Netaji Shubas Chandra Bose 237, New Society 120, Nicky

Morgan 226, Nigel Farage 218, Nigel Lawson 56, Nigel Relph 206, Nirala Restaurant 70, Noor Miah 185, Notun Din -129, 139, 140, 141, 142, Nurul Huq Councillor 74, Nurun Nessa 25, 43,

O

Odeon 69, Oliver Letwin 49, 50, Omar Faruk General Manager Biman 84, Omarjan Bibi Begum 25, 107, 108, Oswald Mosley 65, Our Lady Fatima Cambridge School 27, 28, 32, 33,

P

Pakistan Overseas Express 83, Pandora Arcade 81, Pankaj Bakshi 139, Paul Jones 177, 183, Paul Rayner 177, Paul Scully MP 226, Peter Hitchens 115, Phil De Launey 28, 29, 30, 31, 32, Phillip Cole 115, 119, Pola Uddin Baroness 11, 64,

QR

Queen Mary University 205, 206, Rabindranath Tagore 237, Rachel Lichtenstein 64, Rafique Hyder 195 Raja Girish Chandra Roy 41, Rashmi Ahmed 14, 54, 60, 61, 92, 99, 100, 101, 229, 231, Ravi Shanker 236, Rayner's Bakery 175, Ready Meals 178, Richard Branson 91, 92, Richard Hughes 184, Rishi Sunak 42, 71, 215, 239, 240, Rokiya Begum 25, 234, Ruksana 59, Rupa Huq 11, 63, Rushanara Ali 13, 63,

S

Sabina Saree Centre 88, Safwan Choudhury 27, Sagheer Qurashi 131,132, Shahnaz 178, Shahagir Bakth 53, 89, 116, 195, 214, 225, Sajid Javid 228, Sajjad Hayat 27, 39, Salauddin Ahmed Director Marketing Biman 84, Salim Salique 167, Satish Advani 231, Sayeeda Warsi Baroness 223, 226, Sean Carey Dr. 121, Sector Base Scheme (SBS) 111,

112, SELTEC 259, Shabana Begum 65, Shahajalal 25, Shamim Azad 65, Shamim Uddin 27,Shanti Lal Barshi 125, Shefali Ghose 71, 90, Shelim Hussain 185, Sherlock Holmes 45, Simon Gaskell Professor 205, Sister Mary Annett 31, Sister Mary Joan of Arc 30, Sister Mary Josepha 30, Sokina Begum 46, 48, Somerset Maugham 31, Stephen Gomes 167, Stephen Watt 64, Suella Braverman 226, 228, Sundar Pichai 239, 240, Surma Travels 84, Swami Vivekanada 237, Sylto Plc 130, 131, 132, 133, 145, 147, 149

T

Tahera Rashid 27, 28, Tara Miah 129, Theresa May 229, Tipu 86, Tony Blair Sir 217, Tassaduk Ahmed 64, Tayebur Rahman 65, Tracey Emins 169, Tulip Siddiqui 11, 63, Tobias Elwood 226,

UVW

Vasant Kumar 231, Vince Cable 185, W.H. Davies 243, Wage Earner Scheme 55, 85, 86, Wali Tasser Uddin (Dr. Hon.) 197, William Hague 225,

XY

Yashvir Sunak Dr. 240, Yasmin Sabina Ahmed 48, Yousuf Ali, General Manager Biman 84,

www.ingramcontent.com/pod-product-compliance
Ingram Content Group UK Ltd.
Pitfield, Milton Keynes, MK11 3LW, UK
UKHW052245010425
456947UK00001B/1